Graphology
A Guide to Health

Graphology
A Guide to Health

MONICA O'HARA-KEETON

ROBERT HALE · LONDON

ISBN 0 7090 6445 4

Robert Hale Limited
Clerkenwell House
Clerkenwell Green
London EC1R 0HT

2 4 6 8 10 9 7 5 3 1

Typeset by
Derek Doyle & Associates, Liverpool.
Printed in Great Britain by
St Edmundsbury Press
and bound by
WBC Book Manufacturers Limited

Contents

Dedicated to the memory of my late father Dr Denis Harding, GP, police surgeon and forensic graphologist who taught me my craft and to my husband Joe Keeton, who encouraged the development of it.

Acknowledgements

I am deeply grateful to all those brave volunteers who agreed to become involved in this project and I respect the wishes of those who preferred to remain anonymous. Special thanks therefore go to Kevin Donnellon, Simon Weston, OBE, and Swasie Turner, PLSM, for subjecting themselves to in-depth scrutiny; to Faith Brown and Dr David Stevenson for their long-term friendship and co-operation; and to Dr Richard Mould for the novel idea of a blind trial.

Thanks, too, to members of the Mouth and Foot Painting Association, to Mrs Estella Hoskin for her co-operation with the samples of Charles Fowler, the Beaumont Society and the Tourette Syndrome (UK) Association, to the editors of the *British Medical Journal* and other publications for complying with requests for unusual samples, and also to Mrs Joan Strange and Mrs Diane Wainwright, JP, for their invaluable contribution.

Much love and gratitude go to Joe, who painstakingly printed out every page of the book, ensured that the illustrations were in the correct order, photocopied them and broke off from his own duties to supply me with constant refreshments. Nor must I overlook the insistence of Ronnie and Tilly Mint, my canine companions, that I take twice-daily fun and frolics in the park. And finally, a great big thank you to Mr John Hale for his patience, perseverance and encouragement throughout the preparation of this book.

Introduction

Graphology, the study of handwriting, can prove invaluable for assessing personality and character traits, and also for pointing out indications of ill-health. It is important to stress at the outset, however, that non-medical analysts should never attempt to make a diagnosis.

For example Sally[1] was fourteen years old when her father was involved in a fatal road accident just before Christmas. She was the eldest of a large family and as one might expect, the shock of his death at such a time had a profound effect on her mind.

When I was given a sample of Sally's writing shortly after the tragedy I was not in the least surprised to see the change it had undergone. Mental trauma was clearly manifest on the written page. Whereas before, her style of writing had been a fast cursive script, relaxed and natural apart from the usual episodes of adolescent scrubbing out, now it was slow, laboured and totally without spontaneity. Furthermore, it had ceased altogether to be a script, having taken on the form of printed letters. The fact that the change in Sally's writing had occurred immediately after her father's accident was evidence of its direct link with the event. Allow me to explain.

Sally had been very close to her father and was obviously devastated by the catastrophe. Unable to release her pent-up feelings of loss, confusion and pain, she may have felt unconscious anger towards him for dying so prematurely, together with guilt for even allowing such thoughts to enter her head.

The printed form of writing was a psychological mask to cover her shame at harbouring such feelings and her inability to cope with them. The very legibility of the sample hinted that deep down in her psyche there was a desperate need for understanding.

Those who knew Sally maintained that she had always been a gregarious type of girl who enjoyed games and parties. Since the death of her father she had become morose and generally withdrawn, spending her time at home reading and listening to moody records.

The switch from normal handwriting to print was an unconscious decision. Rejecting her friends was a conscious one. Both represented withdrawal and occurred simultaneously.

Printed handwriting is unusual but not rare. The analyst's first impression might be that these writers are protecting their privacy or being secretive for reasons best known to themselves, but that does not necessarily follow. There are many reasons why people print, not all of them sinister. The simplest explanation is often that the writer suspects that his[2] script is such a scrawl as to be almost illegible to those who are unfamiliar with it.

Teachers and journalists sometimes adopt a semi-print style for their own reasons; teachers are in the habit of writing clearly on a blackboard or flip-chart, while in the days before new technology, a considerate sub- or copy-editor marking up typewritten folios would have wanted to ensure that compositors understood the instructions for setting copy.

However, even when a form of print is used instead of conventional handwriting it is still possible to analyse it. This is done by checking such aspects as how the writing is placed on the page, whether pen pressure is light or heavy, the presence or absence of margins, whether the baseline is level or drooping, whether the os are open or shut at the top, whether the t-bars are light, heavy, short or long, and whether the legs of some letters trail beneath the line.

When putting pen to paper, a writer often starts off being guarded, but begins to relax towards the end, and that is often the best place to begin an analysis, whether of printed or scripted samples.

Nothing should escape the eye of the graphologist. It is important to examine how the words are laid out, whether they slant to the right or the left, or whether they stand up straight; whether the lines are well spaced out or all muddled and entangled with each other.

The most casual observer of handwriting might recognize and identify certain shapes and forms, and distinguish the flashy from the inhibited, the tidy from the untidy, the clever from the slow-witted. But without making a long and protracted study of the subject, these observations are in danger of being too generalized, even inaccurate. If someone's personality is to be completely mapped out, all the features must be taken into consideration. Each must be seen to show a separate relationship with the character as a whole. Like pieces of a jigsaw they must all fit into place before the total picture can emerge.

It has long been established that no two people's fingerprints are the same; it may not be so well known that nor are any two people's handwriting – not even those of identical twins. And each person's outlines are basically the same, regardless of how they have been written. A person unfortunate enough to have lost the use of a hand, and who has had to learn to write with the other, will develop a similar style to the original once the technique has been re-established. Likewise, if both hands are missing or immobilized and the writing instrument is held in the mouth or by the foot, the outlines will be more crude but the angle and formation of letters and words should not have changed. The same applies even to someone by the sea, writing in the sand with a toe.

Three things which do not show up in the script are left-handedness, age and gender. Whereas some graphologists claim to be able to state categorically which hand has written the sample before them, and there are indeed left-handed tendencies in some scripts, I do not believe there is a foolproof method of determining whether the writer is right- or left-handed.

In most people the right hand is dominant; some 90 per cent of the population is right-handed.

Illness or injury may make a naturally right-handed person left-handed (as in the case of Admiral Nelson). So too might a misguided parent or teacher who believes it is harmful for a child to write with the 'wrong' hand.

Some naturally left-handed people, encouraged to write with their right hand, manage to do so efficiently, becoming ambidextrous and coping well with both hands. Others are equally clumsy whichever hand they use, but the introduction of force results in stress.

Children who have been made to change their writing hand from left to right against their will are likely to develop all sorts of problems. The stress of struggling to get it right can manifest itself in the form of headaches, poor academic progress and general nervousness. Bed-wetting and stammering are also commonplace in this group. The effects of making a child switch from natural left-handedness can be severe and long-lasting.

Age is difficult to determine because some people are old at 20, whereas others are young at 80. Naturally, very immature hands can be recognized as such, and so can those of the elderly and infirm because the script, like the body, deteriorates with age and illness. But between those two extremes it is not possible to establish a writer's age with any accuracy.

Gender cannot be established because we are all androgynous creatures; females have male hormones, producing certain male traits and characteristics, and males have female hormones. A dominant, aggressive woman therefore, could have an abundance of 'male' signs in her writing, whereas an effeminate man might have very few. However, *sexuality* can show up in writing, as we shall see.

We are all individual and unique, and our handwriting reflects this. By studying an individual's handwriting, therefore, an analyst can evaluate physiological patterns and detect personality traits and behaviour disturbances. An in-depth character assessment is thus possible.

Graphology can also provide insights for those working with disturbed children and adolescents, and it can make an important contribution to the associated fields of medicine and psychology. Just as X-rays can penetrate the head to produce clear pictures of the skull, a graphologist's reading can penetrate the writer's thoughts to see what lies behind them. With a few pen strokes, and without even realizing it, people can disclose the deep symbolic meaning of their thoughts. The example of Sally has shown how conscious actions can be controlled by unconscious mechanisms. The hand may be holding the pen or pencil but it is the brain which directs the writing instruments around the paper.

A blind trial

Academics have long been interested in the potential of graphology. When the scientist Dr Richard Mould came to Liverpool to be interviewed about his latest book[3] in 1984 I invited him, as I invite all interviewees, to sign my review copy. We had just had lunch, the mood was jovial, and the doctor's signature was so fascinating that I provided him with a free graphology reading over the coffee and brandy.

It was all a bit frivolous because the conditions were not conducive to serious study, but the findings intrigued Dr Mould and whetted his appetite for more. A physicist, statistician and then honorary Senior Lecturer at Westminster Hospital in London, he wanted to set up some sort of official means to test my methods. When he suggested a blind trial I was all in favour, because I had never been involved in anything like that before.

So with the help of his historian friend the late Harold H. Winter, the trial was organized. They removed from the handwriting samples any signatures, addresses, dates and other clues I might be likely to pick up on. I was also given a very limited time to conduct the readings, because the two men felt that if I were a real expert (their words) two or three lines should be enough and it should not matter whether the person was dead or alive at the time of the readings.

In due course, I was presented with seven samples and only when the test was completed were the identities of the writers revealed. All were leading men of history, and included Lord Nelson. The anonymous note from him contained only the words 'Dr Fisher, Christ's College, Cambridge'. What could I make of that?

I began my analysis by noting that the script was written in a strong, upright style, of muddy pen pressure. The writer was proud and fiercely independent, a divergent thinker, but moody. He was, I added, the sort of man for whom time was precious and not to be wasted on non-essentials; there was important work to be done and he was the one to do it.

He was also the sort of man who was likely to say something along the lines of 'Bureaucracy be blowed' because one had the distinct impression that he felt that people who mattered would have to take up where he left off.

The muddy look of his script I attributed to his emotional state. He also showed signs of being myopic. His sexual activities appeared normal, if spasmodic.

Dr Mould seemed quite impressed with all of this. 'The graphology reading for Nelson is remarkable,' he observed when the writer's identity was revealed.

'Bureaucracy be blowed' recalls the incident of the telescope to the blind eye and the Nelsonian remark, 'I see no ships.'

That Nelson was proud, independent and difficult to work with is not open to doubt. The comment about the one-eyed admiral being myopic is very good.

A graphology reading is relevant to the date at which the sample was written. In Nelson's case this was 5 September 1805 which, according to the *Encyclopedia Britannica*, must only have been a mere ten days before he sailed from Spithead for the Battle of Trafalgar.

Regarding the comment that Nelson's sex life was normal if spasmodic, the doctor concluded: 'As an eighteenth-century sailor, it would have had to be spasmodic, at least with Lady Hamilton!'

When I was shown the full sample, I saw that the signature was 'Nelson and Bronte' (Nelson had recently been created Duke of Bronte). Admiral Lord Nelson is known to have varied his signature to suit the circumstances; signing himself sometimes as on Dr Mould's sample, sometimes as Horatio Nelson, sometimes simply Nelson.

After the Spaniards shot off his right hand during an attack on Santa Cruz in 1797 (he had already lost the sight of his right eye, in Corsica), he learned to write with his left hand. His signature changed from a rightward to a leftward slant as Figures 1 and 2 illustrate.[4] Figure 3 shows another version of the left-handed signature.

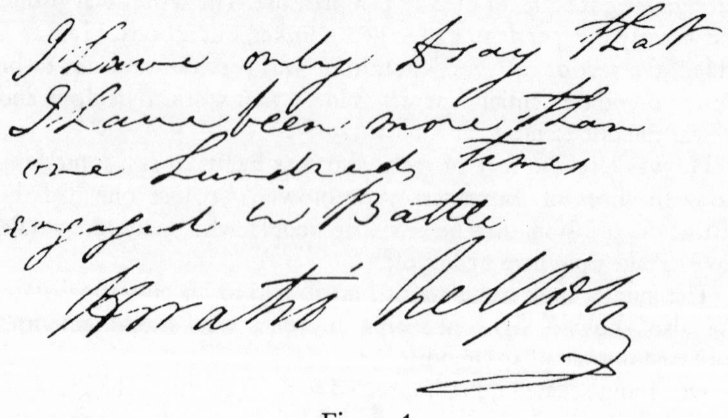
I have only to say that
I have been more than
one hundred times
engaged in Battle
Horatio Nelson

Figure 1

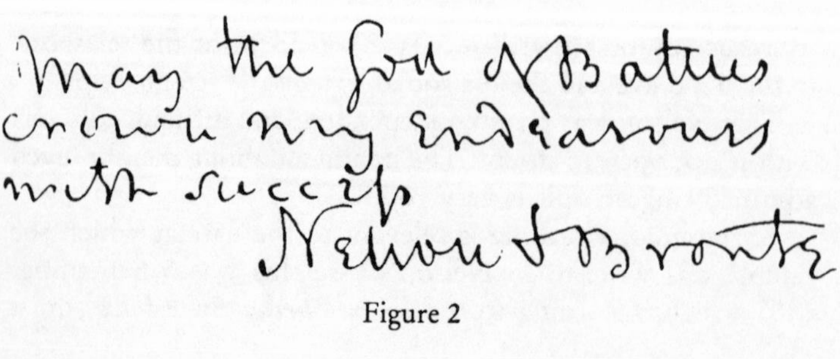
May the God of Battles
crown my endeavours
with success
Nelson & Bronte

Figure 2

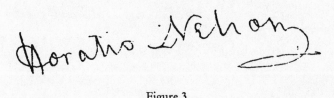

Figure 3

Dr Mould, delighted with the results of his blind trial, devoted an entire chapter to it in his next book.[5]

And Sally? Yes, she did eventually adjust to the loss of her father. Now an adult and a parent herself, she has recovered from her traumatic experience and once more writes with a natural cursive style.

The purpose of this book is to focus on the health aspects of graphology: to examine, through this medium, the state of the writer's mind and, by association, the body. We shall see how aspects of the personality are reflected in the writing and how changes in the personality are also registered.

Notes

1 Not her real name.
2 Throughout the book, I use the general term 'he' to refer to individuals when the gender is not known, in order to avoid the more clumsy 'he or she'.
3 Mould, Richard F., *Mould's Medical Anecdotes* (Adam Hilger, 1984).
4 Hattersley, R., *Nelson* (Weidenfeld and Nicholson, 1974).
5 Mould, Richard F., 'Is Graphology Accurate? Ask Lord Nelson and the Duke of Wellington' in *More of Mould's Medical Anecdotes* (Adam Hilger, 1989, pp. 139–47).

Note

For the purposes of reproduction, many of the handwriting samples illustrated have been reduced. The percentages shown next to the figure numbers are approximate.

Part I
Theory and Practice

1 Background

The history of writing

Most forms of writing as we know them today have been traced to Egyptian hieroglyphics, a mixture of animal figures and abstract symbols which produced a language understood by our ancient ancestors. Once those abstract symbol meanings were generally accepted, they took on the form of written language, and the invention of alphabetical characters is usually attributed to the ancient Egyptians.

Over the centuries, these early forms were modified, reshaped and altered until they developed into our modern alphabets. Each race modified the symbols in its own way, but all were probably offshoots of the same system. Alphabetical symbols came to the British Isles with the Roman conquest, which accounts for the fact that our alphabet is based on early Roman, or Latin, lettering.

Roman letters as we now know them are based on the Trajan alphabet, designed in honour of the Emperor Trajan, who lived in the first century AD. Between the fourth and fifth centuries, a new alphabet was formed, called the majuscule. As the name indicates, the letters were large. This alphabet was used by early Christians for scriptures and other sacred texts. Celtic scribes working on the Isle of Iona, however, preferred the minuscule alphabet, in which they specialized during the sixth century.

Greek and Latin manuscripts developed two distinctive styles: bookhand and cursive. Bookhand was stiff and formal, and was used by professional scribes; cursive was rapid and simple, and was used for the private correspondence and diaries of the literati.

Then came the Gothic style, which was considered eminently suitable for formal and religious scripts until the Vatican developed Chancery Italic. It must be appreciated that in those days, religion figured prominently in the lives of the people and at a time when the

Papal Curia was Europe's high court, monks and priests were the mediators of literacy for the laity.

A disciplined yet flamboyant style, Chancery Italic was full of lovely swash capitals with extending strokes. It became the standard script for secular texts like medical and legal documents and musical manuscripts. In time, however, italic script gradually developed into a more natural and less ornate style. Unlike some of the more complex writing forms which followed as a result of the Renaissance, this style has no looped ascenders or descenders.

In the sixteenth century, books began to be printed in copperplate and the form of writing so named was adopted. The roundhand which followed was simple and more straightforward, while printscript, which was introduced in the early days of the twentieth century, made for easy legibility.

The main difficulty with this form of writing was that it did not readily adapt to cursive or spontaneous writing. Teachers in traditional schools preferred copperplate – an offshoot of the nineteenth-century style – finding it ideal for the sharp, pliable pens of the day. Written carefully, it was aesthetic and stylish but at speed it could degenerate into a scrawl.

When Gothicized italic was reintroduced, a curious discovery was made. Whereas in the early days the only people able to write were men, it soon became apparent that, with their more precise hand control and nimble fingers, the best scribes were women.

Children normally learn writing by copying from models, helped along by their teachers. At least they did until 1935, when Marion Richardson, a British educationalist, published a book which was to revolutionize the whole concept of letter formations. An art teacher, she based her system on the natural inclinations of a child to make rhythmic patterns with oversimplified letters.

This new form of writing was readily adopted in British schools because it was the first time children had ever been encouraged to use a free-flowing hand, which meant that they no longer needed a teacher guiding their little hands through every move. The trouble with this style was that not all children matured simultaneously; Miss Richardson's form of writing was a real help to the slow learners, who could now move along more quickly than before, but brighter children soon became bored with it.

Over the next ten to fifteen years, old-fashioned styles began to be taught once more and the early 1950s marked the reappearance of italic writing. Careful and slanted, it was made up of letters based on sixteenth-century writing but much more simplified. Although free and cursive, it proved difficult to master and write at speed and, like copperplate, frequently slipped into illegibility.

Thus was a series of writing patterns established over the centuries. A sound knowledge of the history of writing is useful for the would-be graphologist; with a rough idea of when the writer was born, the analyst should be able to establish which method of handwriting was taught and so decide on which set of letter forms to base the analysis. Armed with this knowledge it is possible to appraise style and assess legibility, spontaneity and personal identity.

Writing implements

Our ancestors first wrote with reeds on sheets of papyrus. Finding this to be a very fragile material which did not stand up well to use, they moved on to the more sturdy parchment and vellum, both of which were made from animal skins. It is, therefore, on those two surfaces that most ancient manuscripts still in existence were written.

As writing styles and surfaces developed, writing instruments also underwent a series of changes. Around the thirteenth century, the reed gave way to the quill, which in time alternated with the brush. Brush strokes made medieval letters heavy, compressed and very dramatic.

Moving on a few hundred years, we find rather more contrast in tone with roundhand writing. This style, produced by seventeenth-century writing tools, resulted in lines varying in thickness from a mere hairline to a stroke so heavy as to be almost brushlike.

With the demise of medieval brushes and quills, pens began to appear. The name, incidentally, comes from the Latin *penna*, meaning feather. Early varieties were of steel, with pointed tips to dip into the ink. Then came ones with wooden bases and detachable nibs.

To write with these so-called dip pens, one had to press very lightly on the upstroke to avoid making holes in the paper. The result was an artistic style of thick and thin lines, which could look very attractive in Victorian ledgers but which often resulted in writer's cramp for the unfortunate clerks having to pore over their entries from dawn until dusk.

Fountain pens have been in use since the beginning of the twentieth century, but dippers of one kind or another were used in classrooms until after the Second World War.

For many people, the arrival of ballpens marked the beginning of the end of stylish writing. With these pens, devised by the Hungarian László Biro, people's handwriting ceased to be the art form it had been with the use of flexible nibs, and became relaxed to the point of carelessness.

Felt and nylon-tipped pens appeared in the 1960s and rolling ball pens were introduced during the following decade, but in recent years we have seen a return of the fountain pen. This is good news for graphologists, because writing produced by a fountain pen is not only aesthetically pleasing, it is also very much easier to analyse.

The history of graphology

The origins of handwriting analysis are clouded in obscurity. Eleventh-century Chinese philosophers are believed to have used a form of it, and various renowned men of history are said to have tried penetrating personality using its techniques, among them Aesop, Aristotle, Caesar, Cicero, Robert Browning and Sir Walter Scott. Shakespeare and Disraeli were also said to have had more than a passing interest.

However, it is generally believed that the instigator of the science as we know it today was Dr Camillo Baldi, a seventeenth-century professor of theoretical medicine at the University of Bologna in Italy. During the next hundred years or so, the idea of drawing connections between personality and handwriting was tested by numerous scientists throughout Europe, but it was not until the end of the nineteenth century that handwriting analysis was shown to have a possible relationship with psychology and physiology. In Germany, Doctors William Preyer and Hans Busse produced several fascinating periodicals on the subject and were later joined by two more medical men, George Meyer and Ludwig Klages.

In the late nineteenth century, Abbé Hippolyte Michon of France, who is acknowledged as the father of modern graphology, published his first book on the subject. He it was who introduced the term graphology.

What graphology is and how it is used

The word 'graphology' comes from the Greek *grapho*, meaning to write or create symbols. Graphology bears no relationship to astrology, or any form of fortune telling. Nor has it anything to do with palmistry, which involves examining lines in the hand, or calligraphy, the art of producing beautiful scripts with a pen or brush. It is not a party game, a cult practice or a means of predicting the future. It is a precise science, capable of recording the activities of the writer's mind and body.

Given that the brain operates like a highly complex computer with a vast warehouse of data inside, it is not difficult to imagine the enormous capacity it must have for absorbing, processing and feeding back information. Like a computer, the brain receives and gives out information, through pathways known as sensory systems. It is through these systems that messages pass from the brain to the hand. They do it by registering in nerve and muscle movements, so although the hand may be holding the instrument, it is the brain which is responsible for moving it around the paper. The result is something as individual as a fingerprint and a shade more revealing.

There is nothing aimless or haphazard about the way we put our thoughts on paper. A slipshod sample, casually executed, is often of far greater value to the graphologist than one where the writer has quite literally watched his p's and q's. Likes and dislikes are reflected in the hand; so are interests, hobbies, states of mind and general health. Personality also shows in the hand, as do creative talents and gifts. As I have said, age, gender and left-handedness cannot be deduced, although sexual inadequacies and disorders are clearly manifest.

Moreover, despite the remarkable changes in writing styles which have taken place during the last fifty years or so, the vagaries of human behaviour continue to be reflected in the hand. In today's literate age, when almost everyone is able to read and write, the scope for graphology grows increasingly wide. If we accept that our entire personality is embodied in the way we express ourselves on paper, handwriting analysis can be very revealing indeed. The professional analyst can help in areas such as career guidance, personnel selection, marriage compatibility and the detection of crime.

Having established that people's entire personality is embodied in the way they express themselves on paper, it follows that graphology can also prove a useful diagnostic aid for medical and allied professions by pointing out indications of ill health, physical as well as mental.

Acute anxiety states show in the hand, as do many chronic

emotional disturbances and sometimes such problems as speech impediments and impaired hearing. What may not be well known is that organic illness can also reveal itself. Alcoholism is often identified by hand tremor and a scrawl, because large quantities of alcohol consumed over a prolonged period impair the brain, resulting in aberrant or irrational behaviour. But tremor can also appear in the writing of people suffering from Parkinson's disease. That is why it must be stressed at the outset that the lay practitioner should only ever point out indications of ill health and *never* attempt to diagnose disease, which must always be left to those who are qualified to do so – the controversial practice of 'grapho-therapy' will be investigated later in the book.

Because of the need for precision, it is a mistake to try to learn graphology from books without additional assistance from someone experienced in the craft. Information from books should form just one part of the picture; but personal observations over a long period are even more important. Other essential qualities for the would-be graphologist are an interest in handwriting, an analytical mind, curiosity, common sense, acute awareness, an ability to see beneath the surface and good eyesight. The equipment needed is minimal, the only requirements being some folders in which to keep a collection of interesting samples, a strong magnifying glass with which to study them properly, a pen and pad to make notes of every little detail – and the confidence to go ahead.

2 The Basics

As children, we are taught to write in a certain way, but as we grow up and mature so does our writing. Our interests and hobbies take us off at a tangent and our writing does likewise. Some of us are practical, down-to-earth types, others are dreamers. Some of us enjoy a life filled with activities, others are stuck in a monotonous rut. Some have questing minds, others simply cannot be bothered.

Having established that the brain controls the reflexes which cause the movements necessary to write, it follows that we stamp our individuality on the paper with every line, angle and curve. Each little dot and stroke gives its own clue to the graphologist.

If, as some people maintain, their style of writing changes from time to time, how can one say that the outlines remain the same? Is this not a contradiction in terms? The fact of the matter is that there is nothing unusual about a normal script which alternates between tidy and scruffy, speeding up, or slowing down. In the absence of any sinister signs in the hand, the reason for these changes is simply because the writer is an adaptable sort of person who likes a little variety in his life. Just as we do not wear the same clothes every day, so we do not make exactly the same signs and symbols either. For example, a mother might wear her best outfit to visit her children's school on prizegiving day, but if she were going jogging she would wear something more casual. So it is with writing. Many of us adapt the style to suit the occasion (the 'when in Rome' syndrome). A note to our friend might be more relaxed than a formal letter of application for employment. But the basic outlines remain constant.

If, however, our note were so casual that it became slapdash and virtually illegible, it would give our friends the impression we did not much care for them. They would feel let down; it would be like

25

inviting them to our home for a dinner party and greeting them in hair curlers and carpet slippers, showing that we did not think enough of them to bother with any preparations.

It helps to have several samples of writing from the same person because only then can it be determined whether any unusual aspect of the writing is a dominant factor of the writer's hand.

The analysis of handwriting, like any other science, has its own theory, its own terminology and techniques. Writing is made up of three zones – upper, middle and lower – which must be examined. Other factors to take into account are the various forms of lettering, slant, size, speed, spacing, baseline, pen pressure, letter connections, rhythm (and regularity), form level and general layout.

Zones

All three zones must be looked at closely to determine whether they are equally balanced or whether any of them is exaggerated. Fundamentally, the upper zone tells us about the writer's intellectual and imaginative thoughts and his spirituality. Figure 4 shows a dominant upper zone.

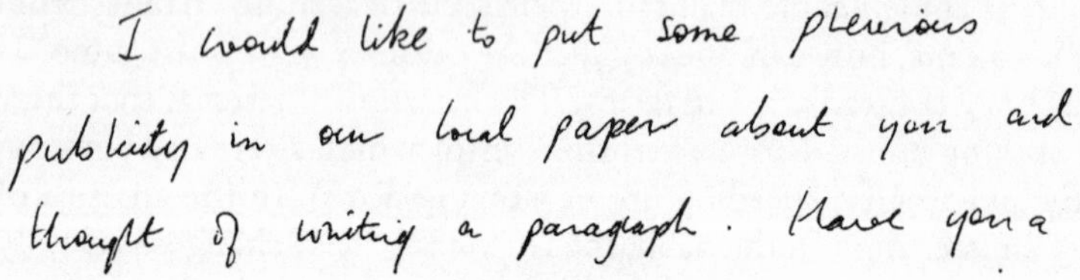

I would like to put some plentious publicity in our local paper about you and thought of writing a paragraph. Have you a

Figure 4 (50%)

Emotional writers emphasize the middle zone and their large, round lettering reflects awareness of physical charms and attributes. Figure 5 shows a dominant middle zone.

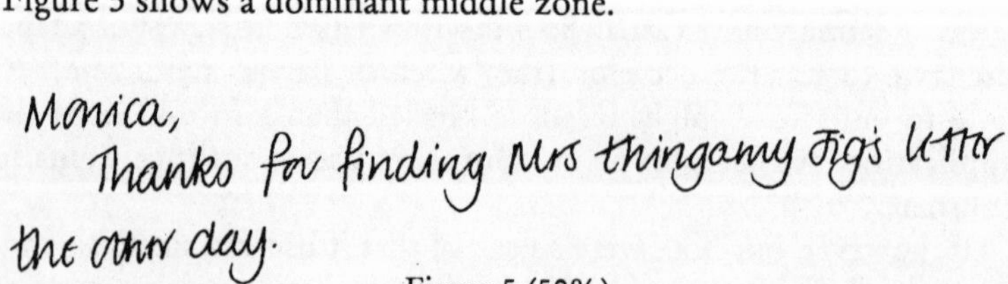

Monica,
Thanks for finding Mrs thingamy jig's letter the other day.

Figure 5 (50%)

Clues about instincts, appetites, energies and sexuality are manifest in the lower zone. Sports enthusiasts usually have a dominant lower zone (figure 6).

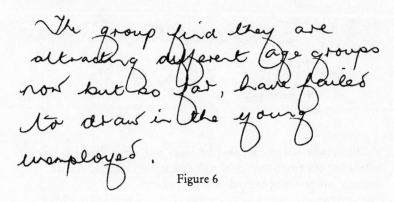

Figure 6

A script which is virtually without loops denotes indifferences. It can indicate that the writer has little or no interests outside himself or his immediate environment. But again, one must be wary. When other signs and symbols are taken into account, an entirely different interpretation might result. Corroborative evidence could show the 'loopless' writer to be physically disabled.

Here, as in every other aspect of grapho-analysis, it is vital to balance positive with negative, to add up all the pros and cons and never jump to conclusions.

Forms of lettering

There are four main forms of lettering, or writing styles: angular (figure 7), garland (figure 8), arcade (figure 9) and thready (figure 10).

As a general rule, the angular writer (with sharp and jagged letter connections) tends towards aggression, or at least self-assertion.

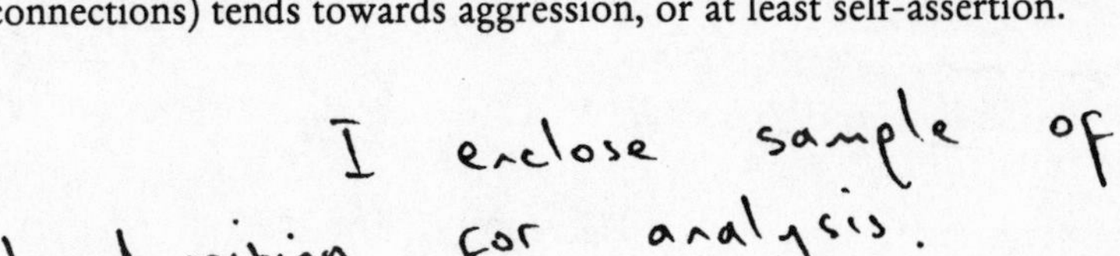

Figure 7 (65%)

The garland writer is warm-hearted, affectionate, tolerant and altogether more adaptable. Garland letter connections swing along like 'garlands', often turning 'm' and 'n' into a 'w' and 'u'.

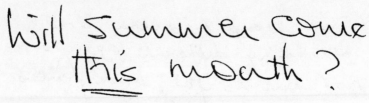

Figure 8

The arcade writer can also be kind and warm-hearted towards others but his emotions are usually kept well hidden. Arcade letter connections produce arched or rounded tops.

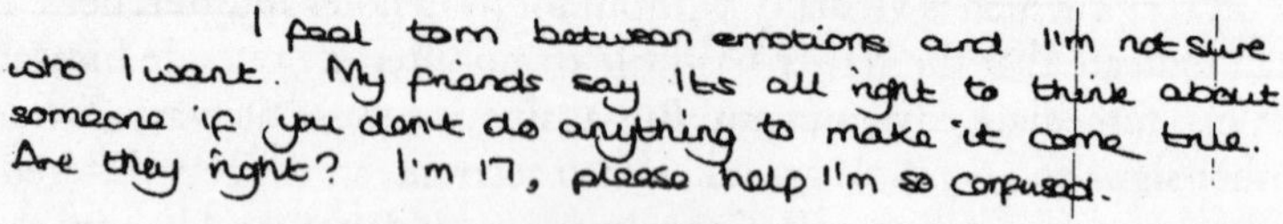

Figure 9 (50%)

The thready script is self-explanatory. It snakes along the page, often degenerating into an illegible scrawl because of the writer's tendency to neglect individual letters in his haste to write the word itself at speed. This type of writer is mentally alert, diplomatic and very talented, but under certain circumstances manipulative.

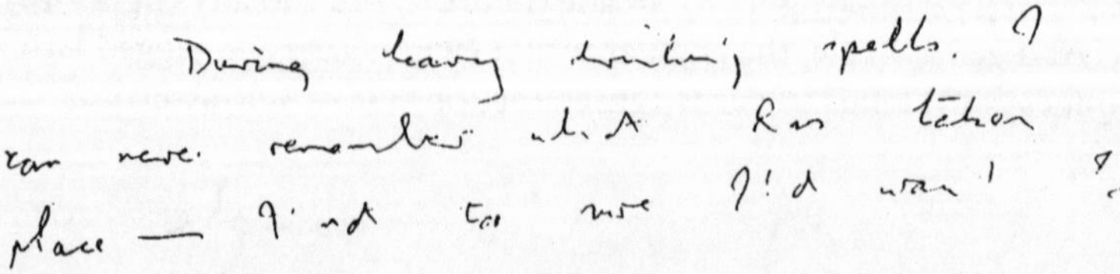

Figure 10

Slant

The slant, or angle, of the writing is how graphologists assess a writer's emotional trends.

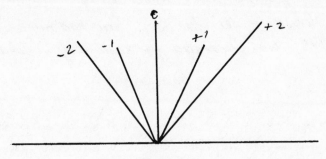

Figure 11

Vertical writing (0 in figure 11, illustrated in figure 12) or writing which slants only slightly to the right (0/+1) shows good judgement. These writers are cool, independent and totally in control of their feelings. They might have great depth of emotion but would seldom if ever show it. The more the writing slants to the right, the more emotional the writers is.

The writer with a pronounced rightward slant (+1 – figure 13) would respond sympathetically to the troubles of others and be very expressive himself. He might, for example, cry with sheer emotion on hearing the music of Brahms or watching a sad film.

An extreme rightward slant (+2) indicates extreme emotion. It is the mark of a writer who relates strongly to others, races around in circles, then comes to a sudden and dramatic halt, completely burnt out.

The writer with a backward-slanting script (figure 14) is the exact opposite. This person will hold back at all costs, forever putting brakes on emotions; the degree of the slant equates with the extent to which he is holding back.

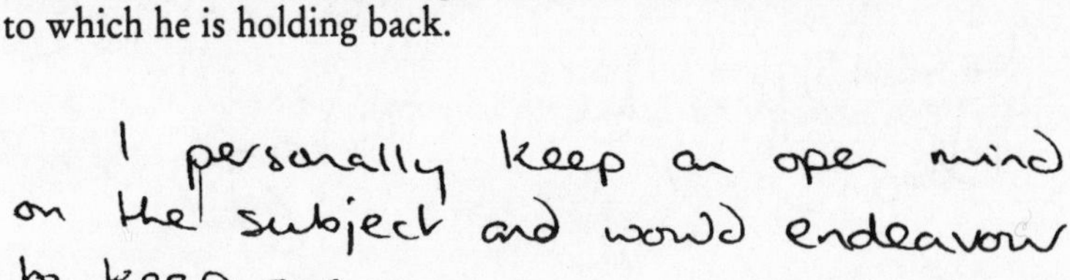

I personally keep an open mind on the subject and would endeavour to keep one.

Figure 12

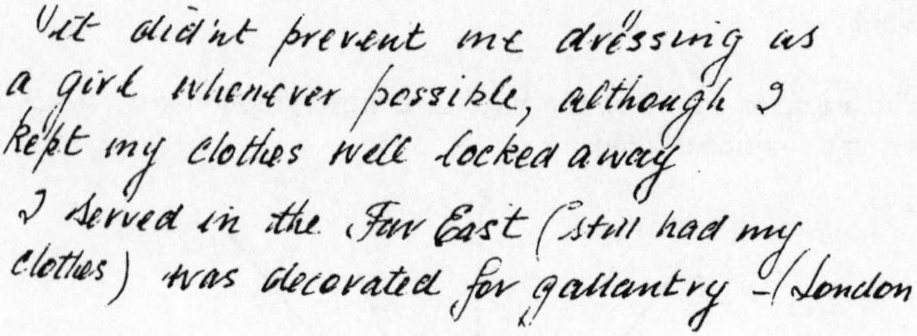

it didn't prevent me dressing as a girl whenever possible, although I kept my clothes well locked away. I served in the Far East (still had my clothes) was decorated for gallantry –(London

Figure 13

disapointed to find nothing in it helps me at all. The reading, of the help it gave to different People

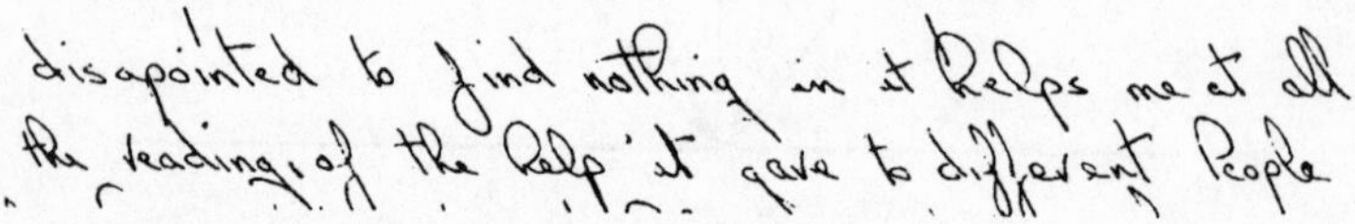

Figure 14 (65%)

Size

Lettering can vary tremendously in size. Large writing usually comes from someone who is active, self-assured and used to being the centre of attention, but not always. The writer of the sample in figure 15 is not at all confident, as is obvious from the overwriting and tumbling baseline.

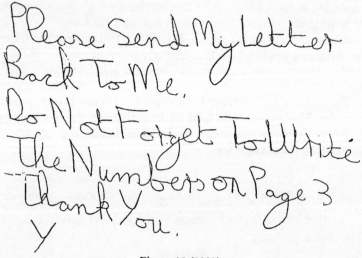

Please Send My Letter Back To Me, Do Not Forget To Write The Numbers on Page 3 Thank You. Y

Figure 15 (50%)

30

Medium-sized writing (figure 16) indicates a practical person.

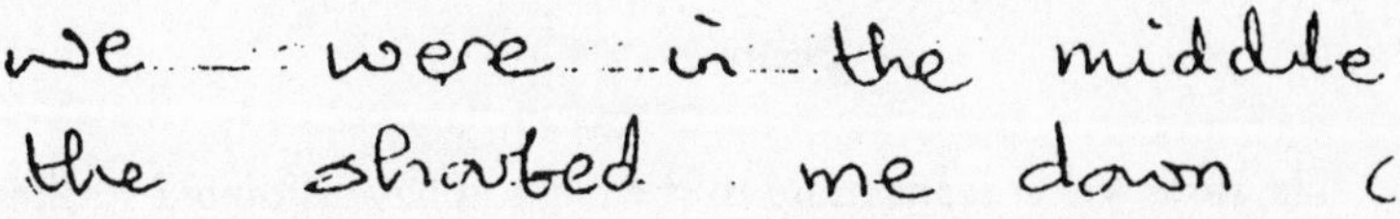

we — were in the middle
the shaoted me down (

Figure 16

A small script (figure 17) reflects shrewdness. It indicates a deep thinker. Very small writing shows excellent scientific or analytical abilities.

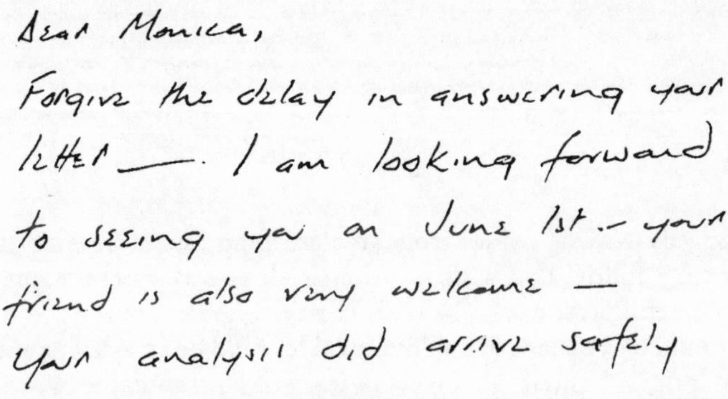

Dear Monica,
Forgive the delay in answering your
letter —. I am looking forward
to seeing you on June 1st. - your
friend is also very welcome —
your analysis did arrive safely

Figure 17

If a page of text begins with large letters and ends with small ones, it probably means that the writer has begun carefully but his real tendency has emerged towards the end.

The same conclusions may be drawn if the writing begins slowly but speeds up, begins smoothly with rhythm and balance but goes off course later or starts legibly but ends in a messy scrawl.

Speed

The signs of fast writing are a tendency to the right, a smooth unbroken stroke, rounded forms, possibly with words connected to each other, in some instances with the final letters trailing off to little more than a squiggly line. See figure 18.

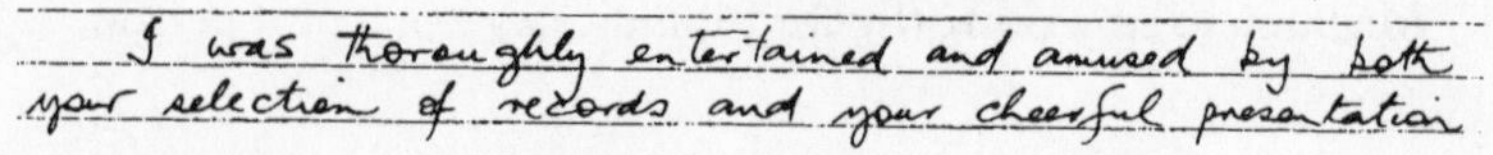

I was thoroughly entertained and amused by both your selection of records and your cheerful presentation

Figure 18 (50%)

The slow writer leans more to the left and has disjointed strokes, and the whole product is ornamental and flourishy (see figure 19). This writer is likely to break off to touch up letters, double-cross the *t*s or turn i-dots into little circles.

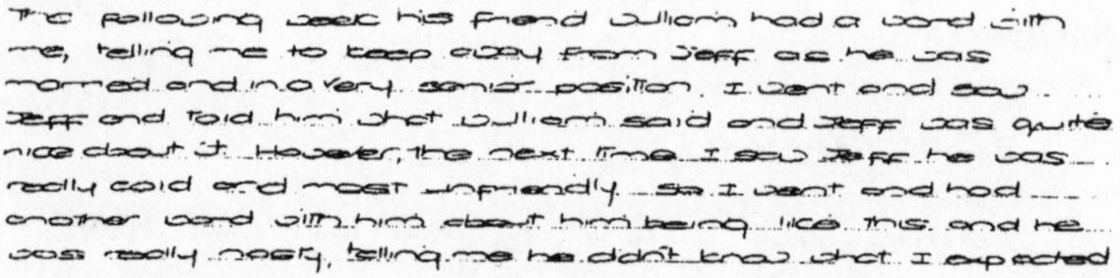

The following week his friend William had a word with me, telling me to keep away from Jeff as he was moody and in a very senior position. I went and saw Jeff and told him what William said and Jeff was quite nice about it. However, the next time I saw Jeff he was really cold and most unfriendly. So I went and had another word with him about him being like this, and he was really nasty, telling me he didn't know what I expected

Figure 19 (50%)

Speedy writing comes from an alert mind, but it does not automatically follow that a slow writer is slow-witted. He might be a very careful person who believes in paying great attention to detail. He could be a pedant or an illiterate. He could be an artist or a scribe who prides himself on every neat, carefully executed word. He could even be a confidence trickster. On the other hand, one must not rule out the possibility of his being physically or mentally disabled. There are no simple answers to these complicated conundrums. Every single pen stroke has its own meaning and all the constituent parts must be added up to complete the picture.

We each have our own individual style of writing. For some of us it is much as it was when we were children: a tedious chore, taking time and concentrated effort. For others, the pen becomes a race-horse, galloping at speed along the page.

Slow writing usually suggests a lack of spontaneity, while fast writing is the more natural style. The graphologist must be able not only to distinguish between them but also to say why one is fast and the other slow. Not all fast writing is spontaneous. There are occasions when it might have been penned by someone who normally writes at a slower pace but is rushing to catch the post.

We must consider too whether the fast writing has come from a mentally alert and quick-witted writer or one who is careless and untidy. Equally, not all slow writing is unspontaneous. It might be the work of a speedy writer hampered by an inferior writing instrument or rough paper.

In addition to the signs indicated above, rapid writing is also suggested when the i-dots and t-bars are placed high above and to the right of the letter, when i-dots are made into inverted commas or omitted altogether, or when the slant and width of the left margins shows a marked increase.

This type of writing usually comes from someone who lives life at speed. The race against the clock is reflected on the paper, i-dotting, punctuation-inserting and page-turning are often considered a waste of time. This writer's thoughts run ahead at such speed that he must commit everything to paper before he loses track of what he is trying to say. So he stays on the page as long as possible, sometimes even scribbling sideways up a margin and filling in any space left at the top (as in figure 20).

The graphologist must determine whether the slow writer is impeded by a poor grasp of language, whether he has deliberately slowed down in an attempt to impress, whether everything he does is meticulous and time-consuming or whether he is handicapped, physically or mentally.

Some slow writers are slow thinkers who cannot or will not be hurried. Their reasoning and knowledge are sound enough but their thought processes are held back. On the other hand, of course, there may well be a mechanical cause for slow writing, like an unfamiliar pen, an uneven writing surface or an aching wrist. No one sign in the writing will determine any of this. For a fair assessment, many considerations must be taken into account and balanced against each other. To complicate the issue further, not all the same signs have the same meanings. Certain marks which manifest themselves in slow writing might suggest something entirely different in the hand of a speedy writer.

Spacing

It is important to determine whether the words run straight into one another as they progress along the page. To get a feel for the spacing, we need to examine the page as a whole, taking into account the gaps left between lines, between words and within words, and the positioning of the margins.

We can view the written page as the writer's environment, the spaces between and within words as the distance he keeps between himself and others and the spaces between lines as the way he expresses his emotions. Therefore, people who shun social contact tend to leave wide spaces between the lines of their writing.

Baseline

The baseline is the line on which the words have been written (whether it is actually printed on the paper or not) and here we really see the importance of symbolism. A script which stays more or less on the baseline, fluctuating only slightly, indicates someone who keeps his feet on the ground. A rising line indicates enthusiasm, optimism and a happy disposition. Drooping lines hint at tiredness, depression and despondency. A wavering or disturbed alignment has very serious connotations.

Pen pressure

Is the pen pressure light, heavy or pasty? (Pasty or pastose pen strokes are thick and heavy and look as if a brush rather than a pen has been used.) Is there an emphasis at the beginning, suddenly in the middle, or only at the end? Is there an increase or decrease in pressure anywhere else? It is important to establish right at the outset whether the general style is spontaneous or not, whether it is simplified or embellished and whether it consists mainly of positive or negative traits.

By studying the pen pressure on a page of text, it is possible to identify the writer's energy level, personality traits, emotional trends and other facets of his character.

In high-quality writing, heavy pressure is usually the mark of an energetic writer (for the simple reason that it takes more energy to press hard on the page than to slide over it). In low-quality writing, however, the interpretation is completely different. Here, the energy expended in producing the script may well be because of unfamiliarity with the written word. Slow learners often press hard in their determined efforts to produce results. But again, other factors must be taken into account. People suffering from certain types of disability press hard on the page, yet may not be in the least energetic.

The high-quality writer whose pressure is light is likely to be sensitive and artistic. The low-quality writer with light pen pressure might simply be lazy. Again, one must always look for other signs and symbols.

Letter connections

Are the words separated or joined together, with several words written in one stroke, as in figure 20? When letters are linked together as the hand progresses along the page, a firm sense of purpose is indicated. The writer's mental processes are seen to be equally continuous. Here we have a systematic and razor-sharp mind, a writer whose thoughts are always clear and logical.

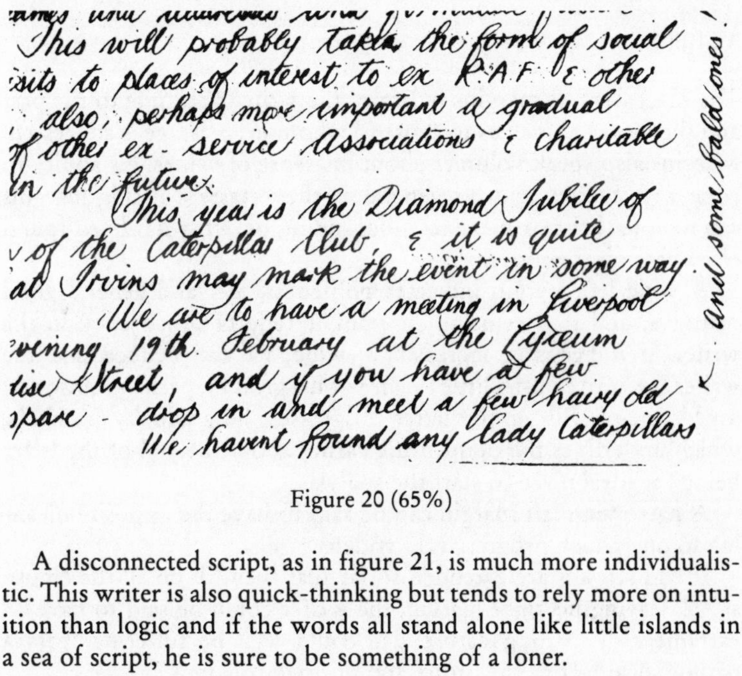

Figure 20 (65%)

A disconnected script, as in figure 21, is much more individualistic. This writer is also quick-thinking but tends to rely more on intuition than logic and if the words all stand alone like little islands in a sea of script, he is sure to be something of a loner.

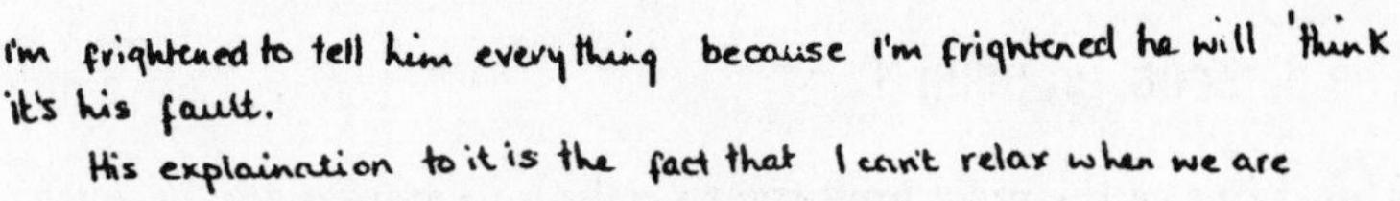

Figure 21 (70%)

35

Width

How narrow or broad are the words, how large or small are the letters within them? Broad writing is the work of someone who likes to spread himself over a wide area (in everyday life as well as on the written page). He thinks big, spends big, wines, dines and indulges himself. He may border on eccentricity, but remember to check the other signs, particularly size and pen pressure.

Narrow writing may be the work of someone who is unable to release his feelings and bottles everything up inside. Narrow writing with wide gaps between the words comes from someone who is likely to be shy and wary of forming personal relationships, particularly if the pressure is light.

Margins

The placement of margins indicates the writer's attitude to the past and the future as well as to those to whom his message is addressed. Margins also speak volumes about his sense of values, his ability to cope with money and his general aesthetic taste. Missing margins can denote thrift or meanness, depending on what has been found elsewhere on the page.

A wide left margin indicates politeness, tact and general good manners, and if it remains constant it reflects consistency in the writer. If it becomes increasingly wide, we can deduce that the writer has started off a little unsure of his ground, perhaps tense and on his guard. But as the letter progresses, he gradually unwinds, which underlines the point made earlier about the end of the letter being the ideal place to start the analysis.

A narrowing left margin can be said to have the opposite meaning to one which progressively widens.

If end strokes are extended so far that they fill up all the empty space, leaving no right margin, the writer could be said to have an extremely distrusting nature. He could well be suffering from a pathological fear of the future and his own role in it.

The personal pronoun 'I'

This is one of the most important symbols in graphology because it projects the writer's ideas about himself.

The structure of this letter alone can tell you about the current state of an individual's mental functioning. It can also, amazingly, give clear indications about early relationships with parents. Its structure is a very important graphological symbol, and for that reason it will be studied in more detail later. Suffice it to say here that it varies greatly from culture to culture. A simplified American version would appear ornate to British eyes.

Other factors

All the positive and negative aspects must be studied in depth and balanced against each other in order to determine whether the sample being scrutinized is regular or irregular, rhythmical or arhythmical, and of high, medium or low form-level.

3　The Main Signs and Symbols

Obviously, a graphologist cannot deduce the colour of someone's skin, his salary or what he was wearing at the time he penned his note. Nor can we be dogmatic about his profession or occupation. Tell-tale signs are sometimes seen in the hand, however, when 'tools of the trade' are incorporated into the text or signature.

A treble or bass clef might appear in the hand of a musician for example; one might notice a football here and there in a soccer player's writing, or a paintbrush in that of an artist.

The signature

Liberace, the flamboyant pianist, when signing his name, left no one in any doubt as to the nature of his profession – see figure 22.

Figure 22

Evil Knievel, the motor-cycle trick rider shows considerable flair and imagination in the signing of his name (figure 23). Note the symbolic wheels and handlebars on his 'flying' machine (which looks equally impressive if turned upside down, as indeed the machine itself must have been on many occasions).

Figure 23

Franz Anton Mesmer, the eighteenth-century Austrian physician, was the father of modern hypnotism, or mesmerism as it was originally known. With the huge, symbolic 'zzzzzzzzzzz' underlining this signature (figure 24), one can almost visualize a swinging watch or pendulum moving to and fro until the observer is overcome by sleep!

Figure 24

Faith Brown, the TV personality, comedienne and impressionist is best known for her brilliant 1980s impersonations of Margaret Thatcher, the then British Prime Minister. In terms of personal appearance, she is also known for her generous cleavage.

It does not stretch the imagination too far to see that magnificent bust in her signature and text (figure 25), both of which are big, bold and sensuous. We also see the mark of the comedienne in the little smile symbol. But most significant of all is in the way Faith has gone to such pains to erase her own identity in a subconscious decision to 'become' the characters she impersonates. The scoring through of a signature is very important graphologically. Normally, the erasure of self is one of the most negative signs a graphologist is ever likely to encounter, but here it is entirely positive, because the signature itself is such a happy one.

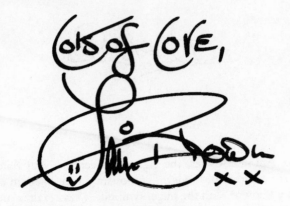

Figure 25 (50%)

I have seen similar sketches accompanying the signatures of Lewis Carroll, author of *Alice in Wonderland*, Rolf Harris, the artist, singer and TV personality, and Ken Dodd, the Liverpool comic.

The writing on a page of text represents the writer's attitude to others, but his signature reflects upon himself, providing an insight into his inner functioning. If the style of the signature and text are the same, the indications are that the writer is honest and straight-forward. If it differs dramatically from everything else on the page and it has been established that the same person has written both, the assumption must be that the writer presents one image to the public at large and another to those sharing his private life. For example, a huge signature combined with a small text would suggest that the writer gives an impression of being a big, showy sort of individual when in fact he is basically an intellectual. A small signature and huge text indicate the reverse.

Similarly, a strong, right-slanting signature and upright or back-slanting text suggests that the writer's outgoing public image is a mask, covering a nature which is reserved; possibly even shy.

Within the signature, the first (or given) name represents the personal ego, the second attitudes to family and society in general (enlarged or reduced, depending upon how the signer sees himself in relation to others). An enlarged first name indicates self-importance, self-assurance and independence. A diminished first name suggests low self-esteem and submissiveness.

When forename and surname are of the same size and slant, harmonious family relationships are indicated. But when they slant in opposite directions, vary in size and pressure and show other contradictory tendencies, the opposite may be the case.

The placing of the signature is also relevant. If it is to the left of the page, the writer is hesitant, uncertain and not very happy in either his domestic or his working life. A centralized signature would suggest a reasonably normal and happy outlook. A signature written on the right might indicate someone who (like the writer who leaves no right margin) is rather frightened of the future and distrustful of others.

Joining the first and second names together shows strong devotion to one's partner and family pride. A married woman who writes her surname larger and stronger than her forename reveals her attachment to her husband and her pride in his achievements. The fact that her own name has reduced itself means that she sees herself as being less important than her husband.

Underlining a signature is a sign of self-importance. If it is followed by a dot (full stop), the person is someone with whom it would be unwise to argue. He is likely to be dogmatic and unwilling to listen to the other person's point of view.

I-dots and t-bars

The correct positioning of i-dots and t-bars shows a writer who attaches a great deal of importance to correct behaviour and accuracy. To dot the *is* and cross the *ts*, he must interrupt his flow, and because these symbols are unconnected with the letters which precede or follow them, the writer can place his dots and bars wherever he chooses. And where he does place them gives the graphologist some fascinating insights into his personality.

However, before launching into a full-scale investigation of these signs it is important to establish whether the script being analysed is of high, medium or low form-level and also to determine its speed and pen pressure.

In a script of high form-level, low-placed i-dots can suggest first-rate powers of concentration, but in a low form-level script, they can indicate depression and despondency. Likewise high-placed dots can be the work of a writer with high ideals, or they can suggest imaginative processes bordering on fantasy. Dots to the right of the letter can be the work of a fast thinker or a tense one.

However, in general terms, i-dots shaped like acute accents are the mark of a perceptive writer, smile-shaped ones suggest a sense of humour and the heavy black blob variety indicate bluntness. The little circles sometimes seen in large, round scripts have different interpretations, depending on whether the writer is male or female. In the case of the female writer, they show a longing for attention and a wish to be different. In the hand of a male, they suggest artistic ability.

The undotted *i* also has different interpretations. In a slow hand, it shows carelessness, forgetfulness, unreliability and a lack of attention to detail. In a fast hand, there are no sinister connotations because speed is probably the reason for the missing dot.

The writer who connects his i-dots or t-bars with the following letter has a superior intellect. He is clever, thinks quickly and enjoys exercising his mind.

The placement of the t-bar can be interpreted similarly. The copybook method of writing the letter is by running the stem from top to bottom, ending with a slight upward curve. The cross-bar, which should be fairly near the top of the stem should run from left to right.

Obstinacy and a quick temper are suggested when the letter or its bar begin or end with an irritated little tick. If the t-bar is placed to the left of the stem the writer could be said to be unhappy in his present environment, particularly if i-dots are similarly placed.

The letter *f*

It may seem rather simplistic to suggest that *f* is a particularly significant letter because of its association with an obscene four-letter word. Nevertheless, the 'f-word' which was once acceptable in everyday language but is now classed as obscene, retains its original meaning in our subconscious minds and therefore in our scripts.

By its dominance or sublimation on the page, this one letter can provide real clues about the writer's sexuality. It is also important to check whether it appears in copybook form or deviates in any way. The upper loop gives clues about the writer's attitudes to and thoughts about sex; the lower loop relates to the act.

An inflated upper loop or curve might indicate lively thoughts about sex, and if the loop in the lower zone is of the same size and style, the writer could be said to lead a lively and active sexual life. Conclusions can therefore be drawn from letter structures about where there is disharmony between the two.

Constricted loops speak for themselves in that they suggest that the writer has some sexual hangups. Letters in which the lower loop is incomplete or does not return to the baseline speak of sexual performance. Other meaningful signs include loops which have been blacked out (suggesting writer has blacked out the whole concept of sex from his mind), scored through or slant in the opposite direction to every other word on the page. When the loop is replaced by a little tick, suspect irritation and frustration, possibly related to impotence, sterility or frigidity.

The under-loops of *g*s and *y*s

Other significant letters for graphological investigation are *g*s and *y*s. These, too, are full of sexual symbolism and the same principles apply as to the analysis of the letter *f*. A writer's basic urges, instincts and desires are all clearly manifest in the lower zones of these letters. Suspect trouble if they appear as blacked-out smudges, are overwritten, slanting in the wrong direction or entwined around themselves in a thoroughly confusing manner.

Figure 26

An upstroke which prematurely crosses the downstroke as in figure 26, indicates celibacy – either voluntary or enforced through impotence, sterility or frigidity. If enforced, it may be because some chronic illness, such as diabetes or kidney failure, has rendered the writer incapable of sex. Another possibility is alcoholism. Whenever the upstroke does not return to the baseline the implication is that the writer is not sexually active. This formation of the *g* is frequently seen in the script of older people.

Normal writing is full of healthy-looking loops, with soft, round, firm strokes. Where the lower loops are thin and entangled – particularly if the pressure is light and hesitant – weakness, disability, age or nervous exhaustion are indicated. Obsessive or compulsive behaviour patterns are manifest in a *y* formed as in figure 27 or figure 28.

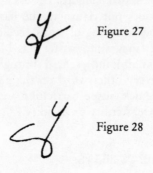

Figure 27

Figure 28

Figure 28 is rather similar to the phenomenon of the double leg-lock, where a young woman will cross her legs in such a way that one becomes locked around the other, as in figure 29.

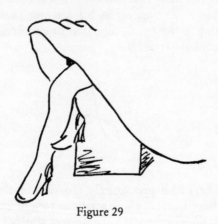

Figure 29

Both the letter and the leg-lock suggest a very defensive attitude. Shyness and timidity are indicated by this posture. Penning under-lengths thus is a subconscious statement that the writer is only at ease when she has retreated into her shell.

Figure 30

A hugely exaggerated underloop, as in figure 30, indicates an inflated ego. Someone who consistently writes such large lower loops is the sort of person who takes centre stage in public but is inadequate and unhappy in private. The writer of this type of letter is never quite what he seems; superficiality is suggested.

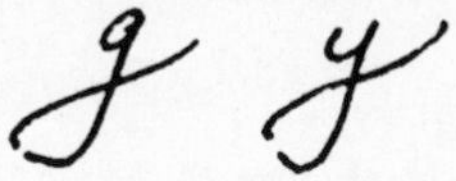

Figure 31

A g or y with a break at the bottom of the loop (figure 31) may suggest virginity but may also point to a sensitive, apprehensive writer who finds sexual practices offensive and against his strict code of behaviour. But rather than jump to conclusions in this as in every other instance, it is wise to examine the rest of the script to ensure that these breaks do not appear in other letters and throughout all three zones, making them a regular pattern of the writing. In that case suspect some sort of trauma to the system or even an irregularity in the heartbeat.

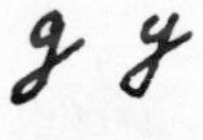

Figure 32

A letter which is regular and of the correct shape, but which appears in miniature (as in figure 32), hints at repression and tension.

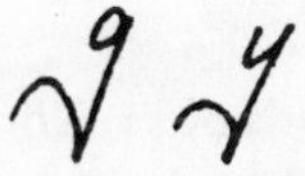

Figure 33

45

The claw sign depicted in the g and y in figure 33 is almost always negative. It has many interpretations, among them greed and the avoidance of sexual and other responsibilities. It is also frequently seen in the hands of writers with very little self-value and sometimes in the writing of women who have suffered the loss of a baby (recognized in graphological circles as the 'upturned cradle').

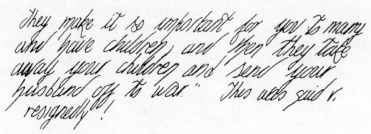

Figure 34 (65%)

With the bizarre letter structures seen in figure 34, one might expect to find equally bizarre lower zone formations, but it is not so. All the lower zones in this career woman's writing tell us is that, for reasons best known to herself, she is not terribly interested in sex.

The next writer (figure 35) says his problem is of a private nature. But very little is hidden from a graphologist, and the clue to his problem lies in the fractured bottoms of his lower loops.

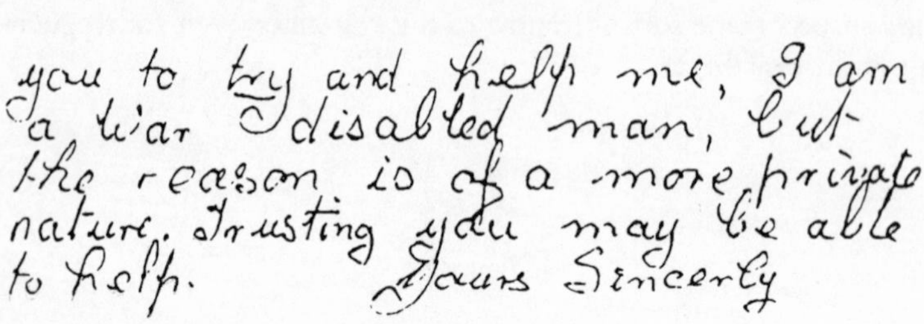

Figure 35 (65%)

Capitals

Printed capitals are the work of someone who likes simplification and has the ability to grasp a situation in its most basic form. This is particularly so if capitals are combined with a simplified script. Such

46

writers are clear-minded and articulate and they attach considerable importance to making themselves understood.

Starting and ending strokes

Within words, the writer must adhere more or less to standard shapes and forms, but outside the actual words, he is free to form letters however he pleases. When he stops to write a new word, he can choose to delay starting, or he can linger over the entire message in order to prolong his endings.

The beginnings and endings of words are therefore more significant than one might imagine. The longer the starting stroke, the longer the writer likes to pause before getting down to the task in hand. Caution is indicated, although he could be just a ditherer, too fond of procrastination. The writer who holds on to the ending stroke shows tenacity, but he is also likely to be someone who lingers over his farewells.

Other signs and symbols

To see how people function as individuals, we must examine the handwriting for various other signs and symbols. We need for example, to establish whether the lower-case *a*s and *o*s are open at the top (writer is a social type) or closed at the top (writer keeps confidences) and if any letters have been overwritten, scored through or omitted altogether (these last three suggesting stress). Something else which needs to be established early on in the analysis is whether any of the letters stand out and therefore have special significance, and whether they are confused or torn apart.

Fluctuating styles

An individual who appears to have several different styles of handwriting could be said to be mercurial. If the style is consistent but the letters within fluctuate from left to right, a moody nature is indicated.

Writers who have fluctuating styles of signature could be said to have problems of personal identity, unless one of these styles has been deliberately cultivated for business purposes in order to avoid forgery.

These are only guidelines, however. For an accurate reading, every little detail must be taken into consideration, every little section pieced together jigsaw-fashion before the completed picture can emerge. Corroborative evidence is essential every inch of the way.

Potential problems

Some graphologists claim that one cannot conduct an analysis except on writers of their own nationality, others that one needs several samples from the same person and others that readings from pencil, ballpoint or felt-tip scripts are not possible. I reject all of these claims.

Take American handwriting, for example. Most of what we see today originated from the nineteenth-century Spencerian system. No pressure is required in this system, so it is often *easier* to analyse than many British hands, and when pressure does appear, it is that much more significant.

The analysis of writings in other languages is certainly more difficult, particularly if the analyst has not been given any idea of the writer's nationality, so as to establish upon which letter structures the script is based. It is not quite so easy to penetrate the mind of the writer if the instrument of penetration is, as it were, blunted. Without knowing how a letter is supposed to look, one cannot easily determine how it might have deviated from the norm, if at all. So some of the more subtle nuances may be missed. But it can be done. If I can draw a parallel, it is like the difference between a medical and a veterinary examination. In the first case, patients are able to provide verbal clues, in the second they are not. But the mode of examination is not very different. In any case, analysts who place emphasis on interpreting strokes will find that the texture of the writing is what matters, and the language is of secondary importance.

Similarly, having several samples of writing does make it easier to build up a comprehensive personality assessment. However, an adequate reading can often be produced from a single sample, provided that it is pointed out that the analysis can only be based on the state of the writer's mind (and body) at the time he actually produced it.

As for blaming the tools, with a little effort it is possible to write well enough for a spot analysis with virtually anything. Quick scribbles can sometimes be very meaningful.

While the style of writing produced by a fountain pen does lend itself more easily to a full analysis, the careless flow from an 'inferior' instrument is often more relaxed because spontaneity is its strength. A writer who is tense and nervous invariably holds back something of himself. When penning a letter, he begins carefully, stopping occasionally to collect his thoughts. So the writing starts off by being guarded. As the letter progresses and the writer begins to get into the flow, so does his script. By the time he reaches the end of the letter, he is relaxed, and so is his writing.

Analyses

'Spot' analyses are always popular with the media and with audiences following luncheon or after-dinner talks, but they can only show general trends. The conscientious analyst will take an entire day or more to conduct an in-depth reading, particularly if the purpose is to check for indications of ill health.

Every little detail speaks multitudes, which is why good lighting and strong magnification are essential for successful psychographology. The magnifier can often pick up tiny clues missed by the naked eye.

For best results, the writer should have a reliable pen, use one side of the paper only and produce a page of text plus a signature. In my own case, if the sample has been written specifically for analysis, it helps considerably if it is accompanied by a few free-flowing drawings and doodles.

In the 25 years or so I have been working as a professional graphologist, I have found that the higher the intellect of the writer, the easier it is to conduct an analysis. The explanation is simple: the higher the intellect, the more attuned the individual is to his own unconscious mind.

The handwriting analyst must always dig deep below the surface, study his findings closely, weigh up the evidence and work out all the permutations. Only then is he in a position to tailor the results to suit the needs of the individual.

Those of us who specialize in health aspects are entering the very deepest regions of the writer's mind. We are delving around in a real

Pandora's Box and extracting as much as we possibly can. Depending on the state of the 'box' and its contents, rummaging around in there can be a thoroughly exhausting exercise. The more troubled the mind, the more draining the probe.

This book is not a graphology primer: its purpose is to concentrate on issues of health, and, it is to these issues we now turn.

4   Dominant Health Signs

When a single feature in the writing prevails over all others by the marked frequency of its occurrence, thus dominating the entire psychological image, that feature is described as 'dominant'. Certain dominant themes have particular health implications.

Loop breaks

The scene was a college lecture hall, the time a year or two ago. I was giving an informal talk to a group of medical students and nurses, with a few doctors thrown in for good measure. At the end of the talk I offered to do a few informal readings. Because people do like to be told something of themselves and because the mood had become relaxed, the response was overwhelming.

Among the scraps of paper passed to me was one I could not resist. A fast, spontaneous script, it was clear and articulate – the work of a concise thinker whose mind was logical, whose judgement was sound and intellectual. Manual dexterity was not in doubt, but it did contain one tiny sign of vulnerability which warranted further investigation, if only to satisfy myself about the writer's state of health.

Although the entire piece only ran to a few paragraphs, I was in no doubt as to the cause of its dominant theme. But I still wanted a word with the writer, if only to prove my findings. Waving the sample aloft, I asked if whoever was responsible for it would mind identifying himself. Intrigued, a rather amused grey-haired man at the back of the hall said the sample was his. He was one of the college lecturers, a medical man.

'Tell me, doctor,' I began. 'Did you suffer from scarlet or rheumatic fever as a child?'

The smile was replaced by a look of astonishment as he admitted: 'I had scarlet fever when I was ten.'

'And you have an irregular heartbeat?'

'Right again.'

'Would I be right in suggesting extra-systoles?'

'Bang on!' said he, pensively scratching the top of his head. 'But . . . how the deuce can you tell something like that from my writing?' I had the feeling he suspected collusion of some sort.

'Because the signs are there in your script.'

'Go on then, tell us all. What *are* they?'

Having spent the previous hour or so listening to what I had to say about the brain controlling those of the body's reflexes which cause the movements necessary for writing, the doctor was quite happy to accept my comments about how we stamp our individuality on the paper with every line, angle and curve.

He was also happy with the concept of unconscious mind and writing being intimately related, knowing full well that one was born of the other. What puzzled him was the nature of this so-called dominant theme I had referred to. He re-examined his brief sample of writing but could detect nothing unusual about it.

It was a tiny, but regular break appearing at the same point in every one of his upper loops, leaving them slightly weaker than all the other pen-strokes. This very minor fragmentation suggested a phenomenon familiar to any analyst who has ever investigated the health aspects of graphology – how imperfections of the body (as opposed to those of the mind) show up in the hand by manifesting themselves in the appropriate part of the writing. Imperfections produce erratic and weakened movements in the areas of the script representing those parts of the body. For example, a flow of writing interrupted in the upper zone would represent a problem in the upper region of the body, in the middle zone weakness or pain in the trunk area, and in the lower zone a problem in the hip, knee or foot.

The flow interruption in the doctor's script occurred in the upper zone, in the region representing his heart. Once I had led him back along the route to the origin of the interruption he could immediately see how irregularities of beat might manifest themselves on the written page and was perfectly happy with the findings. He conceded that suddenly it all made sense.

He even went on to explain in more detail why it should be so. Extra-systoles, he confirmed, could follow an attack of scarlet fever, rheumatic fever or diphtheria – all of which serious infectious illnesses were commonplace when he was growing up in the 1940s but had virtually disappeared thanks to the discovery of antibiotics.

Extra-systoles are an irregularity of rhythm often found in otherwise normal hearts. They occur when the heart contracts following an impulse arising outside the norm and are no real cause for concern unless associated with diseases of the cardiovascular system. In fact, they often pass unnoticed by the patient. And sure enough there it was on the written sample, the split-second 'jump' of the heart resulting in the split-second 'jump' on the paper, hence the giveaway breaks in his loops.

However, it cannot be overemphasized that before examining possible complicated reasons for any changes in pen pressure or breaks in loops, it is always advisable to eliminate the possibility of a bad writing instrument, uneven surface or other external factors.

Incidentally, in mentioning the condition of extra-systoles I was not diagnosing an illness. The writer who produced them was not ill. All I was doing was demonstrating how a split-second break in the heart's rhythm could produce a split-second break in the hand's movement. The fact that I happened to be familiar with the medical term for this break is irrelevant. The point is that when a sample of writing is characterized by the regular appearance of an unusual sign or symbol, there is a reason for it.

The sample referred to above is unfortunately no longer available, because the doctor insisted on keeping it as a souvenir, but it was something like figure 36.

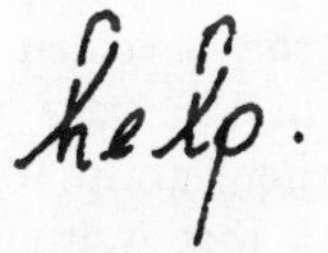

Figure 36

Resting dots

The extract in figure 37 was written in 1918 by a 17-year-old student teacher.

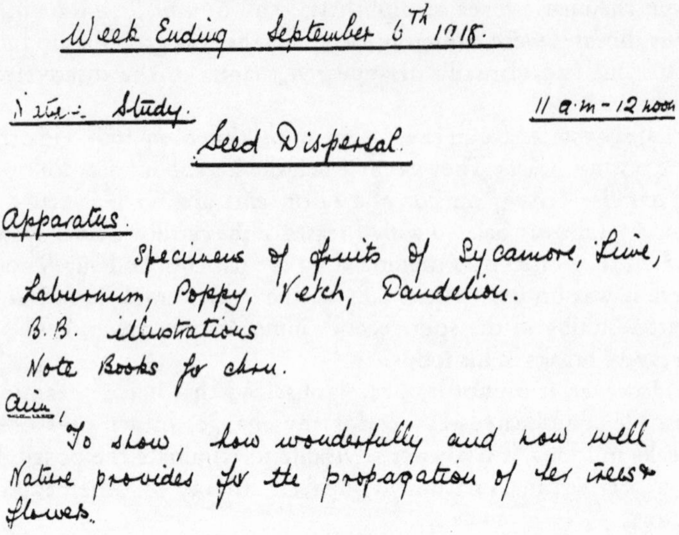

Week Ending September 6th 1918.

Nature: Study.   11 a·m - 12 noon
              Seed Dispersal.

Apparatus.
              Specimens of fruits of Sycamore, Lime,
Laburnum, Poppy, Vetch, Dandelion.
B.B. illustrations
Note Books for class.
Aim.
       To show, how wonderfully and now well
Nature provides for the propagation of her trees &
flowers.

Figure 37 (50%)

The style is flowing, flexible, balanced and rhythmic, indicating a bright, alert mind, even though the upper loops are inhibited and the lower somewhat confused. Nevertheless, when one considers that well-bred young ladies of the period were not encouraged to give vent to their feelings, it is hardly surprising to find sexual inhibitions and confusion. What is surprising is the sight of at least a dozen resting dots – tiny blob-like spots which appear in the writings of individuals suffering from exhaustion.

They are the symbolic equivalent of a housewife whose bag of groceries is so heavy that the only way she can carry it home is by allowing it to drop on the pavement at regular intervals while regaining her strength. In the same way, when the pen drops momentarily from the writer's grasp, it does so because the writer's mental exhaustion is such that writing is not possible without a break, even for a short period.

A healthy young student teacher on the brink of her professional career should not be showing such negative signs in her script. Those dots, the general tautness of the script, the shaky *u* in 'nature' and the blacking out of certain letters (*p* in 'specimens' and *o* in 'flowers') indicate considerable stress. Worry about forthcoming examinations is the most likely explanation. Furthermore, worry could well be responsible for the sharp, pointed peaks of the double *l*s in 'wonderfully' and 'well', which point to severe headaches. Poor thing, what agonies she must have suffered during those years of study.

The postcard shown in Figure 38 comes from the same writer, aged 63.

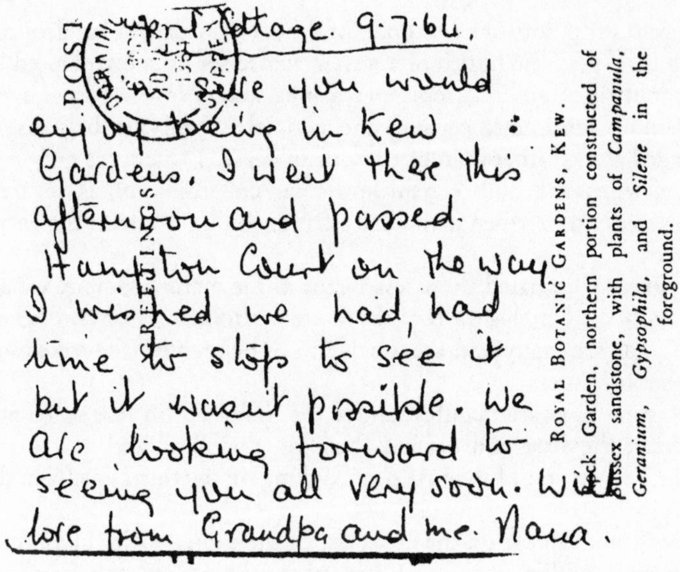

Figure 38

The first change we notice is that the slant has changed from slightly forward to upright. This tells us that however fond of company the writer might have been as a young woman, she was no longer keen on socializing. Also, although her vision does not appear to be defective, nor her judgement impaired, the script has lost its flexibility in maturity. Now the negative signs and symbols are connected more with her state of health than her age.

There is no further evidence of headaches, but there is some weakness of pressure in the upper zone indicating physiological illness. Unlike the doctor's irregular heartbeat described above, this type of weakness is more likely to be related to lung function; indeed chronic bronchitis was subsequently confirmed by the relative who provided the sample. Pressure changes in some letters and furring over of others are both classic signs of chronic disease. And the resting dots are back, but more seriously they are now accompanied by pen trails.

Pen trails

While resting dots are symbolic of a heavy burden being dropped for a brief rest, the health of a writer whose script is interrupted by pen trails is in an even more precarious state. Now we have overwhelming weakness, causing the pen (the symbolic bag) to be dragged along rather than lifted with any ease. These signs only ever occur when the body's neuromuscular co-ordination is severely compromised or when mental stress is such that it affects the entire system.

Having eliminated the stress factor in the mature sample, we are left with the conclusion that the writer's problem is physiological. The signs are many and those which can be seen by the naked eye appear as follows.

Resting dots are manifest above the first 'had' in line seven and between the first and second 'had' on that line, and above and slightly to the left of the first *o* in 'looking' in the third line from the bottom.

Pen trails appear on the cross bar of the capital *H* in 'Hampton' (line six); within the word 'to' (third line from the bottom); running towards the *s* in 'seeing' and over the *s* in 'soon' (penultimate line); and nestling under the starting stroke of the *l* in 'love' (last line).

The findings from this sample are not good. Everything adds up to a picture of muscular weakness, respiratory problems and a precarious state of general health. Not being a diagnostician, I was not in a position to state the nature or cause of the muscular weakness, nor of the respiratory problems (which could be related to asthma, bronchitis, emphysema or a host of other conditions for which only a doctor could give a definitive diagnosis). All I could do was pick out areas of weakness in the script and conclude that this writer was not exactly in the peak of health. I could not say whether she was critically, or even seriously, ill, and even if I could, it would not have been my place to make such a statement. In fact, she was gravely ill at the time of writing the postcard, and she had a sudden and catastrophic stroke shortly afterwards.

The effects of age

I read a detective story recently in which the hero made a 'brilliant' assumption regarding a suspect's handwriting. A young man was alleged to have forged his father's signature and was feeling pleased with himself because he thought he had got away with his crime. The forgery was so cleverly executed that it fooled everyone until the detective appeared on the scene.

Our hero examined some samples of the father's writing, compared them with the suspect document and immediately recognized the forgery. 'Easy,' he told his sidekick. 'It was the work of a young hand, whereas the other signature had clearly been written by an old man.' Problem solved.

Only it was not solved, at least not for me. That sort of situation never occurs outside fiction, because the actual detection of forgeries is considerably more complicated and warrants a book in itself. Suffice it to say that it is virtually impossible to work out chronological age from someone's writing.

However, certain signs do manifest themselves in the hands of the elderly. These signs may include a generalized intellectual decline, loss of vitality and failing eyesight, but I must emphasize the word 'may'. Some elderly people are more sprightly than people half their age, in writing as well as in everything else. To further confuse the graphologist, there is a medical condition known as presenility, which can occur in people as young as 40 and which can have the effect of making a middle-aged hand look elderly. Intellect and emotions can be affected, with the rhythm of a hand accordingly knocked off balance. A jerky hand can reduce what had previously been high form-level writing to something bordering on illegibility.

Neurotic tendencies, hitherto repressed, may come to the fore in old age with the resultant effects on writing. Some elderly people revert to childhood behaviour and their writing also takes on an immature look. 'Trendy' senior citizens, unwilling to face up to their years, might cultivate what they consider to be a 'young' style of writing just as they might adopt a young style of dress and behaviour. So the graphologist who positively states a writer's age is foolish indeed.

'Grapho-therapy'

There are those who contend that by changing one's style of writing, it is possible to change one's character and so eliminate all one's nasty negative trends. It may indeed be possible, but it is surely most unwise. If the writing shows negative trends, then it seems to me that the obvious answer is to find out the cause of those trends and eliminate them. A graphologist (or 'grapho-therapist') who tries to change someone's writing style is simply masking that person's symptoms, and that is never advisable. In any case, it is my firm belief that it is no part of the graphologist's work to *treat* those whose writing has been presented to him for analysis.

To take an analogy, a doctor treating a patient for a sore throat will not have the throat anaesthetized to deaden the soreness. The patient will be treated for the condition which caused the throat to be sore in the first place. In other words, the doctor will tackle the underlying cause of the problem rather than eliminating the symptoms.

So it should be with handwriting. Negative signs should not be changed or removed without a proper investigation of the cause, otherwise they will simply turn up elsewhere. Forcing a writer whose natural style slopes backwards to write with a forward slant is likely to put the writer's mind into a state of utter confusion. In attempting to turn, say, an ugly, scrawling hand into a stylish one, these 'therapists' are in effect trying to fabricate a new identity, and trying to change someone's nature can be a most precarious business.

I once came across a girl who had been 'treated' by an analyst who practised this form of graphology. She told me that having seen her writing, he recommended certain 'improvements' and over a period of several months succeeded in making her acquire a style more to his taste. It was far removed from her natural style and was executed with great effort. As a direct result of this treatment, her flow of writing became stilted, but so too did her speech.

Before she realized what was happening, she found herself beginning to stutter. When the cause of her speech impediment was discovered, she reverted to writing – and speaking – in her original natural and fluent style.

If attempts to change handwriting are to be successful they should be self-motivated. Handwriting is complicated enough without making it more so. The best and most enjoyable way of transforming an untidy hand into a beautiful one is to take up calligraphy.

Mirror writing

Mirror writing runs from right to left and is so called because it forms a mirror image of normal script. Right-handed children often find that when they try writing with the left hand the result is mirror writing. They usually lose the knack as they grow older. Two students of my acquaintance automatically resort to mirror writing as examinations approach. This seems to suggest certain psychological factors in adults who adopt the habit, but that is not necessarily so.

To read the message contained in figure 39 one needs to stand in front of a mirror, but to decipher the signature the sample must be turned upside down. This sample was handed to me as I was about to do a live radio phone-in on graphology. The writer was an alert septuagenarian, perfectly sound in mind and body, but she enjoyed experimenting with her pen, and was blessed with a strong sense of fun.

A consultant neurologist who advises me on complex issues such as this assures me that there is nothing abnormal about the personality of this writer. He describes her as a mental gymnast. 'Some people mirror write for the same reason that others stand on their head,' he explains. 'It pleases them to do so.'

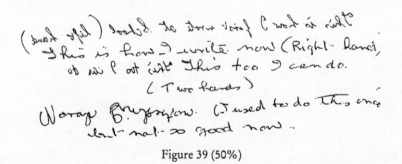

Figure 39 (50%)

Right-handed people who are paralysed on the right side of the body sometimes discover that when they attempt to write with the left hand the letters are reversed. The conclusion must be that once

59

the right hand has grasped the ability to write normally the performance of the same movements in reverse by the left hand is an automatic function of the unconscious.

Part II
Probing Deeper

5 The Personal Pronoun 'I' and Other Ego-symbols

Our grandparents believed that the eyes mirrored the soul. This may well be the case, but eyes can glaze over, become cloudy and give out very confusing messages as they hide behind dark glasses or tinted contact lenses. For my money, the best 'eyes' through which to gain an insight into someone's personality are the personal pronouns. I find the study of a writer's personal pronoun 'I' (PPI) a very reliable method of character assessment. Close scrutiny of that one important symbol enables a graphologist to obtain a strong image of the writer's functioning and behaviour.

The PPI and one's parents

The PPI is an extremely important graphological symbol – it holds the key to our personality and our attitude towards those around us and those responsible for our very conception. In-depth exploration of this one symbol can provide the greatest of all clues with regard to the writer's personal identity. In terms of childhood experiences, it reflects on his basic behavioural patterns.

While the signature has traditionally been accepted as the stamp of self, the personal pronoun has an even greater significance. The structure of the PPI really shows the current state of the writer's mental functioning and goes on to provide clear indications about early relationships with his parents as well as theirs with each other.

Each section of the PPI reflects the part individual parents played in the development of a writer, so male and female symbolism provide potent clues about paternal and maternal influences. An equal balance between the upper and lower sections, for example, tells us that the parents themselves were well matched.

The upper part of the PPI relates to the mother (or mother-substitute), the lower to the father (or father-substitute). With that in mind, we can determine the influences each parent had on the writer during his formative years. If we take the arcs and curves of the upper section to symbolize the very first maternal embrace, then the structure of the lower section must represent basic paternal functioning.

When either section appears in circular form, the encirclement reflects the warmth of the writer's feelings towards the relevant parent. When one section of the letter consists of sharp lines and the other of curves, the basic principles of sharp lines representing aggression and curves representing warmth apply. If either section is missing, the obvious conclusion is that the relevant parent did not figure prominently in the writer's upbringing, if at all.

Figure 40 features a very odd-shaped PPI.

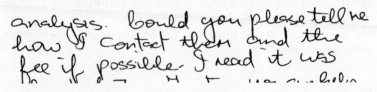

Figure 40 (65%)

While the father symbol is an integral part of the pronoun, taking its normal left turning from the base of the stem, the mother has become a separate entity. It appears to have been inserted as an after-thought. The tangled lines and letters snaking from zone to zone point to emotional disturbance.

Figure 41 shows much warmth towards the mother, but the father is hardly in evidence at all.

In figure 42 we have the opposite situation, with the writer showing hardly any feelings towards her mother, and all the warmth towards her father.

The very sharp PPI in figure 43 speaks of double rejection. The signs show that neither of the writer's parents showed any warmth towards her or each other. Small wonder then that she cannot show any affection for her husband. Such a troubled upbringing is bound to have an adverse effect on her. It is sad but understandable that the writer's marriage has broken down.

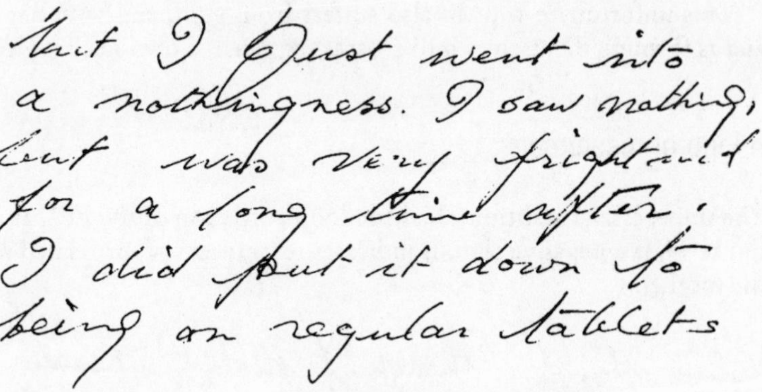

that I just went into
a nothingness. I saw nothing,
but was very frightened
for a long time after.
I did put it down to
being on regular tablets

Figure 41 (65%)

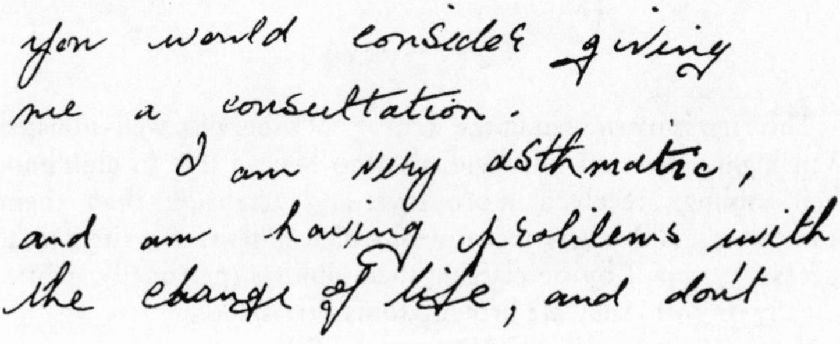

you would consider giving
me a consultation.
          I am very asthmatic,
and am having problems with
the change of life, and don't

Figure 42 (65%)

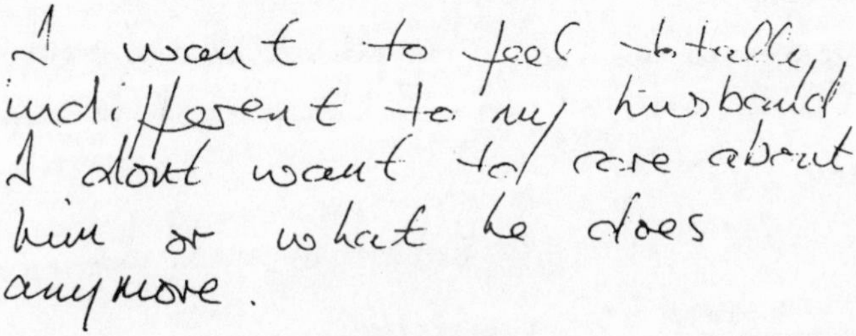

I want to feel totally
indifferent to my husband
I don't want to care about
him or what he does
anymore.

Figure 43 (50%)

We have already interpreted the negative aspects of the 'upside-down cradle' in descenders. The cradle sign at the base of this writer's pronoun is often seen in the hands of those who have experienced or are experiencing marital trouble.

This unfortunate woman also suffers from guilt, and with her *t*s and *f*s forming themselves into crosses the cause is obvious: religion.

A loop of resentment

The unnecessary addition of a little loop at the top of the PPI, as in figure 44, is a negative sign. It indicates resentment of, or related to, the mother.

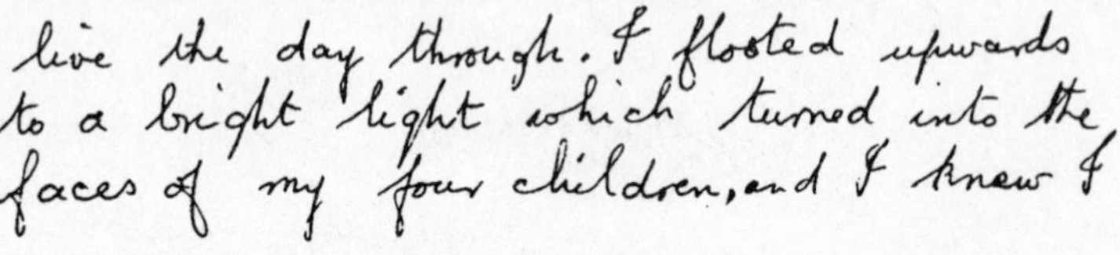

live the day through. I floated upwards
to a bright light which turned into the
faces of my four children, and I knew I

Figure 44 (65%)

This sign is often seen in the writings of otherwise well-adjusted, even highly successful, individuals who believe that in childhood their siblings received more love and attention than them. Sometimes it is this very resentment which spurs such writers on to success. It is as if by outclassing their siblings (personally, professionally or both) they are proving some private point.

Figure 45 also contains a loop-topped PPI.

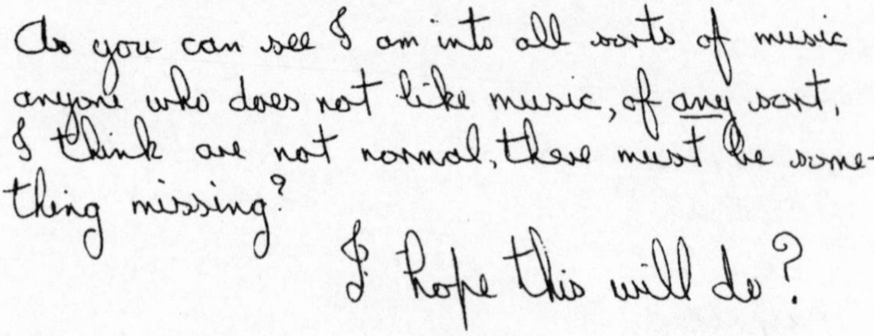

As you can see I am into all sorts of music
anyone who does not like music, of any sort,
I think are not normal, there must be something missing?

I hope this will do?

Figure 45 (50%)

A left-slanting rather inhibited hand, it contains many negative signs, but this man is not the type to let things get on top of him (the writing, like his self-confidence, develops and enlarges as he progresses down the page.)

As he is at pains to point out, all his energies have been directed into the enjoyment of music. It is the one great love of his life – so much so that his PPI begins to take on the shape of a treble clef (figure 46), thus providing us with another variation on the theme of a personal pronoun.

Figure 46

A lack of warmth

Figure 47 features a PPI with no mother symbol and the mere suggestion of one for father. This writer is very verbal and articulate. She is bright (as indicated by the delta-shaped *d*), humorous (smile-shaped t-bars) and cautious (starting strokes before the *f*s and at the commencement of the penultimate line). But the structure of her PPI combined with the slight backward slant of her script and wide spacing between some of the words suggest an uncertainty about the reactions of others.

Circular i-dots show her desire for attention, but in this case only if those providing that attention keep their distance. This enigmatic young woman is liable to reject anyone who attempts to become too close.

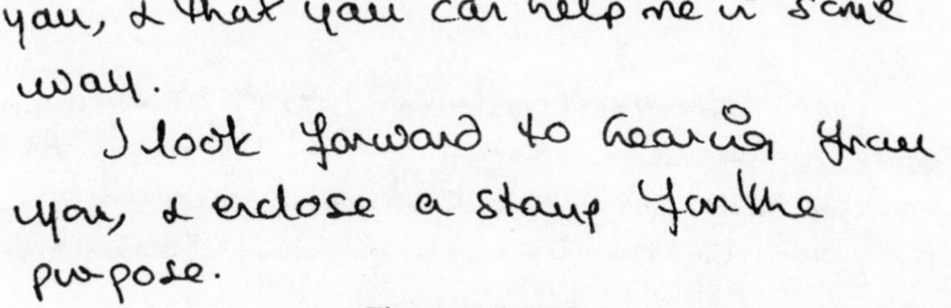

I hope that this letter manages to reach you, & that you can help me in some way.

I look forward to hearing from you, & enclose a stamp for the purpose.

Figure 47 (65%)

Size and style

It is advisable to check the spaces surrounding the PPI to see whether the person feels isolated, or is a loner.

The size of the personal pronoun is also of major importance. If it conforms with all the other capitals on the page the interpretation is that the writer is confident and self-assured, and has no wish to dominate or pretend to be something he is not. A PPI which *does* dominate can indicate an inflated ego or mask feelings of inferiority. Other signs and symbols in the writing must be studied to provide further clues.

Another sign to look out for is a PPI in the shape of an S. The writer who pens his PPI thus is quite likely to be a sensitive, or 'fey' as the Celts might say. He is undoubtedly shrewd and very perceptive, with the ability to see beyond the surface.

Clawlike signs are invariably negative and the interpretation of their appearance is the same as for similarly shaped descenders in other parts of the text. The writer who pens his personal pronoun thus could be said to have a rebellious streak. Greed should also be suspected.

A tall, narrow and congested PPI, as in figure 48, is the work of a repressed and inhibited individual.

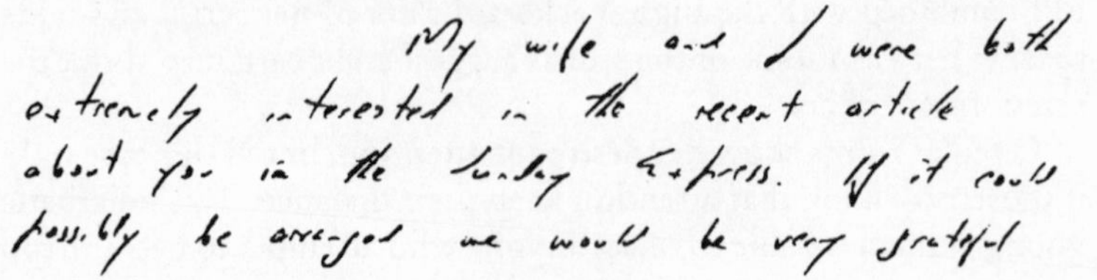

Figure 48 (65%)

A very small structure or one written as a lower-case letter reflects low self-esteem and timidity (see figure 49).

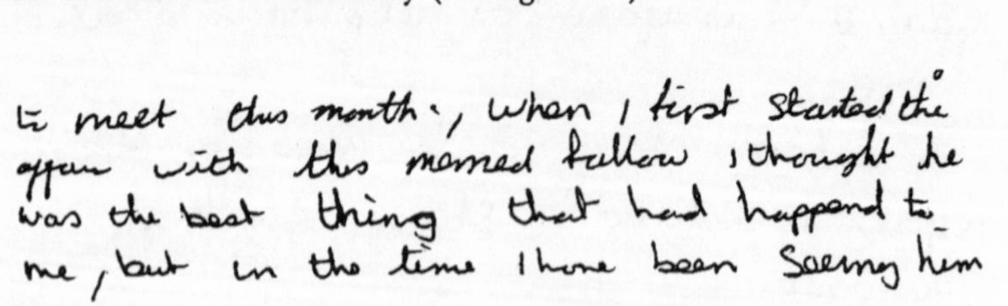

Figure 49 (50%)

The extract in figure 50 is from a letter whose script is typical of the writer's age and development: it was produced by a 14-year-old girl.

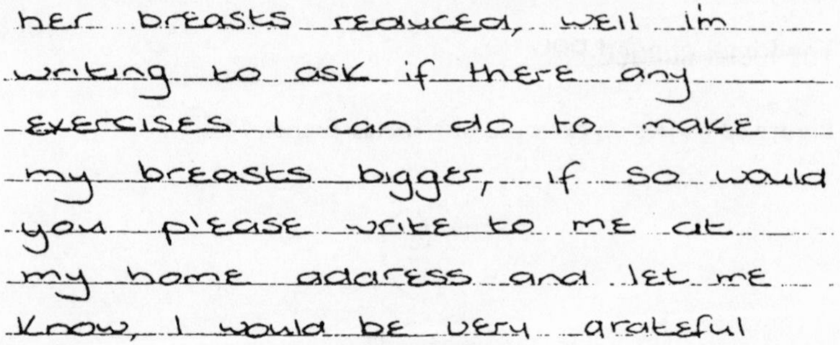

her breasts reduced, well im
writing to ask if there any
exercises I can do to make
my breasts bigger, if so would
you please write to me at
my home address and let me
know, I would be very grateful

Figure 50 (65%)

The emphasis of the large, round script is almost entirely on the middle zone, suggesting strong concern about personal image.

The girl wants her breasts enlarged; but from a graphological point of view, it would seem that if her PPI were larger, the other difficulty would not take on such importance.

Whatever its size, if the letter is sharp and angular, the writer is either assertive or aggressive, depending on the degree of angularity. One which slants in the opposite direction to the main body of the text could well indicate guilt; for confirmation, the structure of the writer's lower loops should be studied, with particular attention being paid to those of the *g* – has the letter itself been stumbled over? Amended strokes suggest neurotic tendencies.

Artificial flourishes and curlicues introduce a note of vulgarity, and the writer who encloses his PPI in circular or oval pen strokes may be something of a recluse, and may also be longing for protection.

If the symbol appears in the form of a number (two, four, seven, nine, for example) an above-average interest in money is indicated. Dollar or pound signs have the same interpretation.

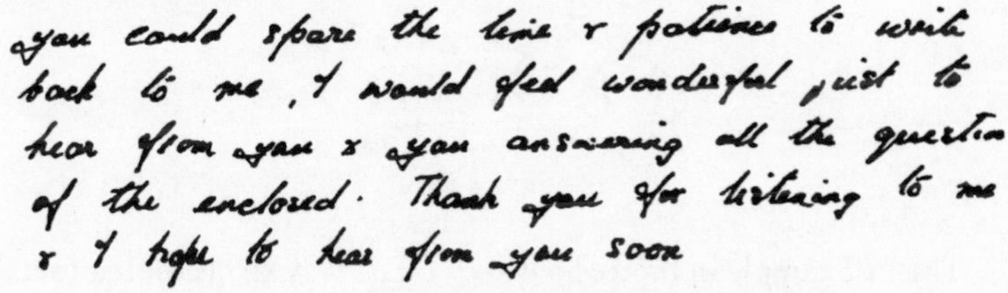

you could spare the time r patience to write
back to me, I would feel wonderful just to
hear from you & you answering all the question
of the enclosed. Thank you for listening to me
& I hope to hear from you soon

Figure 51 (65%)

69

The writer of figure 51 has money in mind, as we see from the way she has shaped her PPI like a figure seven.

The foetal-shaped PPI

Figure 52 shows an example of a foetal-shaped PPI.

Figure 52

It should not be confused with the less complex ear-shaped version (figure 53).

)

Figure 53

The foetal form of the letter shows an unwillingness to mature and cope with contemporary issues. The writer who pens his PPI in this way is self-contained and inward-looking, and has very real problems socializing with his peers. A sensitive immature type, he tends to shut himself away in his own private world and when stressed may well revert to the repetitive behaviour of childhood such as footstamping, nail-biting and refusing to accept blame when things go wrong. This is particularly so if it is allied to the very compulsive *Sacré Coeur* type of doodle, like the one shown in figure 54.

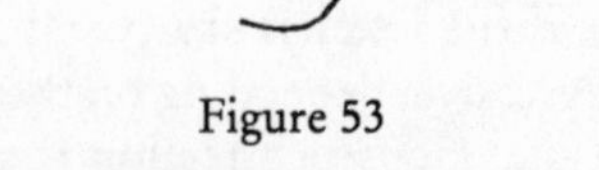

Figure 54

The PPI sample in figure 55 is well on its way to becoming foetal-shaped, with everything that particular structure implies.

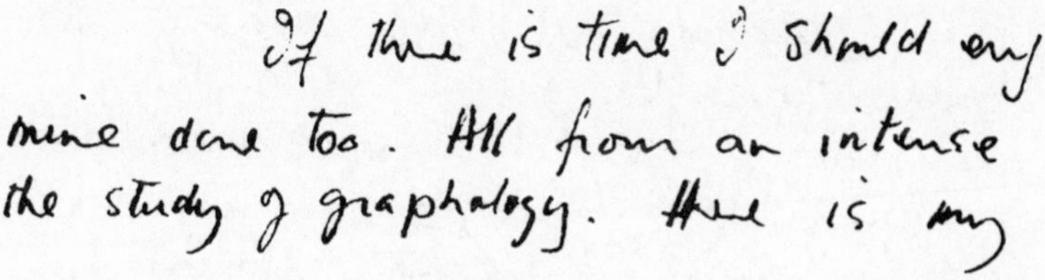

*If there is time I should copy
mine done too. All from an intense
the study of graphology. There is my*

Figure 55 (65%)

Figure 56 is already there.

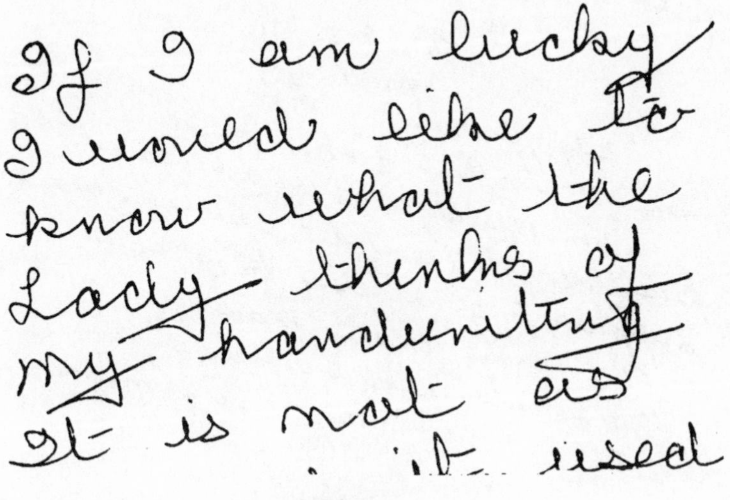

*If I am lucky
I would like to
know what the
Lady thinks of
my handwriting
It is not as
. it used*

Figure 56

The ear-shaped PPI

Hearing-impaired people often provide signs of their disability by making their PPIs ear-shaped! From the hundreds of samples I have collected in order to search for common denominators, I have found that hearing-impairment and this very symbolic sign go hand in hand. The unconscious message appears to be 'Here's my ear, try speaking into it.' Figures 57–64 clearly illustrate the point.

It does not automatically follow that if a writer's hearing is impaired, his PPI will appear in this form but, in my own experience, it is usually the case that if the pronoun is ear-shaped, the hearing is impaired.

71

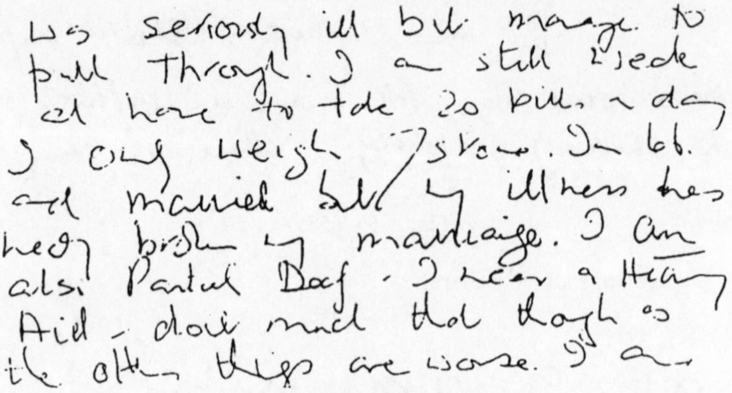

was seriously ill but manage to
pull through. I am still used
at home to take 20 pills a day
I only weigh 7stone. I'm 66.
and married but my illness has
nearly broken my marriage. I am
also Partial Deaf - I wear a Hearing
Aid - don't mind that though as
the other things are worse. I am

Figure 57 (65%)

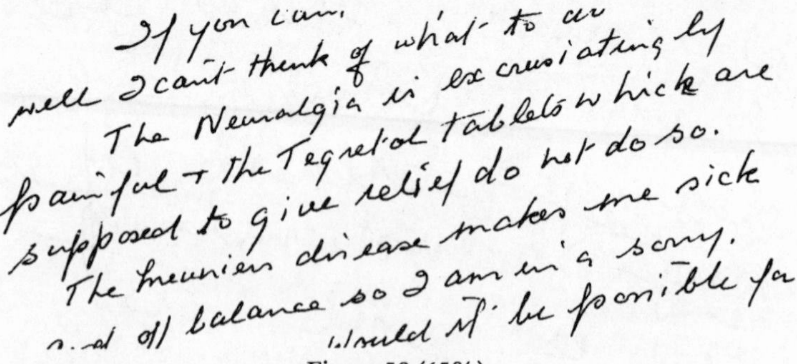

If you can,
well I can't think of what to do
The Neuralgia is excruciatingly
painful + the Tegretol tablets which are
supposed to give relief do not do so.
The Meuniers disease makes me sick
and off balance so I am in a sorry.
would it be possible for

Figure 58 (65%)

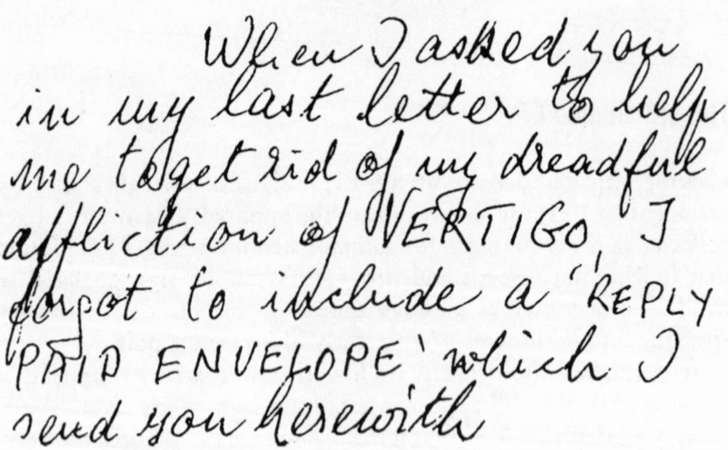

When I asked you
in my last letter to help
me to get rid of my dreadful
affliction of VERTIGO I
forgot to include a "REPLY
PAID ENVELOPE" which I
send you herewith

Figure 59

72

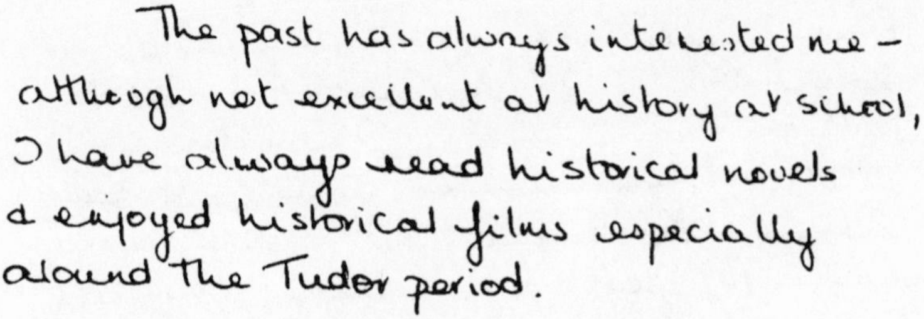

The past has always interested me – although not excellent at history at school, I have always read historical novels & enjoyed historical films especially around the Tudor period.

Figure 60

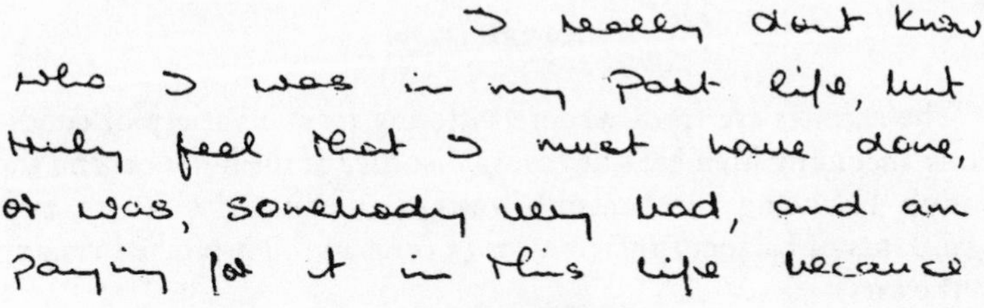

I really don't know who I was in my past life, but truly feel that I must have done, or was, somebody very bad, and am paying for it in this life because

Figure 61 (65%)

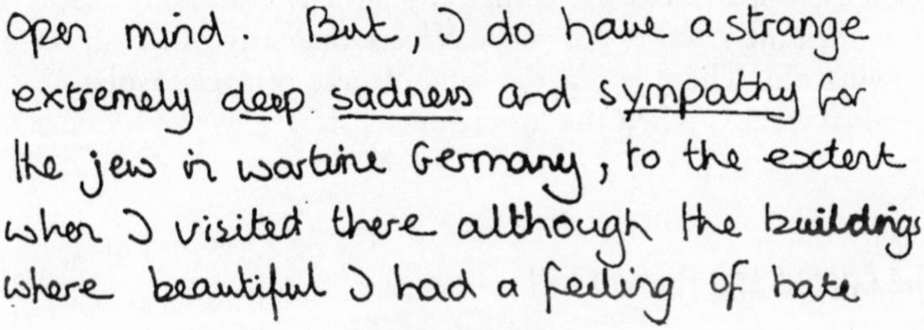

open mind. But, I do have a strange extremely deep sadness and sympathy for the jews in wartime Germany, to the extent when I visited there although the buildings where beautiful I had a feeling of hate

Figure 62 (65%)

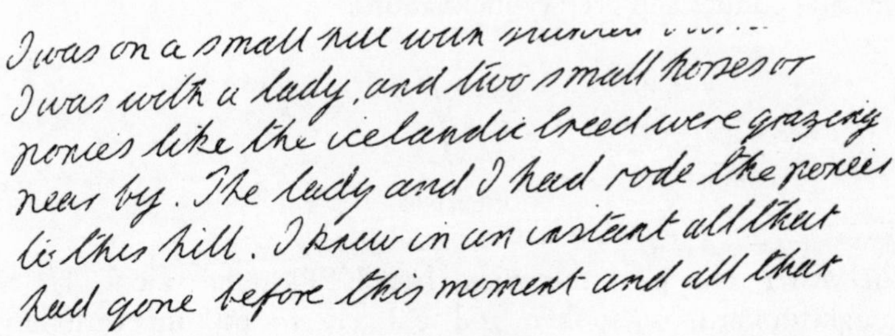

I was on a small hill with summer ..... I was with a lady, and two small horses or ponies like the icelandic breed were grazing near by. The lady and I had rode the ponies to this hill. I knew in an instant all that had gone before this moment and all that

Figure 63 (50%)

73

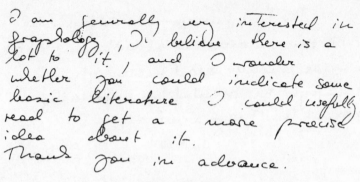

Figure 64 (50%)

The extracts are from writers suffering from a variety of conditions, including Menière's disease (a disorder of the inner ear and the body's balancing mechanism), vertigo (dizziness, sickness and, again, loss of balance) and tinnitus (a constant high-pitched ringing in the ears).

Degenerative age-related deafness does not appear to affect the structure of the PPI in this respect. This makes sense because when the impairment has come on gradually it does not seem to be significantly worse for the sufferers than any other aspect of growing old. There is not the same degree of social isolation or personal trauma when the loss happens slowly over a number of years.

The printed and Roman PPI

The printed PPI (a single stem without any additions, as in figure 65) indicates culture and literary inclinations.

Figure 65

The writer who pens this stick-shaped PPI stands alone. He is straightforward, outspoken and unlikely to put up with any nonsense.

The classical Roman version, with bars above and below (see

74

figure 66) is the work of a writer who possesses all of these qualities and he too is also cultured and literate.

Figure 66

The extra strokes above and below the letter which differentiate the Roman from the printed form tell us that this writer also feels a need to protect his privacy and his individuality.

With the upper and lower strokes, we can apply the sample principles of analysis as we would to a scripted PPI, taking the top to represent the writer's mother and the bottom his father. We can then check whether one predominates.

Reversed strokes

Some people write the PPI with reversed strokes. How does one set about analysing such oddities – and without actually seeing someone write the letter how can one even determine whether it has actually been written in reverse?

The secret of determining where a pen stroke started is that more energy is expended there than where it ended. Reverse strokes sometimes reveal themselves to the naked eye but they always show up clearly under magnification.

The method for determining whether the PPI has been written in this way is to take a piece of tracing paper and go over the outline in the way one thinks its originator did. Then, alongside the traced sample, one should write another PPI, this time in the normal way. Then compare the two.

Constructing the PPI the wrong way round which in a British or European hand means starting on the baseline and working upwards as in figure 67 instead of downwards as in figure 68, and in an American hand means doing the opposite as in figure 69, indicates rebellion. This is an individual whose priorities are the wrong way round. If, in the same sample, the cross-bar of the *t* has been inserted before the main stem of the letter, no further proof is needed.

Figure 67

Figure 68

Figure 69

Different styles of PPI in the same text

The 32-year-old married woman who wrote the extract featured in figure 70 is relatively well adjusted, and although her PPI appears in both printed and Roman versions, each is of normal size.

The printed pronoun appears where she refers to her teenage friend, recalling a time when life was simple and straightforward. In the Roman version, she now shows concern for her personal identity hence the more defensive version.

Figure 71 was written by a teenage girl whose self-confidence obviously needs a boost. She has very real problems, not just with personal identity as indicated by the two different PPIs, but also with her self-image because the printed version is only about half the size it should be.

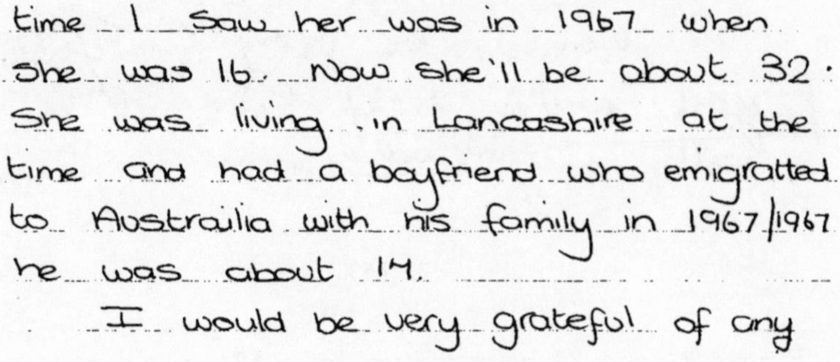

time I saw her was in 1967 when
she was 16. Now she'll be about 32.
She was living in Lancashire at the
time and had a boyfriend who emigratted
to Australia with his family in 1967 1967
he was about 14.

I would be very grateful of any

Figure 70 (65%)

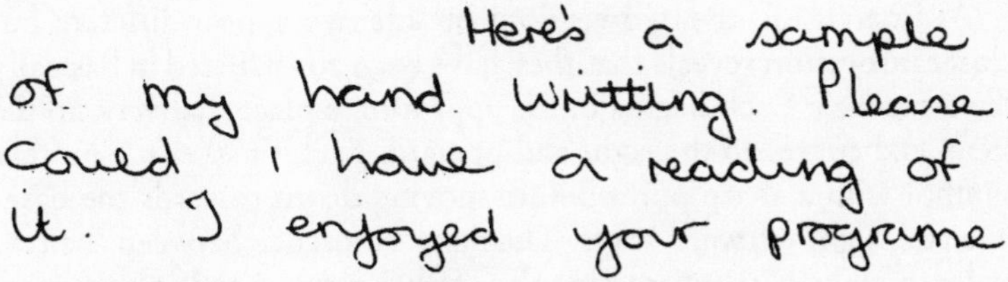

Here's a sample
of my hand writting. Please
could I have a reading of
it. I enjoyed your programe

Figure 71 (65%)

The scripted version soars quite high but there is no real warmth
in either upper or lower section, and here we have the root of the
writer's self-consciousness.

Her difficulty in forming relationships is seen in both the left-
slanted script and the wide gap between the PPI and the surrounding words.

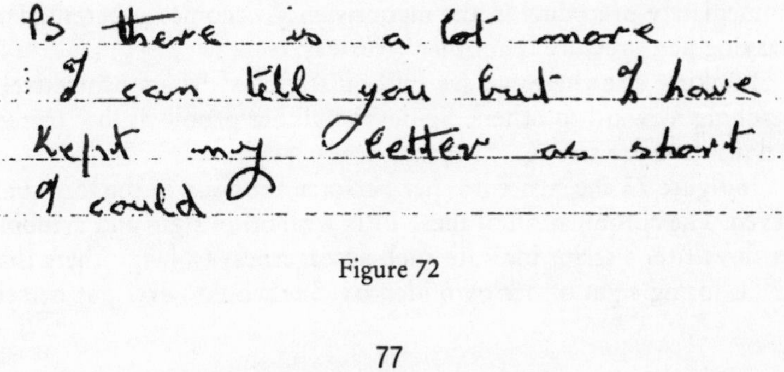

Ps there is a lot more
I can tell you but I have
kept my letter as short
I could

Figure 72

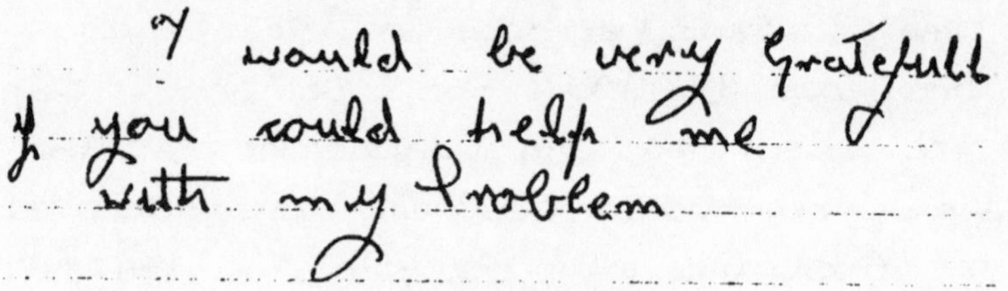

Figure 73 (65%)

Figures 72 and 73 were written by a 58-year-old woman. Although brief, these extracts speak multitudes. Figure 72 contains no fewer than three types of PPI, which hints at very real problems of personal identity.

At first glance, the two versions on line two appear different but closer inspection reveals that they have been constructed in basically the same way. Each begins in the appropriate place, halfway up the stem, and curves to the right and upward. Each finishes the mother symbol with a sharp point before moving down towards the baseline at a slight leftward angle. The main difference between the two is down at the base where the token father symbol ends on the stem of the first but curves to the right on the second.

In the third version in figure 72, the writer makes no attempt whatever to include the father symbol, with the result that this one ends up resembling a figure nine. The shape of the third pronoun suggests that the woman's worries are related to figures (i.e. money). The neurotic retracing of its stem points to anxiety, also related to money.

Examining other components of the script and balancing them against what has already been discovered we find generalized mental confusion, which can be seen in the varying slant of the letters, particularly in that final word 'could'. It is also apparent from the letter sizes: if we compare the *i* in 'is' in line one with the *e* in 'there' immediately preceding it, the inconsistency becomes apparent. The varying pen pressure is another giveaway.

Looking elsewhere we see two outstretched t-bars protectively reaching forward to others. So despite all her problems, her maternal instincts are strong.

In figure 73 she structures her personal pronoun in the form of a seven. The combination of these PPIs with other signs and symbols in the writer's script indicate such an eagerness to help others that she is losing sight of her own identity. She would never put herself first or draw attention to herself in any way.

She is likely to suppress her emotions and isolate herself, something which may well have a detrimental effect on her health. Other inconsistencies in this hand include weak and fragmented strokes as well as disturbing ink dots and pen trails, which can be seen at the beginning of line two and between the *t* and *he* in 'there' in line one respectively.

Harmony and discord

We have already established that if, in the general text of a person's writing, upper, middle and lower sections all harmonize, it indicates a sense of balance in the writer. Nowhere is this more clearly seen than in the structure of the personal pronoun.

There should be little or no difference in pressure between the main text and the ego-symbol. We know that heavy pen pressure indicates high energy and vivacity. If the formation of the PPI is particularly heavy, a sensuous personality is suggested, although in a heavy hand showing mainly negative traits, it may indicate criminal tendencies, the nature of which do not concern us here.

When the personal pronoun is lighter than the rest of the text (particularly in its main downstroke) low self-esteem is indicated. Writers who live in a dream world tend to put very little pressure on their PPIs. Writers who slant it in a different direction from the rest of the rest are moody and tend to take too much to heart (see figure 74).

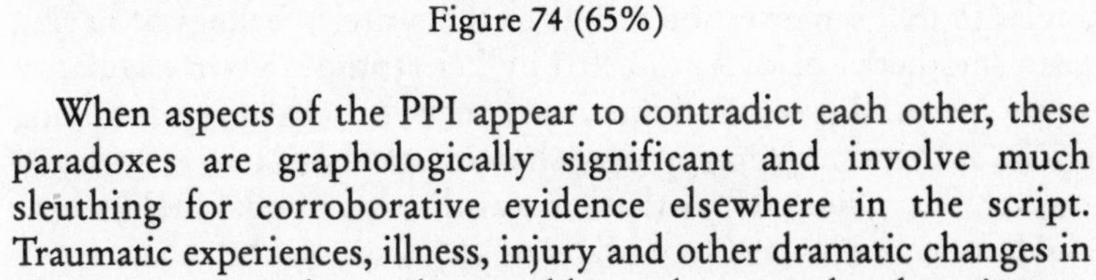

Figure 74 (65%)

When aspects of the PPI appear to contradict each other, these paradoxes are graphologically significant and involve much sleuthing for corroborative evidence elsewhere in the script. Traumatic experiences, illness, injury and other dramatic changes in circumstances can bring about sudden and spectacular alterations to the symbol. This is something else which adds to its importance:

these changes do not necessarily affect other capital *I*s, which are unrelated to the self.

Few of the samples coming to people like myself are harmonious, most contain some discrepancies and contradictions, while some are full of inconsistencies, with numerous interruptions of flow, segmentation of strokes and little or no continuity of movement.

The two *I*s illustrated in figures 75 and 76 are the work of a man in his fifties. A successful and busy executive, he manages a large staff in a rapidly expanding company. He is happy and fulfilled in both his personal and professional life.

Figure 75

Figure 76

In figure 75, mother and father symbols balance each other fairly well, although the mother figure is somewhat stronger. In figure 76 the mother symbol predominates. Its strong upward slant indicates maternal ambition and the writer himself agrees that his mother certainly was ambitious, never having made any secret of her high hopes and plans for him. The angle at the peak of this section suggests that she was dominant. The combination of curves and angles in that same section points to the writer's feelings of having been smothered or overprotected by her attitude. Sharp angularity at the apex of this section hints at strictness, but the upward-curving stroke at the top is a happy sign, showing an abundance of love and respect. Sharp lines tell us that his was the sort of household where children were expected to work hard and abide by the rules.

This writer's love for both parents is not in doubt, nor is their love for each other. Although his identification with his mother is strong, the fact that the bottom section of both samples is more rounded than the top indicates that it was towards his father that he felt most warmth.

We see from the lower section that father was warm, caring and happy with the status quo – the proverbial quiet man. The signs indicate that his acceptance of maternal rule in the household was because of failing health; whereas the top portion of these PPIs is strong and healthy, the bottom is weak and fragmented.

The breaks in pen pressure at the extremity of the father symbol do not appear anywhere else in the writer's script, so they can be discounted in terms of his own health. It is absolutely essential to make such comparisons when analysing the PPI.

In figure 76 the distinct gap between the end of the bottom section and the stem of the letter represents complete severance: i.e. the death of the father. The writer confirms the accuracy of all these findings.

Ambiguity

When writing is difficult to decipher, one must conclude that that was how the writer intended it and that he therefore wished to be ambiguous.

Figure 77 is a fine, sophisticated style, fast and clever with subtle little innovative shapes. It is the work of an intellectual who is only too well aware of his own cleverness.

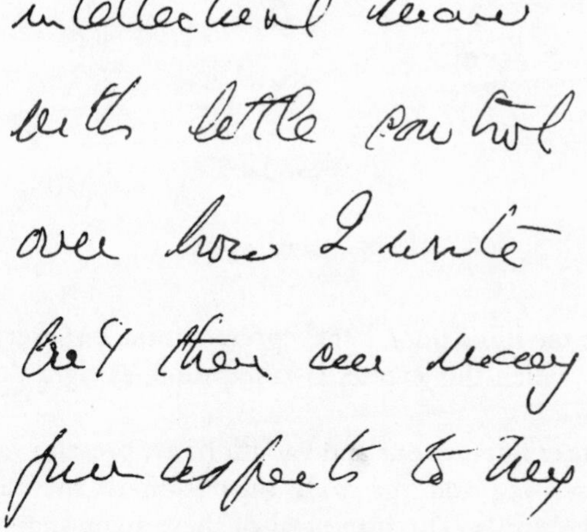

Figure 77 (65%)

It is also an arrogant, self-centred hand, from a writer who does not really care about legibility. The message coming through loud and clear is that if the reader cannot work out what he is saying, then that is the reader's fault, not his.

The mother symbol predominates; so much so, that the *t* in the word 'but' on the penultimate line almost takes on a similar form. It is also a very stressed hand. Magnification reveals several ink dots and pen trails, some of which are even obvious without the aid of a magnifier.

The pressure, while generally light, changes throughout, reflecting constant changes in the writer's energy levels.

But the most dominant feature of this hand is the PPI because it accentuates the warmth and tenderness associated with the mother but displays no feelings at all towards the father or father-substitute. This writer is so mother-orientated that any other woman in his life must surely find it hard to compete.

Neurotic tendencies

The sample featured in figure 78 is full of repression and tension. The writer displays a whole host of negative feelings.

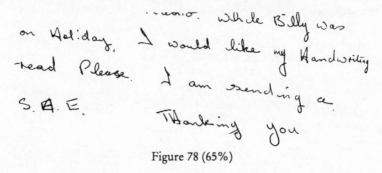

Figure 78 (65%)

Not only is the PPI a poor, bent representation, but every line of the letter from which this extract is taken tumbles right down off the baseline.

Many other fluctuations and variations are present: varying letter sizes, overwriting and the wide separation of the PPI from its surrounding words. The sum total of these signs and symbols is a serious draining of physical and mental strength.

The lower-case *e*

This is another ego sign. *E* is for ego, hence the symbolism, but it should only ever be interpreted in conjunction with the personal pronoun.

We are dealing here with the lower-case form of the letter because it is so much more revealing than the capital. The focus of our attention should be on the main loop or 'eye' of the letter. Tight, compressed *e*s suggest repression and inhibition, as they do with any other compressed loop. When the letter has been completely blacked out, the implication is that the writer is attempting to hide some information about himself, the nature of which is only likely to be revealed by an in-depth study of the rest of the sample.

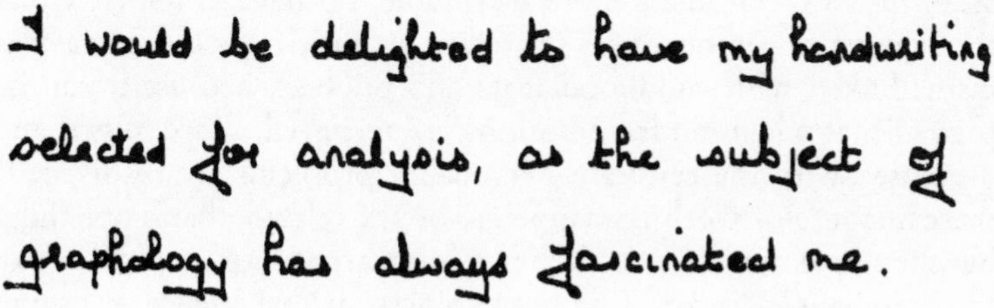

Figure 79 (65%)

What a fascinating selection of giveaway signs and symbols we have in figure 79. On the one hand we have a strong, legible script, and on the other a multitude of blacked-out letters.

Interestingly, the one letter which has virtually no dark shades or blacking out is the *h*, so we must resort to symbolism once more. *H* is for home, where the writer is obviously very happy.

Further proof of that state was picked up from her lively signature (not reproduced because of the writer's wish to remain anonymous). Blacked-out symbols include the mother section of her personal pronoun and several of her upper loops. More significantly, of the ten lower-case *e*s in this three-line sample, she has only left the eye of one of them open, whereas of the six *h*s, she has only blacked out one.

It is worth mentioning in passing that the signature is exactly the same size and shape as the text, with equal emphasis on the first and second names.

83

The writer made a point of inserting the title 'Mrs'. That and the signature's central placement on the page add further credence to the comment about her happy home. It is an altogether fascinating sample because of the many signs and symbols it contains.

The brief extracts shown here and elsewhere in this chapter demonstrate why the PPI and lower-case *e* should never be taken in isolation or viewed as individual features of the writing. They are both of the utmost importance, but only in conjunction with all the other parts which go to make up the whole.

Freud and Adler

Freudian psychoanalysts hold the view that personality is shaped by sexual influences from a very early age, and this affects their analysis of the PPI. But much more acceptable, I believe, is the view that the shaping of personality is related to unconscious defence mechanisms linked with childhood fears and phobias, because it can be proved that when hidden emotions are retrieved, re-examined and dispensed with the resultant personality problems are resolved. If these unconscious feelings happen to be sex-related, that is one thing but they need not be. Indeed, they seldom are at least, not in the way the Freudians maintain. I write from personal experience of having seen hundreds of these behavioural and physical problems resolved by means of deep, regressive hypnosis.

In graphological analysis, buried emotions and unconscious factors are sometimes manifest, but in my own experience, they show up more clearly when spontaneous drawings have been provided alongside straightforward writings.

The Freudian explanation for writing a PPI with reversed strokes, for example, is that those who do so have what they colourfully refer to as an 'anal fixation'. They start at the wrong end of the letter because their parents over-emphasized their potty training.

This seems a pretty daft sort of generalization to me; is it not more sensible to conclude that the writer is simply an awkward type who enjoys kicking against his background, upbringing, family traditions, conventions etc.? I utterly reject the notion of sexual connotations, at least in the absence of other signs in the text which might suggest their presence.

A couple of years ago I was giving a slide-illustrated talk to a group of fellow graphologists. One of the questions raised was whether a particular writer featured in my collection was homosexual.

The question surprised me for two reasons. The first was that most practising graphologists can quickly identify the writing of someone with homosexual tendencies. The second was because the questioner stated categorically and with an air of supreme authority that the sample had clearly been produced by someone with an anal fixation. Surely I had investigated that aspect of the writer's personality?

No, I responded. I did not consider it any of my business. I had not asked my correspondent whether he was a Roman Catholic or a Young Conservative either, because as far as I was concerned, the answers to these questions were equally irrelevant. A writer's sexual, religious and political inclinations are his own concern. Unless there is a particular reason for investigating these matters, I do not see that it is necessary in a general graphological assessment. In any case, I have yet to be convinced that an 'anal style of writing' actually exists.

Freudian graphology is all very illuminating, but I believe that these psychoanalytical concepts are just a shade far-fetched. Trendy and controversial they may be, but the pertinent question is whether they have any real relevance to our daily lives.

Psychoanalysts who pursue this line of thinking also maintain that if there is a vast difference between the size of the top of the PPI and the bottom, it shows an unresolved Oedipus complex (Oedipus, it will be recalled, killed his father and married his mother). How very imaginative. But might a more logical explanation not be that this discrepancy merely mirrors the different attitudes these parents had towards each other and by association towards the writer?

Alfred Adler, the Austrian psychiatrist, was originally a friend and follower of Freud, but severed the connection because he disagreed with Freud's views on infantile sexuality. Today, Adler is best remembered for having devised the term 'inferiority complex', a concept which still figures in studying the PPI.

Adler's conclusion about the ego-symbol was that as well as relating to self-image, parts of it provided clues about deep-rooted feelings with respect to the influences of male and female parents. In the light of what we now know, this line of thinking makes perfect sense, so why complicate the issue with sexual innuendo?

6 Buried Emotions

A computer cannot operate without its programmer, nor can the human framework be activated without some sort of mechanism. The human control system lying deep inside the brain is known as the autonomic or unconscious nervous system (the UNS). The outer surface of the brain, the cerebral cortex, contains the cerebrum and the cerebellum. Some experts maintain that the cerebrum contains the conscious or subordinate part of the mind, and the cerebellum the UNS or dominant part of it.

Carl Gustav Jung a psychiatrist and analytical psychologist who was a contemporary of Freud, compared the two systems to an iceberg, with the conscious as the visible part and the UNS as the infinitely greater submerged section. Like Adler, Jung differed from Freud in his views about the human psyche. While Freud attributed everything to sex, Jung believed that mental disturbance was caused by the patient's inability to deal with a current problem. His contention was that the symptoms of psychiatric illness were signs of disturbed normal functioning and that these need not necessarily have sexual connections.

It was Jung who devised the terms 'introvert' and 'extrovert', both of which have graphological significance. An introvert is someone who is inward-looking and not keen on socializing. His handwriting slants to the left. An extrovert is outgoing, gregarious and enjoys the company of others. His writing slants to the right. While we sometimes find personality problems with extroverts, sufferers of phobias and obsessional neuroses are generally introverts.

Like driving a car or riding a bicycle, writing soon becomes an automatic process. We do it almost without thinking and as the pen works its way along the paper all sorts of messages filter through from the innermost section of our mind.

While the conscious gets on with the business of composing the script and writing the actual words, the UNS takes little or no notice of letter structures, slant, spacing or anything else relating to the minutiae of writing. Nor does it stop to consider the size and shape of the PPI, or any other letter, of peculiar pen strokes or of alterations in pressures. In ignoring all this it produces its own clues in the writing, providing various signs to hint at the messages beaming out from within.

The falling baseline, for example, is a classic sign of depression. Other important messages filtering through from the UNS can warn of weaknesses and deficiencies in the body, many of which are stress-related.

A stressed state of mind and the deteriorating health associated with it manifest themselves quite clearly on the written page, where once again we see the importance of graphological symbolism. In the samples that follow (which, incidentally, were not provided specifically for analysis), we shall see how writers proceed to reveal their problems.

Some of the extracts are taken from letters written to my husband by patients requesting treatment, others are from letters sent to me during my period as an 'agony aunt'.

Obsessional neurosis

Obsessional neurosis is a state of mind in which fears are so numerous and varied that they can dominate one's life. The condition is common among sufferers of stress, whose panic may be linked to the sight of domestic animals, birds, insects or any of a number of creatures which to the rest of us are totally inoffensive and harmless. Phobic sufferers may be disturbed by certain situations, such as the thought of being sick and having to visit a doctor or enter hospital. Their fear may be motivated by the sight of blood or the possibility of dying on the operating table. Cancer phobia is also relatively common. Fire, thunderstorms and the prospect of nuclear war are among other irrational fears.

In attempting to hide their personality problems from others, these writers may become secretive and inhibited, and their script will display classical signs of inner conflict.

Lack of rhythm indicates uncoordinated thoughts. Changes in pressure suggest changes in energy flow. Ink dots and pen trails may also be present. Indeed there are many clues for the graphologist to

pick up. Buried emotions and unconscious factors manifest themselves in a variety of ways, including childlike letter formations,
cramping or over-separation of words and a dramatic switch to
printing.

Post-traumatic stress disorders are more common than most of
us realize, and show up in the form of inhibited repressed loops, the
blacking-out of certain letters and sometimes hand tremor.

Compulsive people perform irrational acts to relieve tension.
Some go in for obsessional rituals such as biting their fingernails
or pulling out wisps of hair on their head. Others might count
everything around them like steps on the stairs, trees alongside a
path, baked beans on their toast. They might also have an irritat-
ing habit like drumming their fingers on the table or clicking their
teeth.

It does not, of course, automatically follow that if someone
does one or more of these things he is suffering from obsessional
neurosis. He may simply be acting out a ritual which has become
a habit. Only those who are medically qualified to do so can
decide whether behavior is normal or neurotic. And as with every
other aspect of handwriting analysis, it is vitally important never
to take any aspect of the personality in isolation. A doctor will
not diagnose a potentially fatal illness on the evidence of a single
sign; he will add up all the signs and symptoms before reaching a
definitive diagnosis. Similarly, a graphologist should not place
undue emphasis on individual characteristics, but should take all
the signs and symbols into account to assess the personality as a
whole.

The life of the writer of figure 80 is obviously dominated by fear,
so much so that he has resorted to printing, in case the scripted form
of his writing might reveal aspects of his personality he would rather
keep private.

Note the trembling execution of the letters, the overwriting of
several strokes and the shakiness of the underscores – these most of
all.

Nervous exhaustion

The script and prints of figures 81 and 82 have both been written by
the same person. This is a much neater, tidier and more controlled
hand than that depicted in figure 80, but it is still very inhibited and

its many changes of pressure and uncertain strokes confirm the writer's own comments about nervous exhaustion. The words 'everything' and 'clear' on the penultimate line of figure 81 are particularly shaky

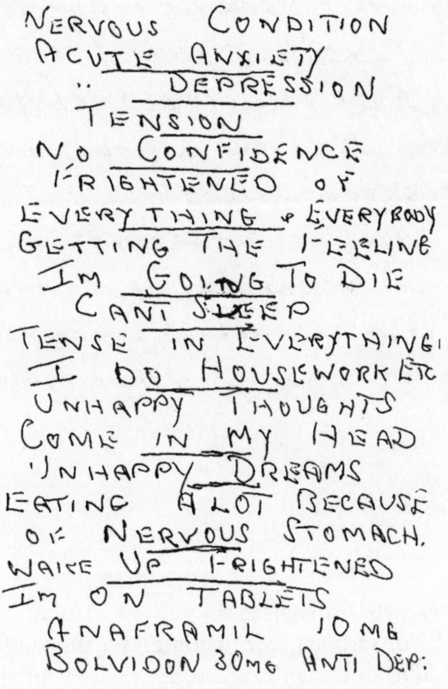
NERVOUS CONDITION
ACUTE ANXIETY
" DEPRESSION
TENSION
NO CONFIDENCE
FRIGHTENED OF
EVERYTHING & EVERYBODY
GETTING THE FEELING
IM GOING TO DIE
CANT SLEEP
TENSE IN EVERYTHING
I DO HOUSEWORK ETC
UNHAPPY THOUGHTS
COME IN MY HEAD
UNHAPPY DREAMS
EATING A LOT BECAUSE
OF NERVOUS STOMACH.
WAKE UP FRIGHTENED
IM ON TABLETS
ANAFRAMIL 10 MG
BOLVIDON 30MG ANTI DEP:

Figure 80 (50%)

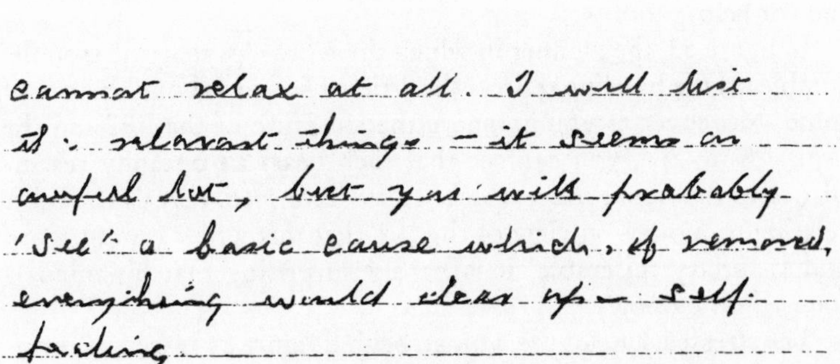
cannot relax at all. I will list
the relevant things – it seems an
awful lot, but you will probably
'see' a basic cause which, if removed,
everything would clear up – self
feeling

Figure 81 (65%)

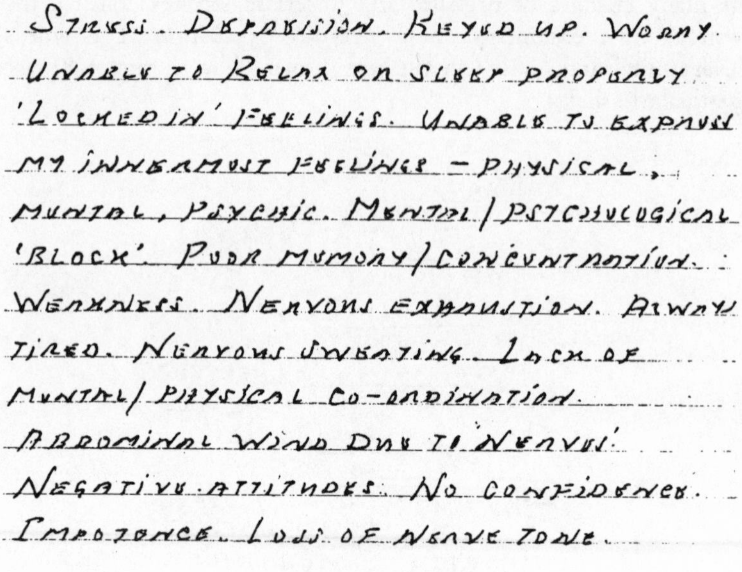
STRESS. DEPRESSION. KEYED UP. WORRY.
UNABLE TO RELAX OR SLEEP PROPERLY.
'LOCKED IN' FEELINGS. UNABLE TO EXPRESS
MY INNERMOST FEELINGS – PHYSICAL,
MENTAL, PSYCHIC. MENTAL/PSYCHOLOGICAL
'BLOCK'. POOR MEMORY/CONCENTRATION.
WEAKNESS. NERVOUS EXHAUSTION. ALWAYS
TIRED. NERVOUS SWEATING. LACK OF
MENTAL/PHYSICAL CO-ORDINATION.
ABDOMINAL WIND DUE TO 'NERVES'.
NEGATIVE ATTITUDES. NO CONFIDENCE.
IMPOTENCE. LOSS OF NERVE TONE.

Figure 82 (65%)

Stress

The extracts featured in figures 83 and 84 display signs of stress. Each script tells of sadness, confusion and a thoroughly depressed state of mind. Without even reading the content of these notes we can deduct from the lack of rhythm and balance and the general 'feel' of the writings that these unfortunate individuals are crying out for help.

In figure 83, the manner in which the words 'psychiatric trouble' tumble off the baseline reflects the writer's feelings about his state of mind. Moreover, if you compare the structure of the PPI and the capital S in 'Sir', you can see that each bears an uncanny resemblance to the figure nine, which, as we have seen, reveals thoughts relating to money. In view of the fact that this writer cannot work and is 'pretty miserable' it is hardly surprising that his mind is focused on money.

The stressed state of the woman behind figure 84 is seen in extensive overwriting, mainly in her PPI, and in the variations of slant.

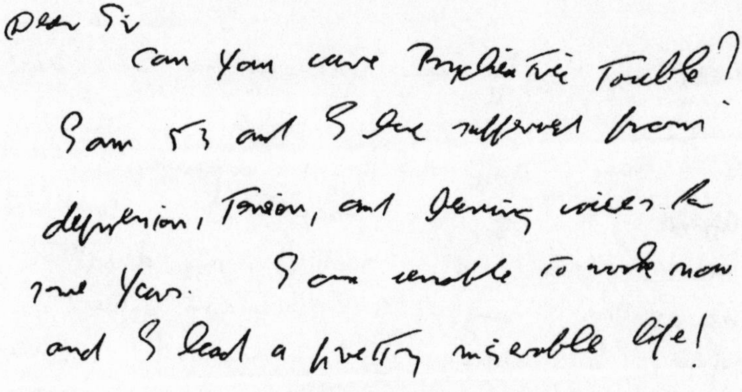

Dear Sir

Can you cure Psychiatric Trouble?
I am 53 and I have suffered from
depression, Tension, and Jerking widers for
two Years. I am unable to work now
and I lead a pretty miserable life!

Figure 83 (65%)

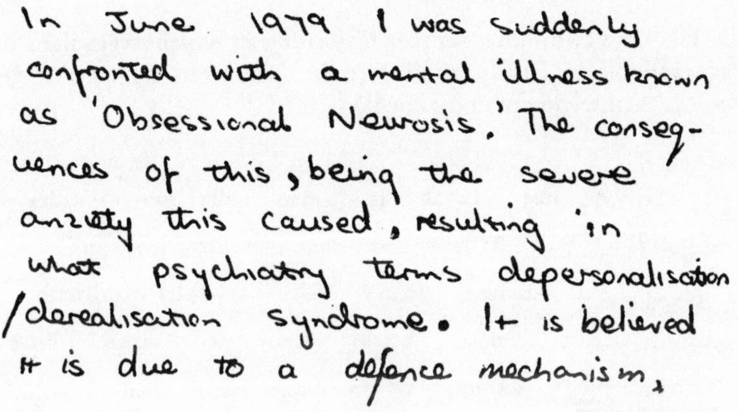

In June 1979 I was suddenly
confronted with a mental illness known
as 'Obsessional Neurosis.' The consequences of this, being the severe
anxiety this caused, resulting in
what psychiatry terms depersonalisation
/derealisation syndrome. It is believed
It is due to a defence mechanism,

Figure 84 (65%)

Agoraphobia

Figure 85 also shows signs of nervous overwriting, added to which
we see many changes of pen pressure. What we have here is an
elderly woman who is frightened to leave the relative safety of her
home. The wide gaps between her words conform her agoraphobia.
Her personal pronouns are particularly well separated from the
neighbouring words.

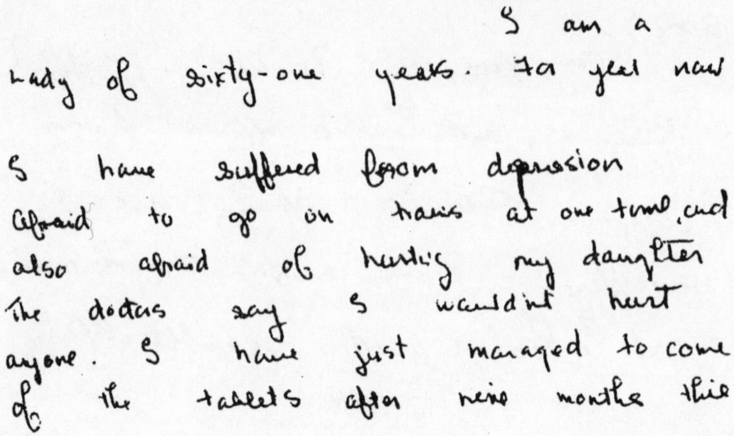

S am a
Lady of sixty-one years. For years now
S have suffered from depression
Afraid to go on trains at one time, and
also afraid of hurting my daughter
The doctors say S wouldn't hurt
anyone. S have just managed to come
of the tablets after nine months this

Figure 85 (65%)

Here are two more samples of writing in which overt signs of agoraphobia are clearly manifest (quite apart from the fact that the words themselves are underlined!).

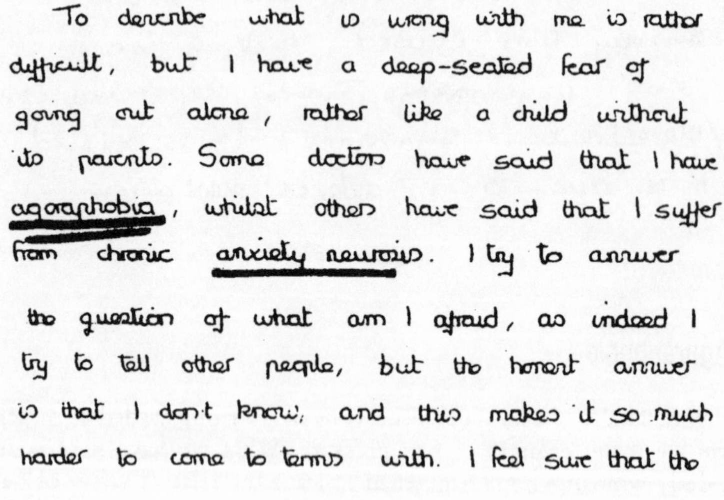

To describe what is wrong with me is rather
difficult, but I have a deep-seated fear of
going out alone, rather like a child without
its parents. Some doctors have said that I have
agoraphobia, whilst others have said that I suffer
from chronic anxiety neurosis. I try to answer
the question of what am I afraid, as indeed I
try to tell other people, but the honest answer
is that I don't know, and this makes it so much
harder to come to terms with. I feel sure that the

Figure 86 (65%)

The writer of figure 86 is a man aged fifty, and for someone of his mature years it is a remarkably immature hand. This man genuinely does not know why he feels as he does, but it seems obvious enough to me. The key letter here is the lower-case *f*, of which there are three examples on line two.

Turning first to the double *f* in 'difficult', we find that although these two letters do hesitatingly venture into the lower zone, their faltering little descenders never manage to return to base, while the *f* in 'fear' is too frightened even to venture down beyond the base-line.

The root of this writer's trouble would appear to be sexual in origin. Note on line seven how he has written the *q* in 'question'. He has taken it down easily enough but once there he has given it a little 'island' at the bottom. And therein lies a further clue. Allied to other signs throughout this man's script the island suggests that he has isolated all his feelings, not only in connection with sex but those of physical closeness generally.

The key phrase appears on lines three and four where he compares his fear of going out with that of 'a child without its parents'.

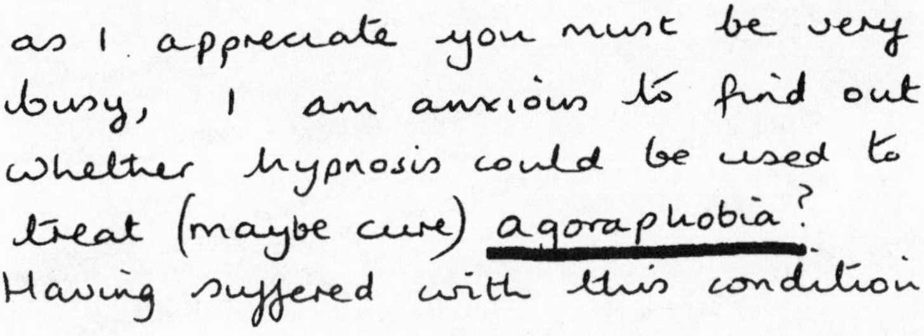

> as I appreciate you must be very
> busy, I am anxious to find out
> whether hypnosis could be used to
> treat (maybe cure) agoraphobia?
> Having suffered with this condition

Figure 87 (65%)

The writer of figure 87 is also middle aged, but in this case a woman. The fact that she too leaves wide spaces between words does not necessarily indicate agoraphobia but it does point to some difficulty in mixing with others. On the whole, however, the script is more mature and better balanced than that in figure 86.

This woman's trouble does not appear to be sex-related. Bruised emotions are the more likely cause. Hesitancy and lack of confidence dominate; the hesitancy can be seen in the pauses before certain letters, noticeably the *y* in 'you' on line one, the *b* in 'busy' and the *t* in 'to' on line two, and the *h* in 'hypnosis' on line three.

Depression

Figures 88 and 89 both show despondency (indicated by the falling baseline). The writer of figure 88 is suffering from a form of depression which doctors refer to as 'endogenous' because the root of the problem is hidden deep down below the surface. Sufferers of this type of depression have consciously forgotten whatever it was that caused their problem, and until the bottled-up memories have been released they fester away at the back of the mind like a mouthful of rotten teeth.

This unfortunate woman's writing shows signs of a major cerebral disorder.

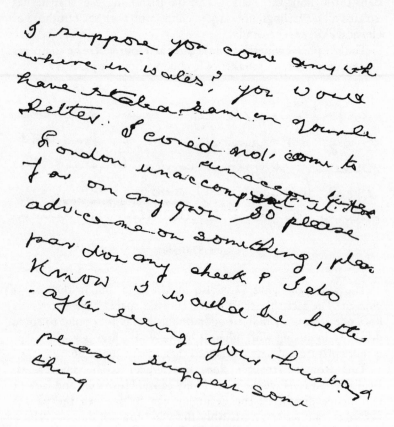

Figure 88 (65%)

Figure 89 was also written by a woman suffering from depression, but of a different type. Doctors call this form of depression 'reactive' because its cause is obvious. The sufferer is reacting to known circumstances and can recall the details at will. She knows why she is depressed – it is because of the potentially life-threatening illness of a close relative.

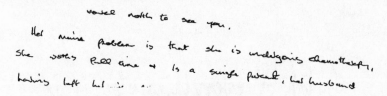

Figure 89 (50%)

Phobias

Figures 90–96 have been penned by phobics. Notice the arhythmic letter formations of the first three and the unduly wide gaps separating the words; the writers are symbolically distancing themselves from other people.

But some phobias can produce emotional dependency, hence the tightening of the words in figure 93. Note, too, the absolute rigidity of style.

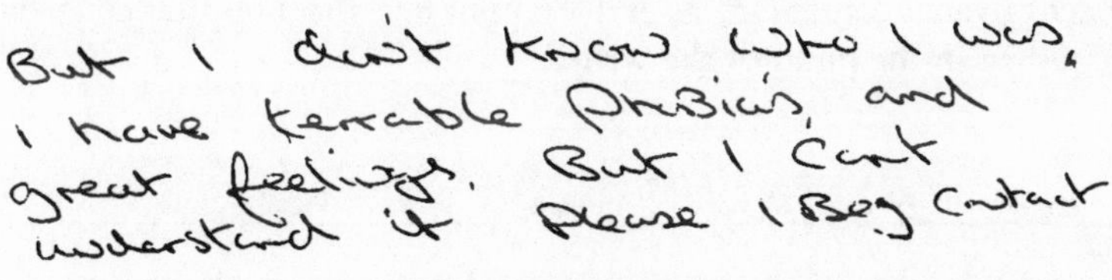

Figure 90 (50%)

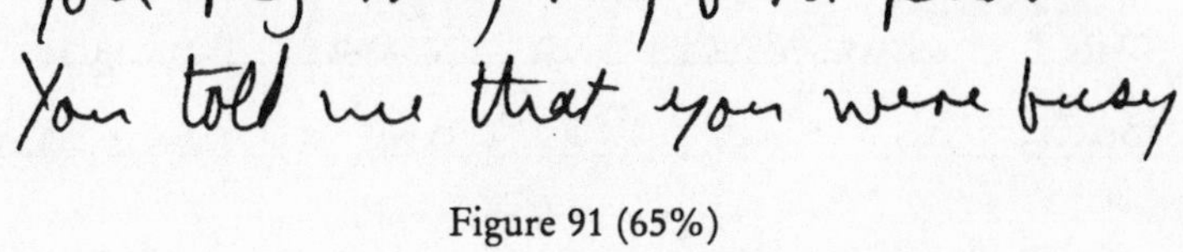

Figure 91 (65%)

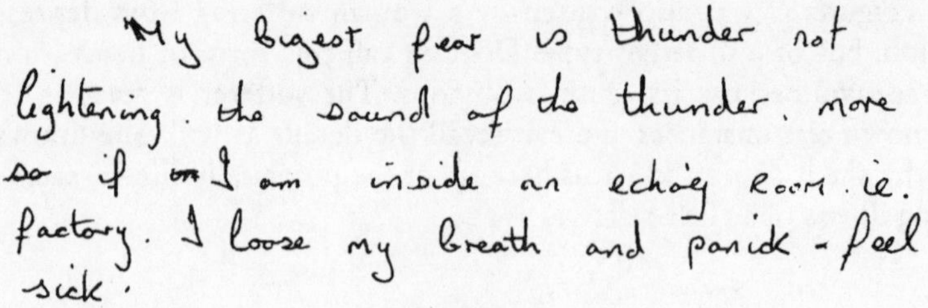

"My biggest fear is thunder not lightening. the sound of the thunder. more so if on I am inside an echoing Room. ie. factory. I loose my breath and panick - feel sick."

Figure 92

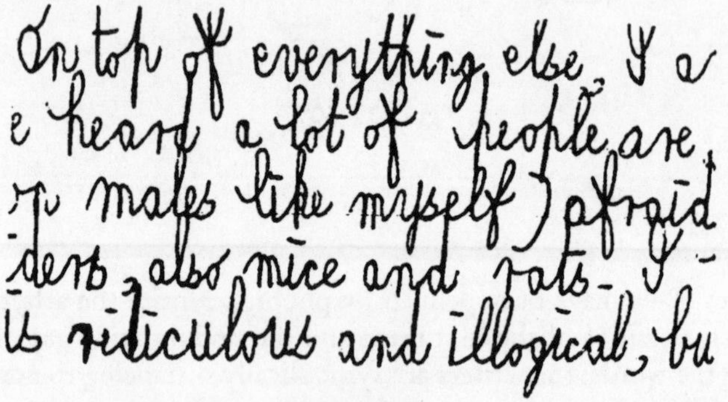

On top of everything else, I a e heard a lot of people are, (males like myself) afraid derk, also mice and rats. I is ridiculous and illogical, bu

Figure 93

Figure 94 shows a similar word separation to that seen in the previous four. Here, it is interesting to see how the word 'fire' has been given a capital *F*, as if to emphasize the importance it has assumed in the mind of the writer.

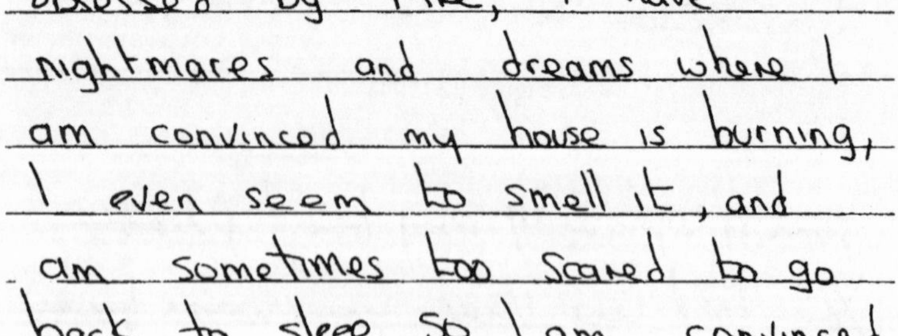

obsessed by Fire, I have nightmares and dreams where I am convinced my house is burning, I even seem to smell it, and am sometimes too scared to go back to sleep, so I am convinced

Figure 94 (65%)

Figure 95 moves swiftly forward as the writer herself would, in view of her fear of being pursued. Light pen pressure points to her sensitivity.

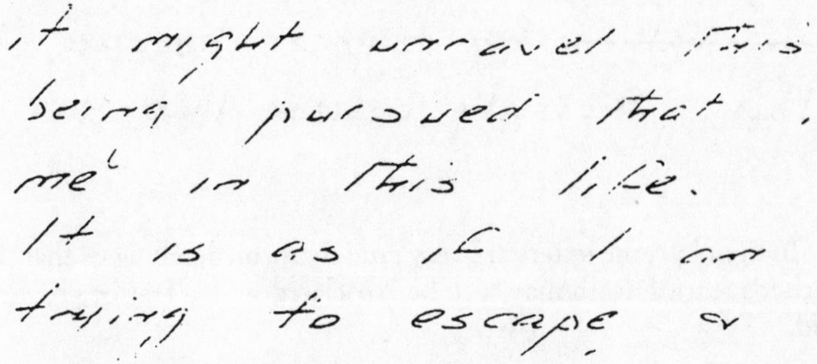

Figure 95

Quite apart from the lack of rhythm in figure 96, its large size, with emphasis on the middle zone, confirms the fact that this writer is unnaturally concerned about her personal image which, in this instance, is related to her weight. Sex – or more precisely the lack of it – is another important factor here. The lower zones reveal that her emotional distress is linked with her attitude to sex.

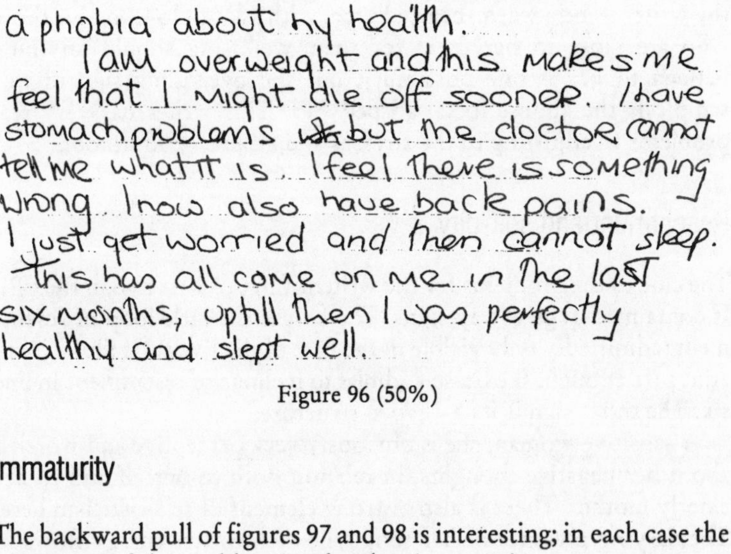

Figure 96 (50%)

Immaturity

The backward pull of figures 97 and 98 is interesting; in each case the root cause of the problem is related to immaturity.

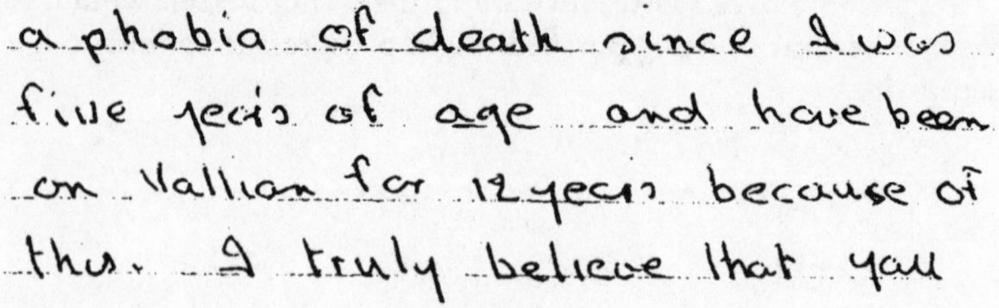

a phobia of death since I was
five years of age and have been
on Vallian for 12 years because of
this. I truly believe that you

Figure 97

In figure 97, the letters are very crudely formed, telling us that the writer's fear of death may well be associated with a fear of growing old.

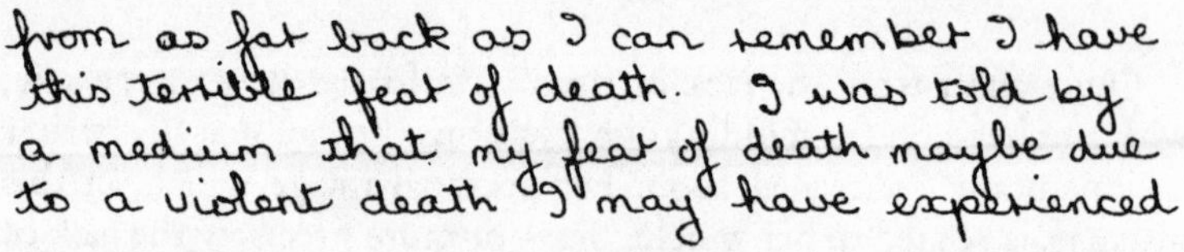

from as far back as I can remember I have
this terrible fear of death. I was told by
a medium that my fear of death maybe due
to a violent death I may have experienced

Figure 98 (65%)

Figure 98 provides two clues. The arcade letter formations show the writer to be a warm-hearted type, with a lot of love to give those who are close to her. Fear for their wellbeing should anything happen to her is one possibility, but the overriding sign of this sample is the almost foetal-shaped PPI. This writer has very real problems of adjusting to the stresses and strains of adulthood.

Resentment and self-pity

The clue to the problems for the writer of figure 99 is also in the PPI. It contains two giveaway signs. The first is the little loop of resentment (admittedly only visible in the first of the five PPIs illustrated). And sure enough, she herself admits to feelings of resentment in line six. The other sign is its S-shaped structure.

A sensitive woman, she is obviously very perceptive and worried about her negative thoughts, in relation both to herself and to her elderly mother. There is also a strong element of self-criticism here. The varying pressure of her script shows how her energy flows in fits and starts.

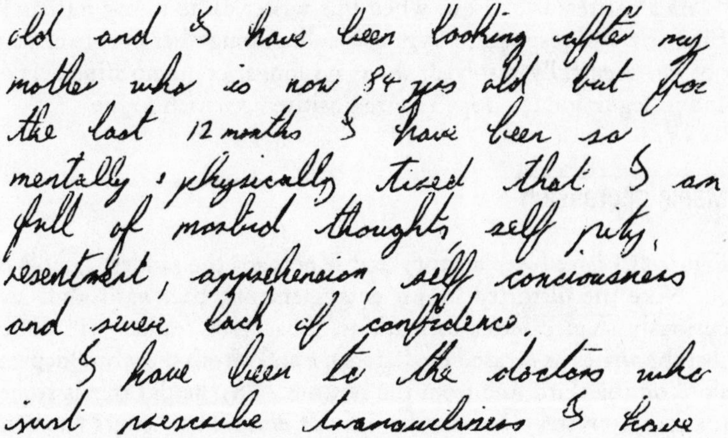

[handwritten text]

Figure 99 (65%)

Suicidal tendencies

Figure 100 was written by a deeply disturbed young woman. The script is full of negative signs, the most disquieting of which is that heavily blacked-out PPI three lines from the bottom.

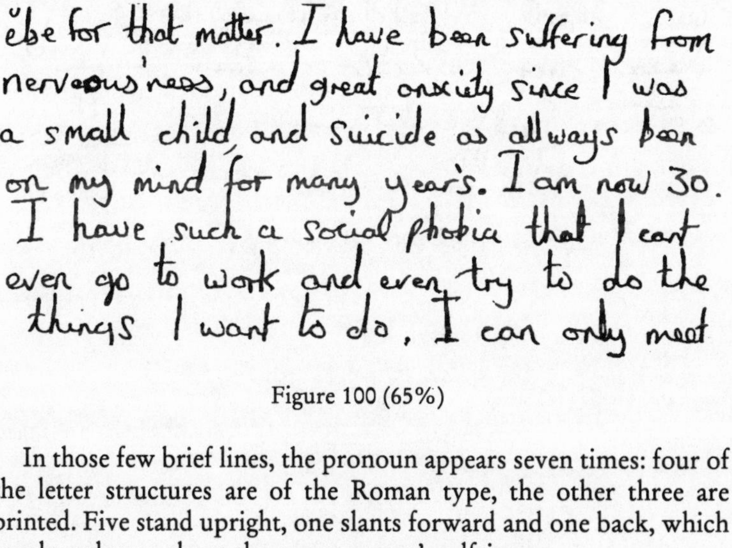

[handwritten text]

Figure 100 (65%)

In those few brief lines, the pronoun appears seven times: four of the letter structures are of the Roman type, the other three are printed. Five stand upright, one slants forward and one back, which speaks volumes about the poor woman's self-image.

As a matter of interest, when this writer came to my husband's clinic, she did respond to hypnosis and although her problems have not yet been fully resolved, she is no longer contemplating suicide and is beginning to adopt a more positive approach to life.

Manic depression

Figure 101 is self-explanatory and is perhaps the saddest sample of all. Note the distorted loops, entanglements, backward slant and curiously shaped letter formations. Observant readers will notice that the writer has erased the letters r, e and s from the word 'depression' on the third line from the bottom. Why he did this is something of a mystery, because he did not erase those letters from the word 'depressive' four lines above it. I cannot begin to understand why he did so.

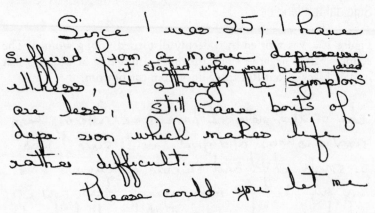

Figure 101 (50%)

7   Different Styles Indicating Different States

Different styles of writing can indicate different mental states, depending on the ways in which the hands differ from those of healthy, 'normal' writers. This can be seen by comparing the samples shown here, starting with a healthy hand.

The healthy hand

The healthy hand is fast and rhythmic, with good, regular pressure and no breaks or strange letter formations. Figures 102 and 103 are prime examples.

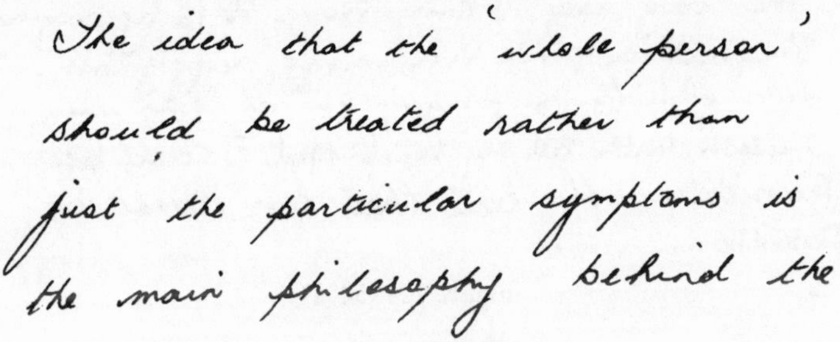

Figure 102 (50%)

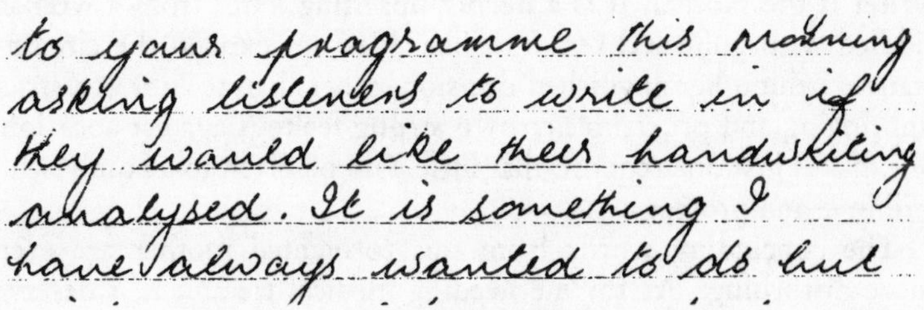

Figure 103 (65%)

These two high quality scripts are enthusiastic, dignified, graceful, building up stamina and speed as they progress along the page. Each is the work of a bright, intelligent writer, easy to read, properly spaced and with much personal style.

Guilt and remorse

Is there anything more heartbreaking than a mother who feels she has no option but to abandon the newborn baby to whom she is manifestly devoted? The few lines in figure 104 are from a letter found alongside a tiny baby girl called Tara.

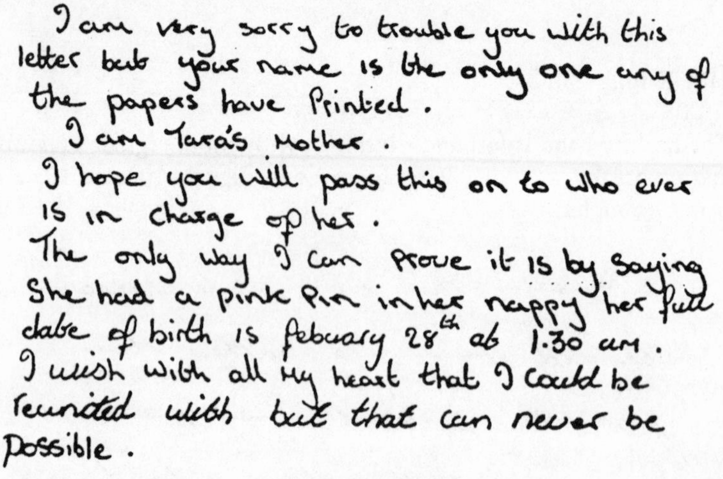

I am very sorry to trouble you with this letter but your name is the only one any of the papers have Printed.
I am Tara's Mother.
I hope you will pass this on to who ever is in charge of her.
The only way I can prove it is by saying She had a pink Pin in her nappy her full date of birth is febuary 28th at 1.30 am.
I wish with all my heart that I could be reunited with but that can never be Possible.

Figure 104 (50%)

The letter goes on to provide other evidence to prove that the writer is the mother. It is a deeply upsetting letter from a woman riddled with guilt and remorse. She does not explain the circumstances behind her anguished decision, other than to hint at a strict upbringing and proclaim her own strong feelings against abortion. She makes just one request: that little Tara be given to a family who will love and protect her.

The concluding words from this tormented mother are even more disturbing: 'As for me needing medical treatment, I deserve whatever happens. The pain may go away, but the loss of Tara and the love I have for her will be with me forever.' The baby and the despairing mother's message of love were found in a public lavatory in Liverpool.

It does not take a detailed knowledge of graphology to recognize the many indications of stress and anxiety in this script. The overriding impression is one of profound sorrow that such a course was necessary but fundamentally, the whole tone of this writing proves what we already know: that the unfortunate woman was distraught.

Her general lack of rhythm and the wavering slant speak volumes. Although written with a felt-tipped pen, it is clear that her hand was shaking as she wrote. Tremulous pen strokes can be seen throughout. Moreover, the slant of the script alters from line to line, within lines, even within words.

There is no doubt about two facts: that the mother really does love baby Tara, and that she considers herself a most unworthy mother. For proof of this latter point comparisons should be drawn between the large *s* in 'she' (five lines from the bottom) with the smaller *m* in 'mother' (four lines above it). Arcade letter formations (rounded letter tops) indicate deeply submerged emotions.

Bearing in mind that the lower zone reflects the writer's attitude to sex, and that the creation of a religious symbol in any letter should never be overlooked, we must turn our attention to the *f* on line six, the stem of which has formed itself into a cross. The writer thus reveals her religious scruples. The fact that it is the *f* – and no other descender – which has been scored through is deeply significant. Unconsciously, she appears to have decided to erase sex from her life. I have seen the same sign in the hand of another writer who made no secret of the fact that after two difficult pregnancies and a failed marriage, she had no further wish for intimate relations.

The hesitation and lingering over writing the letter *g* (at the end of line seven) combined with the cross on the *f* (or scoring through, depending on the viewpoint) indicate another factor – guilt.

Basically, the letter structures in this sample show the writer to be warm-hearted and generous. Although full of conflict, there is not a single sign of aggression to be found. Her problems are all rooted in her own childhood. The personal pronouns show a most unsatisfactory relationship with her parents. The mother symbol is not quite complete, the father symbol even less so.

While her PPIs are not exactly foetal-shaped, they are very immature formations and indicate an inability to cope with the stresses and strains of motherhood. The fact that the writer has blacked out so many of her lower-case *es* reflects erasure of personality, and wide gaps between the words indicate difficulty in relating to others.

Even in this brief extract the slant of the writing swings from upright to forward to backward. It is a disturbing hand, totally lacking in form and consistency.

Hatred and aggression

By way of complete contrast, figure 105 shows an example of hate mail. Most journalists receive a poison pen letter at some stage in their career, so when this envelope was delivered to me, I knew without even opening it what it would contain.

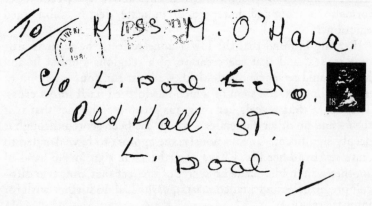

Figure 105 (65%)

Whereas the previous sample displays not a single sign of aggression, this one is full of it and the writer's mental instability can be seen in every pen stroke. Neurotic overwriting appears on every line. Anger can be detected from the heaviness of the pen digging into the paper, depression from the falling baseline and violent changes of mood from the combination of all these factors. This writing is totally without rhythm or balance.

Attention-seeking

When artificial letter forms and signs show up in a script, there is a reason. Their sole purpose is to impress.

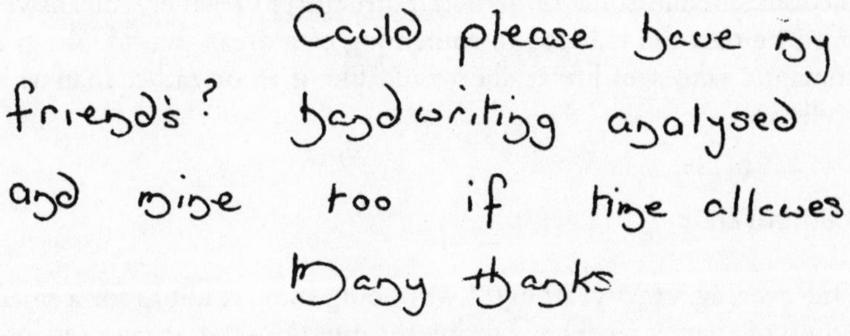

Could please have my
friend's? handwriting analysed
and mine too if time allowes
Dasy thanks

Figure 106 (65%)

The writer of the sample in figure 106 enjoys being different and ostentatious, but what she may not realize is that her stilted style masks a personality problem. The very wide spacing between words tells of her difficulty in socializing, hence the need to impress, to go one better than everyone else and pretend she never wanted to mix in the first place.

The note featured in figure 107 contains what journalists might call the 'aah' factor, an element some might find sickly sweet. Coming from a married woman, I have to say that I find its tone rather twee.

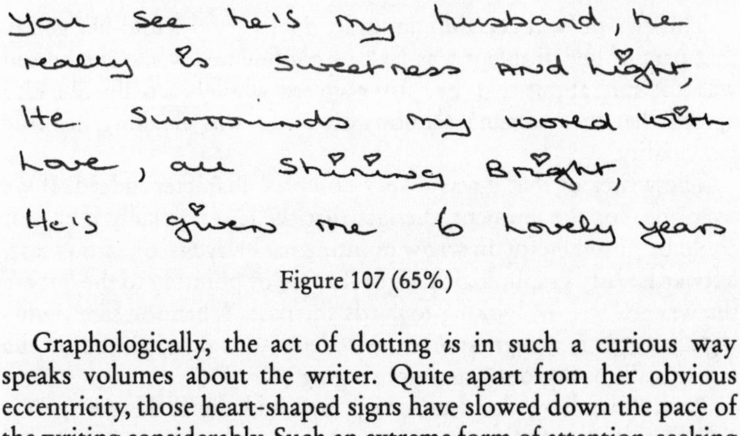

You see he's my husband, he
really Is sweetness And hight,
He surrounds my world with
Love, au shining Bright,
He's given me 6 Lovely years

Figure 107 (65%)

Graphologically, the act of dotting *is* in such a curious way speaks volumes about the writer. Quite apart from her obvious eccentricity, those heart-shaped signs have slowed down the pace of the writing considerably. Such an extreme form of attention-seeking raises questions about the motivation behind it. This whole sample suggests that she 'doth protest too much'.

If, as she claims, her husband is so wonderful that she has an urge to make her i-dots heart-shaped, why does her script tumble off the baseline as it progresses down the page? Why are her underloops inconsistent and some of her letter structures variable? The answer must be that she is living in something of a dream world. She is a romantic who sees life as she would like it to be rather than as it really is.

Flamboyance

One evening a few years ago I was doing some readings for a small group of charity workers. During the question-and-answer session, the most flamboyantly dressed member of the group came forward and asked if I could explain why two symbols in her writing were different from those of everyone else. The first of these was her personal pronoun, which appeared as a lower-case *i*. The other was that she always shaped her lower-case *e* as in figure 108.

Figure 108

This person was certainly an individualist, and I told her gently that part of her problem was lack of confidence. While she herself was not sure about that, her sister agreed wholeheartedly. She also agreed that the woman's flamboyant outfit was cloaking her true personality.

The writer of that *e* was a very complex character indeed. If we overlook, for the moment, the fact that the letter actually *is* an *e*, it could be mistaken for an arrow pointing backwards – or, in this case, leftwards. Any graphological signs leaning or pointing to the left are the writer's way of looking towards the past. When the sign pointing leftwards is an ego-symbol, it reflects thoughts focused on the individual's background and upbringing.

And, as we have also seen, sharp lines and angles denote aggression. The sum of these two factors is an inherent urge to rebel against family background and traditions. However, without seeing a sample of her script and assessing all its other signs and symbols, I was unable to say any more about the writer.

Insecurity

A printed lower-case script often points to insecurity and unfamiliarity with the written word, and although at first glance the one in figure 109 appears straightforward enough, it is anything but. This type of writing is often penned by problem teenagers.

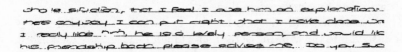

Figure 109 (50%)

Introversion is seen in the writer's hand, as well as a massive inferiority complex, which is manifested rather differently from the previous case. This writer does write her personal pronouns as capital letters, but some of them are so miniaturized that they are even smaller than surrounding lower-case letters.

She too has a great need for companionship, as seen in the cramping of letters within words. Writers with this type of style tend to be over-critical of others and are often alienated as a result.

The anonymous note from which this is extracted was sent to the advice column I used to write. My correspondent was worried that her boyfriend did not understand her. Her own love for him was not in doubt; one has only to look at the word 'him' on the penultimate line. While all the other words stay securely on the baseline, that one is way up on a pedestal: an unconscious statement about where, in her mind, she had placed the man himself. She therefore shows herself to be much more deeply in love with her man than the writer with the heart-shaped i-dots and the romantic turn of phrase!

Executive stress

I recently interviewed a 32-year-old business executive for a newspaper feature on his post with a fast-growing international company. He was relaxed, happy and utterly charming. He showed none of the usual signs of executive stress.

When the interview was over, he said he knew I was also a graphologist and wondered if I would mind having a look at his handwriting. Despite appearances, he said he felt troubled, but had no idea why.

Choosing the first sentence that came into my head, I asked him to write the words 'I am not my brother's keeper'. When he had done so, his writing was full of symbolism. For a start, the word 'keeper' stood out above the others by being darker and larger than the rest. His *k* had taken on the form of a man kicking out at something. Then an even more unusual sign attracted my attention. The word had four rather than three *e*s.

Combined with the odd-looking *k*, the extra *e* provided a deep insight into the working of the man's mind. I had already established in general terms that his was not the hand of a sportsman. He was no footballer, so what was the relevance of a *k* that gave the impression that its writer was kicking out? Was he kicking at, or against, something?

Yes, he said, he most certainly was. One of his directors was making life intolerable, and he had so much work on his plate that he was finding it difficult to cope, though on meeting him no one would have suspected it.

The relevance of the extra *e* might thus be that he had too many eggs in one basket. It was significant that it was the *e* which was repeated. Repetition of the ego-sign suggested his having to put on a brave face. Image, as we all know, is very important for anyone in such a high-powered position.

As for the writing as a whole, had I not seen him produce it I would not have believed that it was his. It was shaky and inhibited and showed a host of negative and disturbing elements. The slant wavered backwards and forwards, there were pressure changes and breaks in the loops, and the general impression was one of complete disorientation. The dominant factors were frustration and aggression, which were totally alien to the writer's character. He was not paying enough attention to detail. His mind was in turmoil, his health was at risk. Despite my first impression, I could see now that he was under very severe stress. Furthermore, he admitted the fact, explaining that he was working a ten- to twelve-hour day, seven days a week. His family seldom saw him.

Fortunately, the story has a happy ending. Having had the root of his problem pointed out to him, he confronted the director in question. As a result, it was agreed that he work fewer hours, take a month's leave and learn to relax. The director was most apologetic – he had not had the slightest inkling of what was happening to his assistant.

Three months later, when I met the young businessman at a press reception, he asked me to have another look at his script. I was delighted to see that it was now completely devoid of hand tremor. The wavering slant, pressure changes, broken loops and many other signs of stress were no longer in evidence. This sample showed him to be in a much calmer frame of mind and much happier.

In view of the fact that he is today a leading public figure and that his writing might be recognized, I have agreed not to reproduce either sample.

8   Stumbling Blocks

When individual words and their associated thoughts stand out in the text they do so for a reason. It is all to do with what I choose to think of as mental 'banana skins' deep down in the mind. The writer encounters one of these, pauses momentarily and tries to by-pass it. Instead, he trips over it and does exactly the opposite of what he intended, by drawing attention to it.

In figure 110, the writer appears to have hit something of a stumbling block when penning the words 'despises' and 'failure'. It is not difficult to understand why.

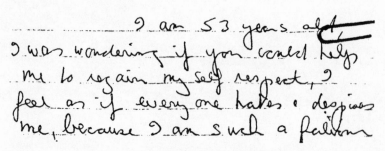

Figure 110 (65%)

The astute graphologist should be constantly on the lookout for the consequences of writers tripping over these obstacles, because a slip of the pen can be even more revealing than a slip of the tongue.

Subconscious stumblings can tell the analyst much about the writer's inner thoughts. These stumblings do not apply exclusively to letters or words dominating a page but can also relate to those paling into obscurity or missing altogether. Their absence means that the writer, deep in his mind, believes they are irrelevant. They may have an unpleasant association or they may represent an issue he is trying to avoid or conceal.

For such psychological hiccups to have significance they must appear regularly in a script. If they only show up once or twice there may be no sinister implications.

Key words

Figures 111–13 show how particular key words are highlighted.

Mrs Appleton
20 Brookdale Rd
Rhyl North Wales.
Being up here for a while
This lady came from Wrexham
40 yrs ago. So I have you on
my mind as you lived this
way too. Hope you & family are
very well. I am staying at Van next week
in Skegness. Left Dad & a friend
there. Here for a week. A little
windy & has been cold.
Very rainy on the way here. The
Sun poor But keeps breaking
Though. Lost your Address
So send with Evelins
Hope your sister is better
& cousin at Hospital OK.

Just found your address now
Can't send on this
So I hope you get
A Concenteeyen
Bit of welsh

Hope you are well
Regards to all Millicent

POST OFFICE PREFERRED
THE MENAI SUSPENSION BRIDGE PT27708

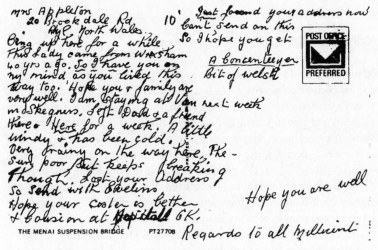

Figure 111 (65%)

The elderly woman who penned the postcard from which figure 111 has been taken is primarily concerned about the welfare of her addressee's cousin in hospital, hence the emphasis on that word.

Figure 112 is from the pen of a university undergraduate about to embark on long years of study. Not surprisingly, his key word is 'succeed'.

or another for the past 5 months without very much Success
Perhaps with your help I may 'succeed'
Yours Sincerely,

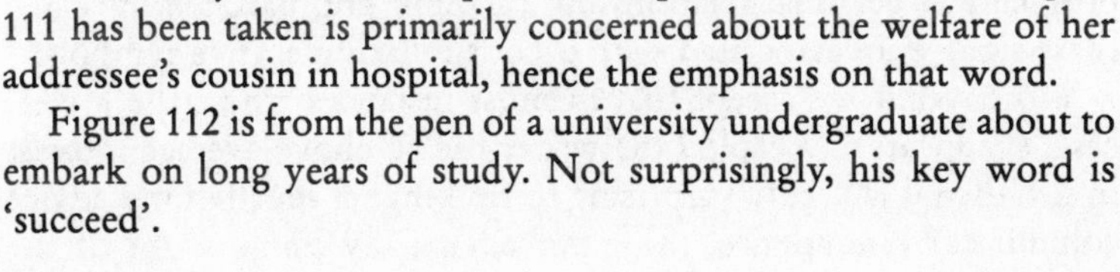

Figure 112 (50%)

The young man who write figure 113 is so worried about his sexual inclinations that he has overwritten the word 'gay' several times.

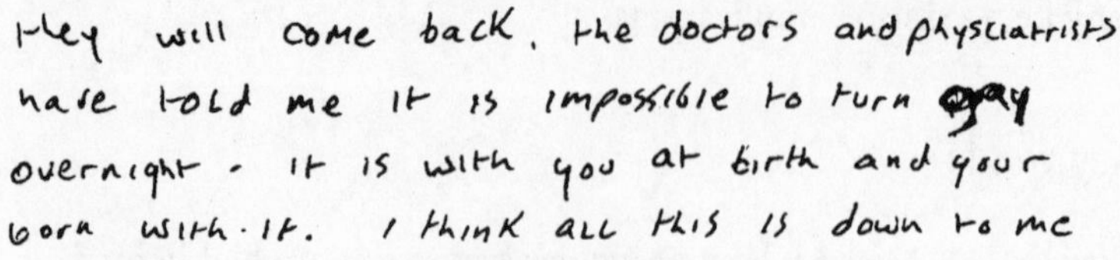

> Hey will come back. the doctors and physuiatrists
> have told me it is impossible to turn gay
> overnight - it is with you at birth and your
> born with it. I think all this is down to me

Figure 113 (65%)

Individual letters

When unusual formations occur regularly and form a certain pattern the unconscious activity behind them should be investigated. As always, however, we must first eliminate the possibility that the pen ran dry, the pencil's lead broke, something interrupted the writer's flow of thoughts or the writing surface was uneven. In the case of one letter I received, the peculiarities of the script were attributed to a kitten pouncing on the writer's pen as it moved along the page.

With all these possibilities excluded, the next step is to search for signs which really are significant. In my own experience of receiving letters from people seeking help from my husband or sent to me for inclusion in my advice column, a common factor manifested itself.

I noticed that the letters most often stumbled over were *d* and *l*. Is it too simplistic to assume that because the words 'dear', 'darling' and 'love' start with these letters, those writers were likely to have problems in personal relationships? I think not, particularly when these signs were associated with other similarly negative symbols.

Moreover if we accept that in most instances where the lower-case 's' appears as a capital the writer has an above-average interest in sex, then it is hardly surprising to find that in much of my advice column correspondence, the letter *S* virtually jumped out of the notepaper.

Above-average interest does not automatically imply over-activity. Under-activity can also bring about enlarged *Ss*. Their appearance simply suggests that, for whatever reason, thoughts of sex have pushed their way through to the forefront of the writer's mind.

There are, of course, exceptions to this rule and it is vital to search for corroborative signs. While symbolism is important in graphological assessment, we must beware of falling into the Freudian trap of making sexual connections where none exist. When the letter *s* predominates, we must look for other sex signs before categorically stating that the writer's mind is preoccupied with such thoughts.

In the letter in figure 114, for example, it would be a very great mistake to seize on the *S* and interpret it as a sex-sign. Careful examination under bright lights and strong magnification (which is how all graphological analyses should be conducted) shows that this is no normal enlarged *s*, but a pound sign, almost identical to the *l* in the word 'letter', two lines above it. Money, rather than sex, is the dominant thought in this writer's mind. Symbolism is very important in psycho-graphology, but only if the interpretation is accurate.

Although one cannot normally determine age the sample is obviously the hand of an elderly person with failing eyesight. Note, too, the irregularity of the inter-linear spacing. And while the writer's mind is still in complete control and she appears to have retained her excellent head for figures, a general wearing down of bodily tissues can be seen in the fractured formation of many letters and the variation in their sizes.

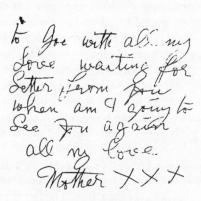

Figure 114

This sample contains a most interesting mix of warm emotions and cold, hard ruthlessness. A former businesswoman, her thoughts are still dominated by money. This is apparent from the following signs: the *g* at the end of 'waiting' (line two) shaped like a figure eight (a symbol which can also have literary implications, hence the need to seek corroborative evidence); the *y* in 'you' (line three) resembling a seven; and the personal pronoun (line four) which could be mistaken for a nine.

Add all these to the £-shaped *s* and we have a clear picture. Triangles replacing loops indicate a good head for figures, and this script contains several. Further triangular shapes can be detected where they would normally not exist: between the *ts* in 'letter' (line three) and on the two occasions the writer has penned the word 'you' (lines three and five).

Warmth is shown in the rounded tops to the name Joe and in most of the upper loops. The fact that those loops are so inflated suggests a fertile imagination, but aggression (in the form of sharp lines and ticks) still comes through strongly. Note the irritable little ticks commencing the first two t-bars (lines one and two).

Elongated bars reaching out over neighbouring letters hint at the mother's protective nature. The backward swing of the *y* in 'my' (line six) is the type of stroke made by writers who believe they are being deprived of affection.

Signs of curiosity can be seen in both the little curl before the word 'mother' and the structure of the small *r* at the end of the same word.

Overlapping loops show muddled thoughts but only in relation to home. The writer was after all in her eighties at the time she penned her note so this is understandable. Despite her age, the *m*s (money) and pound signs are all clear as whistles.

Thrift can be seen in the way she has cut back some of the *m*s to a bare minimum (note how she has actually omitted a stroke in some, almost turning them into *n*s). A sense of humour is indicated by the smile-shaped t-bar in the word 'to' (lines one and four) and i-dots in 'waiting' (line two) and 'again' (line five). Closed and tightly knotted *o*s show her ability to keep secrets.

Despite her obviously failing eyesight, her mental co-ordination is first-rate. There is not the slightest hint of hand tremor, as can be seen in the steady execution of the t-bars. The fact that those bars are shaped like crosses suggests the importance religion has assumed in her mind.

At the time of penning this note, the writer was a shrewd and very astute old lady who lived on in remarkably good health for many years to come.

Sex

While sex can be discounted in figure 114, it is certainly a factor in the next three samples.

The woman who wrote the piece from which figure 115 is taken resorts to the 'leg-lock' type of *y* loop. Sexual scruples are indicated.

Figure 115

The clue in figure 116 is in the g. On that one line the letter appears three times, each structured differently. This writer's attitude to sex is one of confusion, associated with guilt.

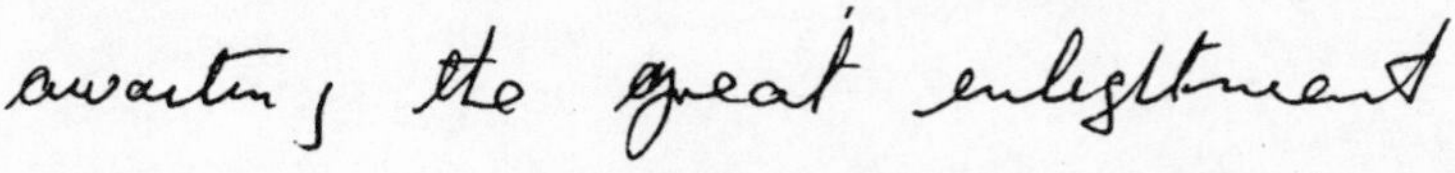

Figure 116 (65%)

The writer of figure 117 says she lies awake at night because of tension and anxiety; to reach the root of her trouble we only have to turn to the word 'afford' and note double *f*. Why that is the letter the writer has stumbled over, rather than any other, can be explained by its sexual significance, as discussed in chapter 3.

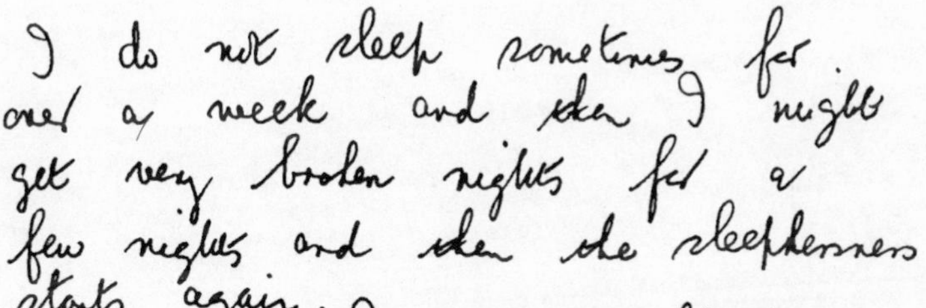

Figure 117 (65%)

The writer of figure 118 could be said to be suffering from what the Victorians called 'unrequited love'. It is such a sad little sample with its symbolic line running down the *y* conjuring up images of a tear running down the face. Note too how much larger that *y* is than any of the other letters in this brief extract, illustrating how much the writer thinks of the person to whom his note is addressed.

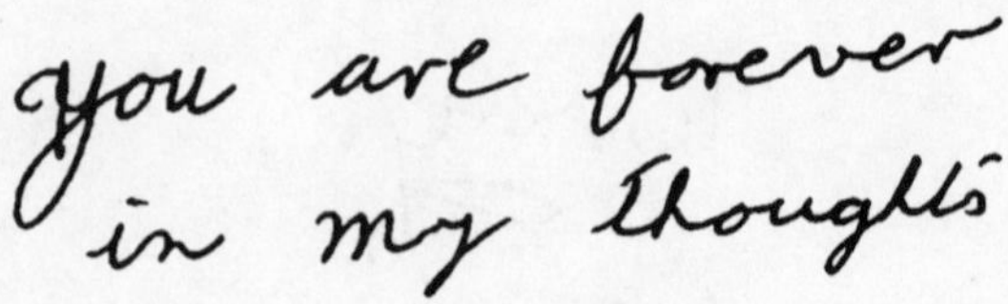

Figure 118

9   Bodily Ills

Those of us who specialize in the health aspects of handwriting analysis look for different signs and symbols from those sought by analysts whose areas of research are in personnel selection or the detection of crime.

The investigation of a writer's health by means of his script involves concentrating on how the three zones of the writing relate to corresponding areas of the body. The basis of this technique is to equate the upper zone with the head, neck and shoulder area, the middle with the trunk region (chest, heart, lungs, abdomen, spinal column) and the lower with everything from the hips down. (However, these areas do tend to overlap.) When particular signs in the writing are stressed, weakened or entirely missing, the interpretation is that the corresponding regions of the body are those in which the writer's problems are located. Handwriting analysis can thus be shown to provide valuable clues about a writer's state of health.

Heart and lungs

The strong-minded, disciplined hand featured in figure 119 was penned by a journalist, author, broadcaster and music critic.

Speedy thought processes are reflected in every movement of his pen: the simplified and many printed letter formations, the joining of words, the angular i-dots and upward-slanting t-bars all crossed on a high level in a single stroke. The words themselves flow quickly and easily, showing that the writer has a literary and quick-thinking mind. The superior quality of his script shows excellent reasoning powers and associated thoughts, the most dominant factor being literary ability.

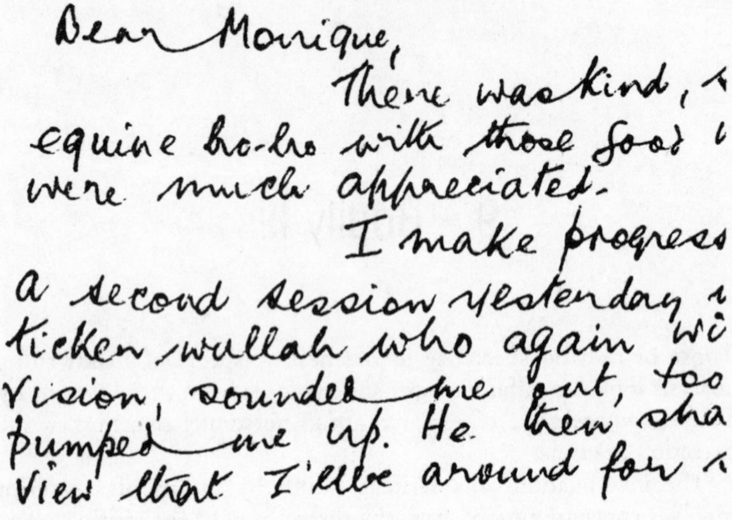

Dear Monique,

There was kind, ↖
equine ho-ho with those food ↙
were much appreciated.

I make progress
a second session yesterday ↖
ticken wallah who again wi
vision, sounded me out, too
pumped me up. He then sha
view that I'll be around for ↖

Figure 119

So much for the mental picture, but what about any bodily signals? To examine the sample more closely, we must take a rule and study it line by line. We will then see that although it begins cheerily enough with an upward slant, it levels off and the next three lines are completely straight across the page.

Line six (beginning 'a second . . .') starts to slope down with the word 'session' then levels off again, hinting at mild, but controlled depression. Likewise the next line. But by the time the writer comes to the final line in the extract, he has straightened himself out again: so much so that for the remainder of the letter, the slant is back on its upward trend.

Switching from the psychological to the physiological, we find changes of pressure in almost every word. The *D* in 'dear' has a jerk halfway down. The *o*, *q* and *u* in 'Monique' have pressure points where there would normally not be any. So too has the bar of the capital *T* the *h*, the *s* in 'was' and so on, throughout the extract. No isolated signs these, there are far too many to be dismissed as such.

These pressure changes and general disturbances in energy flow represent a recurring weakness, indicating a precarious state of health. Despite his apparent cheerfulness, the writer was seriously ill and although he may not have been conscious of the fact, his unconscious knew it because the words themselves give him away. It is when he writes about his sessions with the 'ticker wallah' (heart specialist) that his despondency is most apparent.

My friend was in hospital recovering from a heart attack. There had been no suggestion of any other medical condition. Indeed, the bright tone of his letter suggested that he believed he was well on the road to recovery. Never one to dwell on physical weakness, he hoped to return to his duties, as he explained on the next page of his letter (not reproduced). Its upward slant certainly reflected that optimism. Yet within eight weeks of penning this letter, the writer was dead; inoperable lung cancer had spread throughout his system.

There was no way I could have detected this from his writing. To attempt to do so would have been to enter the field of the diagnostician and as I have repeatedly pointed out, it is something I do not believe in. Some of my more adventurous colleagues claim to be able to pick up cancerous and pre-cancerous conditions in advance of a medical diagnosis, but to my way of thinking, this is very dangerous territory for a lay analyst to enter. Cancer is not just one disease but a whole group. A patient presenting with suspicious signs and symptoms will be given a physical examination by the doctor, who will also take the patient's medical history. He may then order a whole series of tests before coming up with a definitive diagnosis. So how can a graphologist with no medical training claim to be able to pick up something so complex from an individual's handwriting?

The sample in figure 120 has been extracted from a letter written by a patient suffering from a different type of lung condition: bronchiectasis.

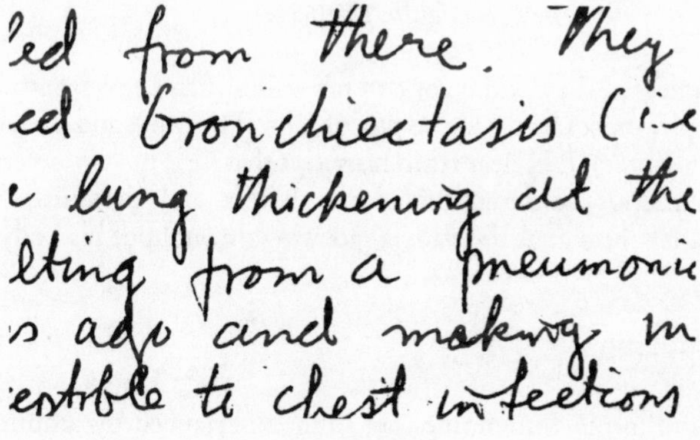
'ed from there. They
ed bronchiectasis (i.e
lung thickening at the
lting from a pneumonia
s ago and making m
eptible to chest infections

Figure 120

Bronchiectasis is usually the result of scarring from an earlier chest infection and it can affect part or all of the bronchial tubes. The damage to and distortion of the tubes results in breathlessness, coughing and the production of excess sputum.

An examination of figure 120 under strong magnification reveals both thickening and weakness in the upper loops. These represent the writer's respiratory tract and his breathing difficulties. In fact, there is a general weakness throughout this sample, which is hardly surprising in view of the debilitating nature of the condition and the intolerable strain it can put on the heart.

The writing itself moves at high speed and its style is not unlike that of the previous sample. This one was written by a general practitioner forced into early retirement because of his illness. His script is the product of a razor-sharp mind with alert and very quick responses. But his body is considerably less healthy than his mind; one can almost feel his difficulties inhaling and exhaling.

Emphysema also affects the lung tissue. It is a condition in which the lungs themselves become over-distended, reducing the ability of oxygen to enter the body and carbon dioxide to leave it. Breathlessness results. The writer of figure 121 is a 70-year-old man whose condition is complicated by dizzy spells, back pain and some digestive problems.

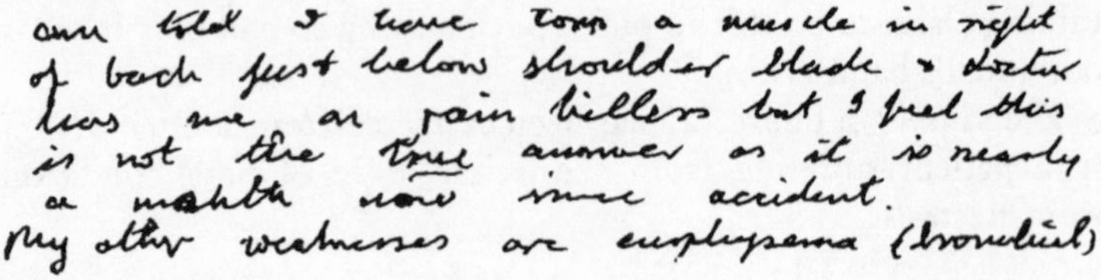
am told I have torn a muscle in right
of back just below shoulder blade & doctor
has me on pain killers but I feel this
is not the true answer as it is nearly
a month now since accident.
My other weaknesses are emphysema (bronchial)

Figure 121 (65%)

Weakness in the middle zone of his writing can be seen throughout the sample, most clearly in the words 'am' (line one), and 'killers' and 'feel' (line three). It is clear from his script that he is in very severe pain. The tremulous construction of the letters and pressure changes throughout show that the pain is radiating throughout his body.

Phantom limb

Phantom limb is a phenomenon often experienced by amputees. It occurs when impulses produced by the severed limb reach the brain and produce the feeling that the limb is still there. Because of the link between severed nerves and pain impulses, people who experience the phantom limb syndrome will confirm that there is nothing imaginary about the agony they are suffering.

The writer of figure 122 is a 47-year-old woman born with a genetic bone disorder which caused small nodules on some of the long bones in her legs. Surgery in childhood removed the worst of them, but the aftermath was a deformed left foot. Subsequent attempts to have it straightened proved unsuccessful, and it was amputated. A year later, lack of circulation in that leg resulted in it also being amputated below the knee.

There was an immediate improvement in the woman's general health and everything would have been fine but for the pain of the phantom limb. At the time she wrote, she was on a high dosage of pain-killers.

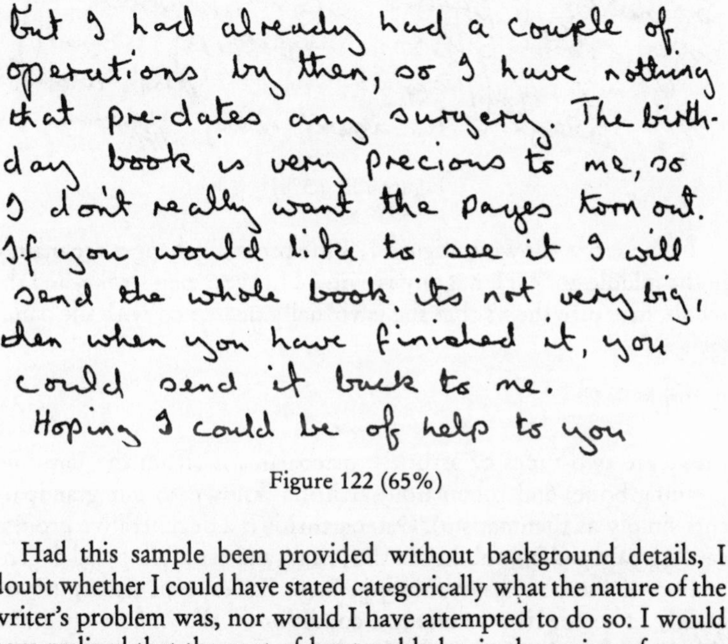

But I had already had a couple of operations by then, so I have nothing that pre-dates any surgery. The birthday book is very precious to me, so I don't really want the pages torn out. If you would like to see it I will send the whole book, its not very big, then when you have finished it, you could send it back to me.
Hoping I could be of help to you

Figure 122 (65%)

Had this sample been provided without background details, I doubt whether I could have stated categorically what the nature of the writer's problem was, nor would I have attempted to do so. I would have realized that the root of her trouble lay in the region of one or both feet, where the pressure shows some slight changes under magnification, but I do not believe I could have been more specific.

This simply bears out the point that graphologists are not diagnosticians, nor should they claim to be. The object of the exercise is simply to pick out strengths and weaknesses in the script and indicate which part of the body has been affected by illness or injury, no more.

Shingles

Shingles is a viral infection closely associated with chicken-pox. Because it mainly affects the nervous system, it is an excruciatingly painful condition. It manifests itself in a rash of little blisters on the trunk, which are burning hot and itchy, and which when scratched bleed and pustulate.

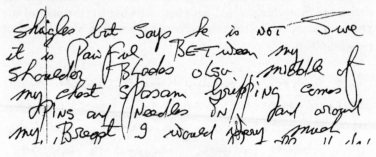

Figure 123 (65%)

In the script shown in figure 123 the pressure changes are mainly in the middle zone. Her agony is evident in every pen stroke, and the whole structure shows that she is virtually demented with the pain.

Arthritis

There are two types of arthritis; osteoarthritis (from the Latin *os*, meaning bone) and rheumatoid arthritis (known to our grandparents simply as rheumatism). Osteoarthritis is a degenerative process causing pain and immobility in the joints, and crumbling and degeneration of the bones surrounding them. Knees, hips and spine are mainly affected. It is a common condition in the middle-aged and elderly, although it can occasionally be a complication of other conditions, including the skin condition psoriasis.

Rheumatoid arthritis is a chronic condition, causing inflammation of the smaller joints of the hands and feet. It can affect people of any age, but is much more generalized than osteoarthritis and can be associated with infection and fever. In rheumatoid arthritis, the joints are painful to move and tender to touch, and may be surrounded by considerable swelling because of the involvement of membranes around the affected joint. Both types of arthritis can seriously impede movement.

The sample reproduced in figure 124 was written by a 60-year-old woman who suffered from an arthritic knee which affected her mainly when climbing stairs.

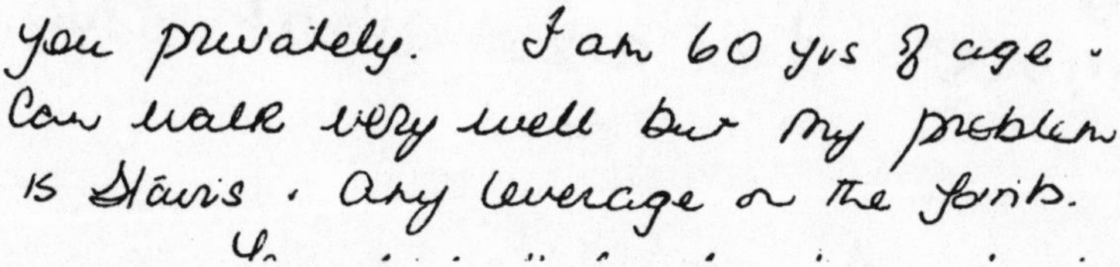
You privately. I am 60 yrs of age.
Can walk very well but my problem
is Stairs. Any leverage on the joints.

Figure 124 (65%)

And one can see the lower zone weakness, which is clearly visible in the way only *some* of these strokes return to the baseline. There are of course weaknesses elsewhere in the script, but then arthritis can affect a variety of bones throughout the body.

The writer of figure 125 is a doctor whose one great love in life is his music. A skilled and highly competent pianist, he could have made his career equally well on the concert platform. How very sad, then, when rheumatoid arthritis set in, crippling both hands so that not only could he no longer tend to his patients, but he could not play his beloved grand piano either.

Although partially controlled with medication, the condition makes hand movements extremely painful, as his distorted writing testifies. With this type of arthritis, it is very difficult to exert fine muscle control.

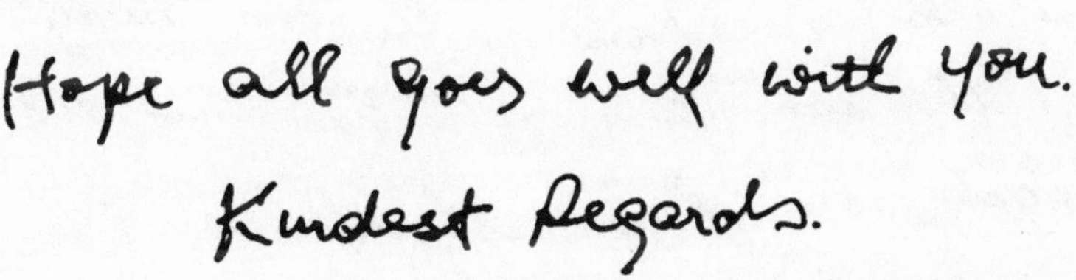
Hope all goes well with you.
Kindest Regards.

Figure 125

The samples in figures 126–9 were also written by arthritics.

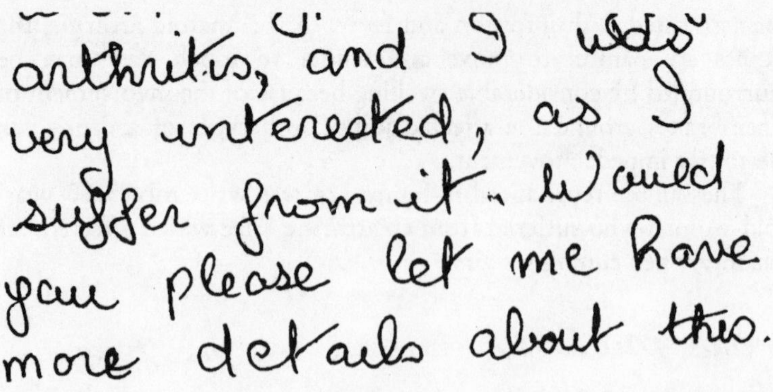

arthritis, and I udo
very interested, as I
suffer from it. Would
you please let me have
more details about this.

Figure 126

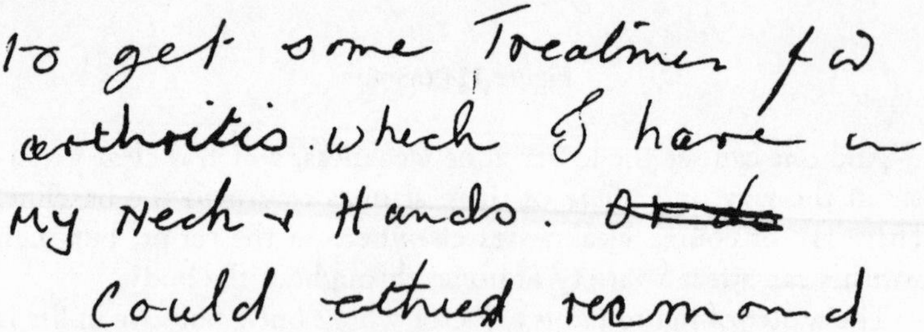

to get some Treatment for
arthritis. which I have in
my neck & Hands. ~~Or do~~
Could ~~ethed~~ recomond

Figure 127 (65%)

help me. I am 50 years
old & 3 years ago began with
arthritis & it is mostly in my
ankles & hands I can hardly
~~w~~lk at times & I've now also
got a frozen shoulder so am
getting hardly any sleep.

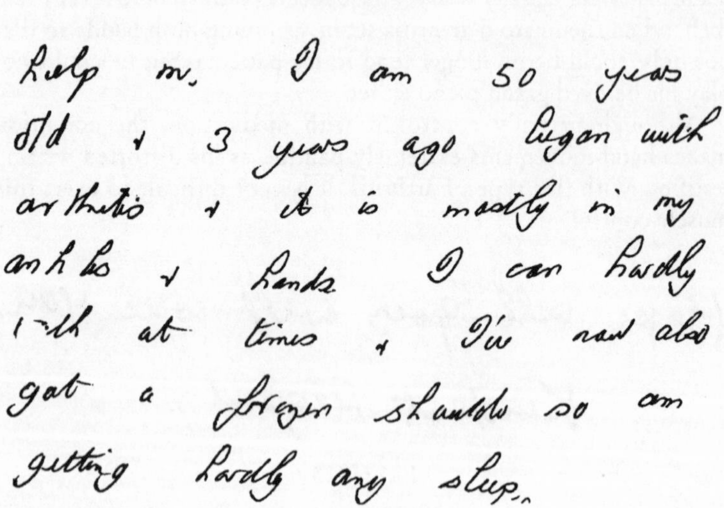

Figure 128 (65%)

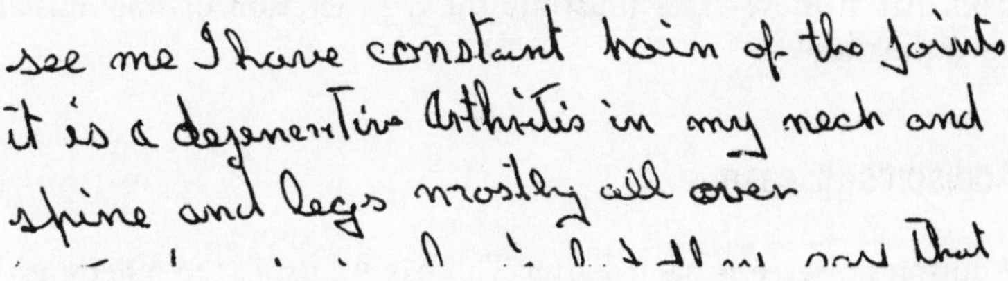

see me I have constant pain of the joints
it is a degenerative arthritis in my neck and
spine and legs mostly all over

Figure 129 (65%)

Trapped nerves

The writers of figures 130 and 131 suffer from trapped sciatic nerves
– the largest nerves in the body, which run from the base of the spine
right down the back of each leg.

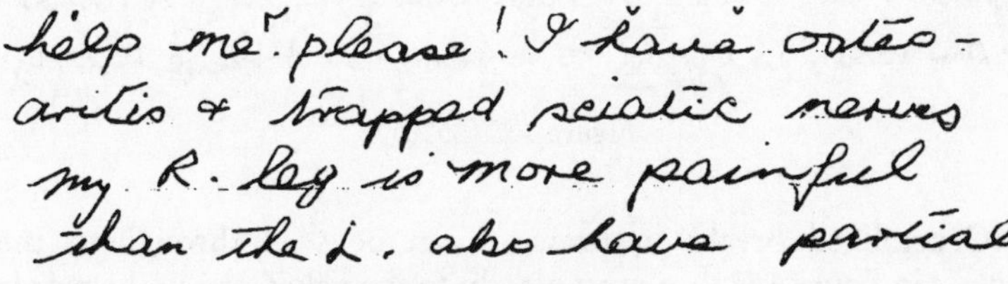

help me please! I have osteo-
aritis & trapped sciatic nerves
my R. leg is more painful
than the L. also have partial

Figure 130 (65%)

In figure 130 the weakness is most apparent in the lower zone but
can be seen elsewhere, as in the base of the *a* in 'trapped' and of the
n in 'nerves'.

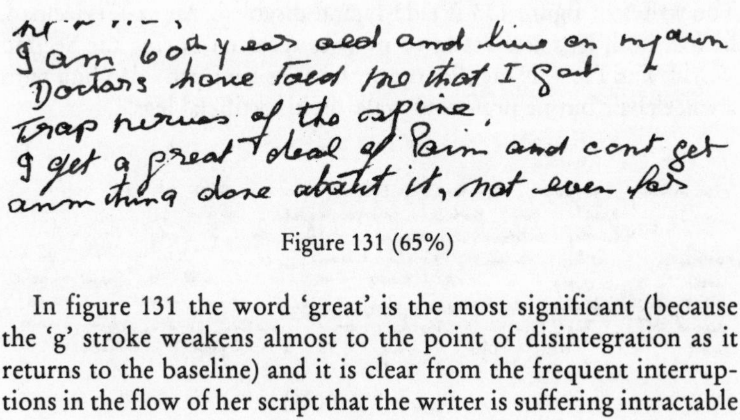

I am 60 years old and live on my own
Doctors have told me that I got
trap nerves of the spine.
I get a great deal of Pain and cant get
anything done about it, not even for

Figure 131 (65%)

In figure 131 the word 'great' is the most significant (because
the 'g' stroke weakens almost to the point of disintegration as it
returns to the baseline) and it is clear from the frequent interruptions in the flow of her script that the writer is suffering intractable

pain. All of these cases illustrate the degeneration of fine muscle co-ordination.

Addison's disease

Addison's disease is named after Thomas Addison, the nineteenth-century English physician who first described it. It is an auto-immune disorder in which the adrenal glands (situated near the kidneys) do not produce enough natural cortisone, and it causes a host of problems in the sufferer.

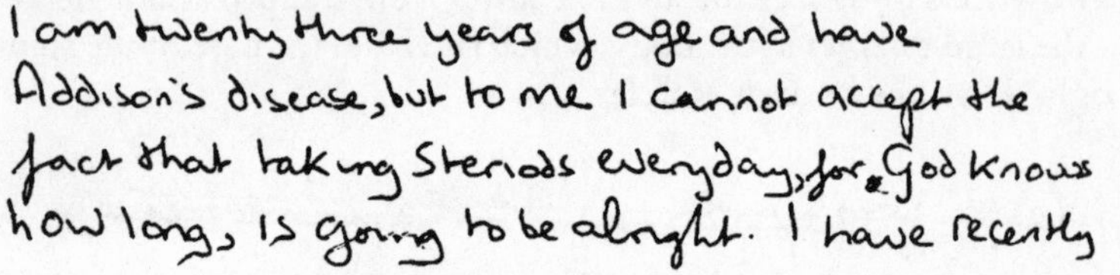

I am twenty three years of age and have
Addison's disease, but to me I cannot accept the
fact that taking Steriods everyday, for God knows
how long, is going to be alright. I have recently

Figure 132 (65%)

Generalized breaks in pressure can be seen throughout the sample in figure 132, but most clearly to the naked eye in the words 'knows' (line three), and 'how long' and 'going' (line four).

Disability

The writer of figure 133 is elderly and disabled. An ex-serviceman, he lost both legs as a result of injuries received during the Second World War. He tells me that the authorities have provided him with a wheelchair but he prefers to walk on his artificial legs.

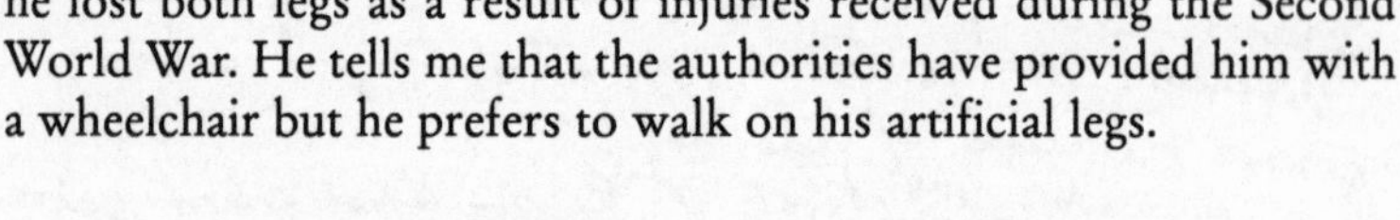

assembly point, where there was 20 to 30 cars
waiting with a police motor cycle escort.
Shortly about 10.30am, the Lord & Lady Mayoress
arrived, who went walk about, and shook hands
with organisers & members to wish all a good morning
and a Have a nice day, then we had a civic
send off, by them both, our police motor cycle escort
took us all the way, to Southport, when we

Figure 133 (50%)

The key to his disability can be seen quite clearly in those abbreviated lower zones.

The writer of figure 134 is an elderly woman, handicapped following a serious illness in her youth. The large size of the script combined with its scrawly presentation also suggests failing eyesight.

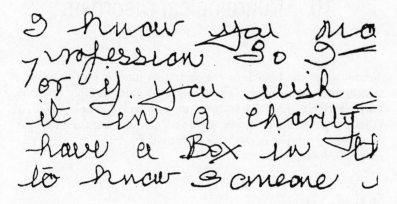

Figure 134

10   Neurological Disorders

Neurology is the branch of medicine that focuses on the nervous system and its disorders. These might include multiple sclerosis, muscular dystrophy, Parkinson's disease and a whole range of others. A general practitioner with patients suffering from epilepsy or inoperable tumours of the brain would also refer those patients to a neurologist.

Multiple sclerosis

Multiple sclerosis is a degenerative disease of the central nervous system. Sufferers often comment on the strange feelings associated

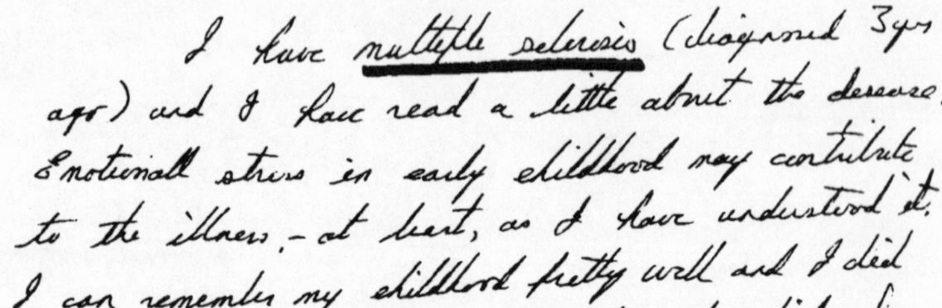

Figure 135 (65%)

with their condition. The waxing and waning of bodily strength and the mixture of sensations associated with it can result in feelings of euphoria one day and utter despair the next. Feelings of wellbeing can alternate with severe visual disturbances, numbness in fingers and toes, weakness in limbs and unpredictable dizzy spells. Figures 135–8 have been written by multiple sclerosis sufferers.

All four demonstrate changes of pressure throughout, the disease being progressively more advanced in each of the illustrated samples. The falling baseline shows depression to be a major factor for the writer of figure 137.

The spidery execution of figure 138 and the generalized tremor suggest that this woman's condition is the most advanced of the four. It is obvious that her hand was trembling quite violently as she wrote.

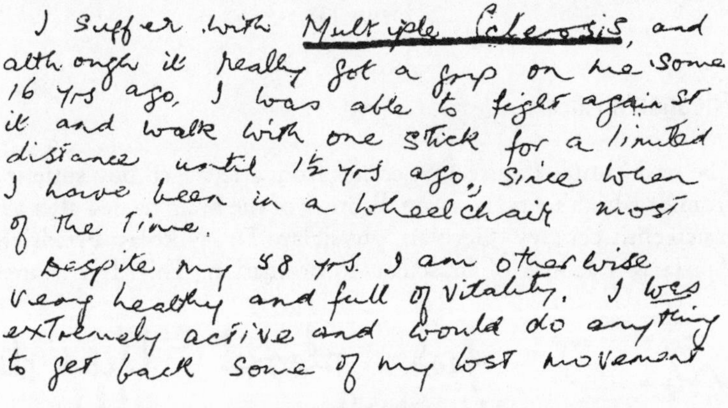
I suffer with Multiple Sclerosis, and although it really got a grip on me some 16 yrs ago, I was able to fight against it and walk with one stick for a limited distance until 1½ yrs ago, since when I have been in a wheelchair most of the time.
Despite my 58 yrs. I am otherwise very healthy and full of vitality. I was extremely active and would do anything to get back some of my lost movement

Figure 136 (65%)

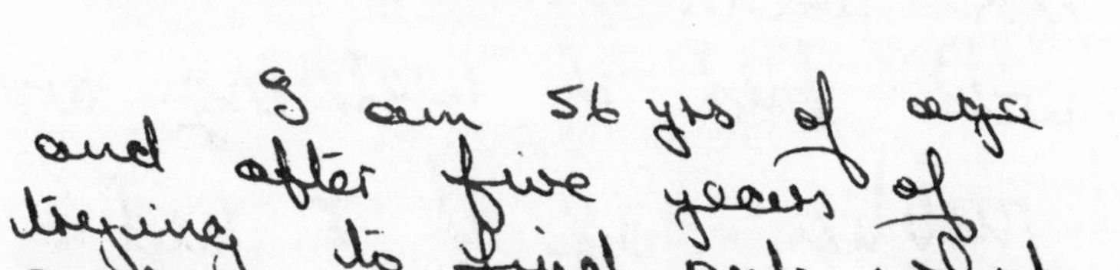
I am 56 yrs of age and after five years of trying to find out what I had wrong with me. Well at last they know, and I do as well. It is M.S. and ...

Figure 137

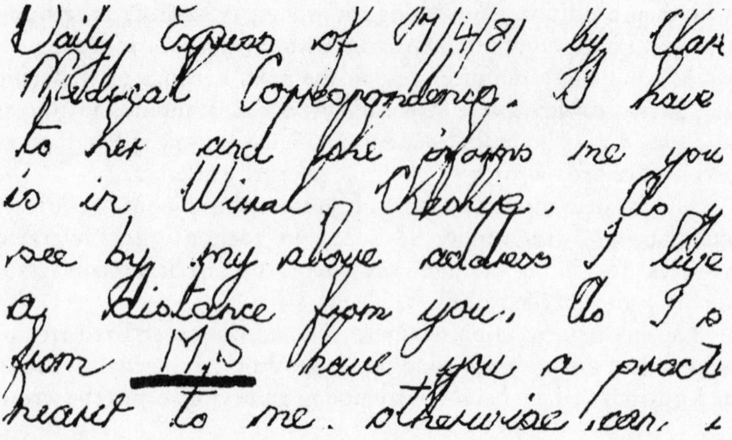

Daily Express of 07/4/81 by Clar
Medical Correspondence. I have
to her and she informs me you
is in Wirral, Cheshire. As y
see by my above address I live
a distance from you. As I s
from M.S have you a practi
nearer to me. otherwise can

Figure 138

Friedrich's Ataxia

The next sample (figure 139) comes from a teenaged boy suffering from Friedrich's Ataxia, a rare disorder of the brain named after the nineteenth-century German physician Dr Nikolas Friedrich. Ataxia is a failure of muscular co-ordination. This degenerative

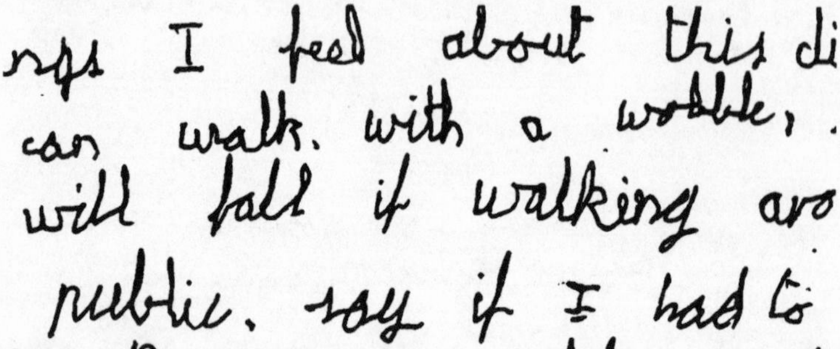

ngs I feel about this di
can walk. with a wobble, .
will fall if walking aro
public. say if I had to
om A TO B in public it ta
mins say. I would walk
ome place going round H-

Figure 139

condition affects the nervous and digestive systems and causes muscle wastage. It can also involve the sufferer's heart and spinal column, and virtually every part of the body.

The severity of this young writer's condition is clearly manifest in the jerkiness and general lack of co-ordination in his script. Muscular control is very poor, with hand tremor forcing many of the letters to break up. Yet, to his credit, the boy who wrote this for me shows no sign of depression or self-pity.

Epilepsy

Magnification shows most of the weakness in the script in figure 140 to be concentrated in the upper zone. The writer has said that he has scar tissue on the left temporal lobe of his brain and suffers from epilepsy.

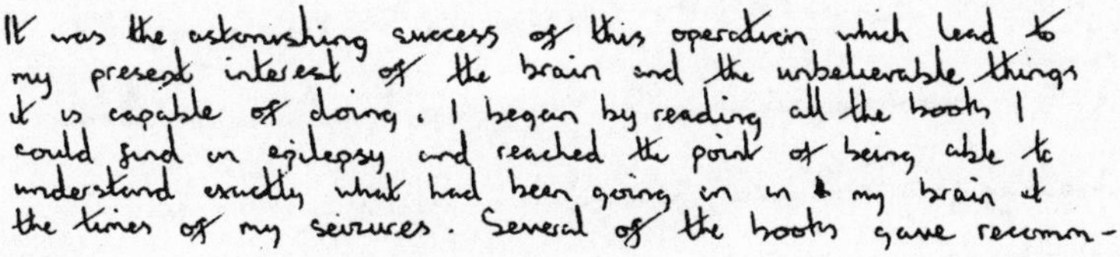

It was the astonishing success of this operation which lead to my present interest of the brain and the unbelievable things it is capable of doing. I began by reading all the books I could find on epilepsy and reached the point of being able to understand exactly what had been going on in my brain at the times of my seizures. Several of the books gave recommon-

Figure 140 (50%)

The key to this man's trouble lies in those curiously slanting t-bars. First, they are weaker than the stems of the letters, and indeed of every other stroke in this brief sample.

More significantly, as they fade away out of sight they break up like the vapour trails of jets sweeping across the sky.

The flyaway strokes suggest that the writer may be losing touch with reality. Note, too, the fracturing of letters in the word 'epilepsy'.

Stroke

The causes of stroke can include atheroma (degeneration of the coats of the blood vessels), arteriosclerosis (hardening of the arteries), athesclerosis (degeneration of the arterial walls), embolism (blood clot) and hypertension (raised blood pressure), with the resultant damage to various parts of the brain. Stroke is the third commonest cause of death in the western world after heart attacks and cancer.

But death is not inevitable and with treatment the quality of life of many sufferers can be restored or at least improved.

Most people who have suffered from a stroke are elderly. When someone under the age of 40 is affected, the cause is usually some form of congenital abnormality of a blood vessel in the brain. The writers of figures 141 and 142 are both in their thirties and the constricted script (the hard, abrupt endings and interrupted letter flows in the lower zone) of each reflects their physical disabilities.

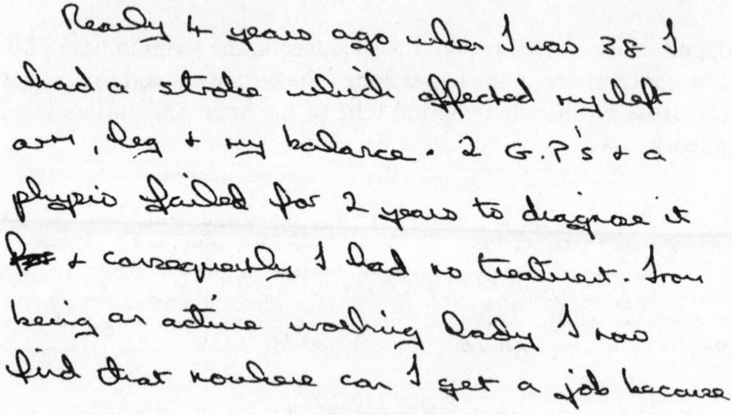
Nearly 4 years ago when I was 38 I
had a stroke which affected my left
arm, leg + my balance. 2 G.P's + a
physio failed for 2 years to diagnose it
+ consequently I had no treatment. From
being an active working lady I now
find that nowhere can I get a job because

Figure 141 (65%)

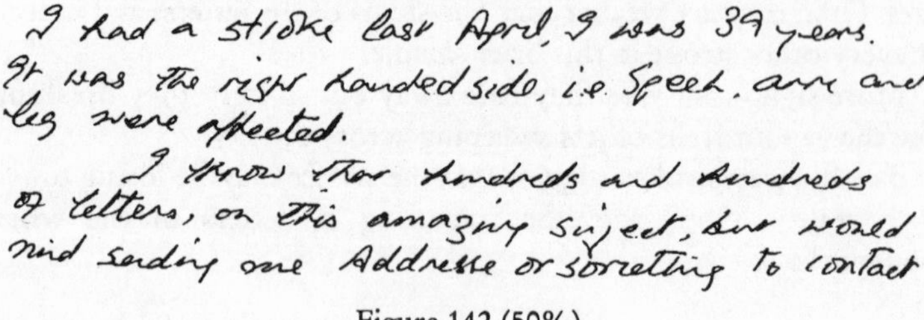
I had a stroke last April, I was 39 years.
It was the right handed side, i.e. Speech, arm and
leg were affected.
I know that hundreds and hundreds
of letters, on this amazing subject, but would
mind sending one Address or something to contact

Figure 142 (50%)

Gilles de la Tourette Syndrome

This disorder, generally known as Tourette's syndrome, is named after the French neurologist who identified it. It is characterized by unusual abnormalities of movement and tends to manifest itself in childhood by recurrent, involuntary, repetitive movements involving many of the body's muscles. These might include blinking, head-shaking, inarticulate grunting and the spontaneous utterance of obscenities.

Those who do not understand it often dismiss the behaviour of sufferers as a bad habit or an attempt to seek attention rather than as a genuine medical condition. Two famous men in history are believed to have suffered from Tourette's syndrome: Dr Samuel Johnson and Wolfgang Amadeus Mozart.

In 1979, Dr T.J. Murray, Dean of Dalhousie University in Nova Scotia, Canada, observed: 'Most authors have thought that Johnson's tics and odd behaviour were either a reflection of his underlying neurotic and expressive personality, or just the expected eccentricities of a great genius.'[1]

No one can say exactly what causes the condition though, according to Dr Michael Trimble, consultant physician in psychological medicine at the National Hospital for Nervous Disease, London, and Senior Lecturer at the University of London's Institute of Neurology, there could be a familial genetic factor, possibly stronger in Jewish families and affecting mainly males. 'It is exacerbated by situations that provoke anxiety and the movements may disappear completely if patients become engrossed in mental activity or pursue such hobbies as drumming or guitar playing.'[2]

Mr RW, a 39-year-old businessman living in the English Home Counties told me he had suffered from the condition since early childhood. In his case, the syndrome first manifested itself in the infant classroom, but was not definitively diagnosed until he was thirty years old.

The movements would begin suddenly and the muscles of his fingers would cease to function normally. Not only did the fact of his having cramped fingers make writing very difficult, but it involved much jerkiness on the page and 'a fair amount of crossing out and rewriting in the pursuit of perfection'. Obsessiveness seems to have been a contributory factor.

He said that in his early writings he tended to dig his pen into the paper and deface the page with sudden pen jerks, adding: 'Writing was a miserable task when I was younger.' Childhood samples are unfortunately not available but the samples in figures 143 and 144 make interesting study. They were written when RW was aged 32 and 39 respectively.

Figure 143 was produced under the influence of drugs intended to control the movements and the obsessive tendencies. 'One of those drugs worked on the central nervous system within the brain as an effective dopamine blocker,' he explained. An unwanted side-effect when it was administered in large doses, he added, was muscular rigidity. 'The reason why my writing is so bad in that sample is because my wrist and hand muscles were so tight. The drugs also caused chronic lethargy and loss of sex drive, and made me feel totally depleted.'

The scoring through of certain words and general untidiness of this drug-induced sample are a clear indication of the difficulties under which it was produced.

Medication has rendered this script virtually illegible. There are major discrepancies of size, speed, direction and rhythm between this and the more lucid example featured in figure 144.

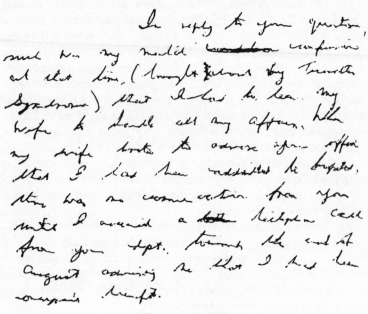

Figure 143 (65%)

Predictably, the tautness of the muscles has produced a tight little script.

Figure 144 is what the writer describes as the letter's 'translation' and constitutes a sample of his current handwriting.

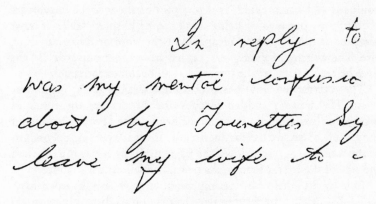

Figure 144

The scoring through of certain words and general untidiness in figure 143 are a clear sign of the writer's difficulty in producing the letter. It can plainly be seen that, under the influence of the medication, the writing in that first sample has almost totally disintegrated. Between it and the sample featured in figure 144 there is a difference in size, speed, direction and rhythm. Placing them alongside each other and taking a detailed look at each, the following observations can be made.

Apart from the size, which has virtually doubled in figure 144 and the fact that it is legible, balanced and has a good rhythmical flow, many of the letters themselves have altered, notably the quivering capital *I* in 'In', which is now strong and confident. Other letters (*p*, *t* and *m*), which are uncertain in the first sample, have become sharp and angular and been written with definite pen strokes in the second.

In figure 143 the word 'at' is shaky and hesitant, and shows an almost complete lack of control; in figure 144 the determined crossing of the *t* creates an entirely different impression. Word structures have also improved.

The letter depicted in figure 144 is more orderly, the writer has control and the entire character of the script has changed.

While the alignment is not exactly perfect, it is good and does add to the general high standard of the letter as a whole. None of the words, or their associated thoughts, have been stumbled over to suggest a similar stumbling block in the writer's mind. In the earlier sample the words 'admitted' and 'hospital' stand out. They are confused and compressed, as if one part of the writer's mind were objecting to the idea of being admitted to hospital while another accepted it blindly, being incapable at the time of doing anything else. The writing becomes very ragged from them onwards. By the time he reaches the final paragraph, it all becomes too much.

The interrupted flow has produced a weakened, jarring movement. The writer's sudden lurches and breaks are the result of disrupted flow from brain to pen. Resting dots appear throughout the sample. Also, we have reduction in size of the personal pronouns as the writer progresses down the page, until the last is roughly half the size of the first. Mental exhaustion is manifest throughout.

One cannot help wondering whether it is the disorder itself which has caused the written page to take on its disturbing appearance or the drugs used in the treatment of it. What does Mr RW think? The following are his comments on my findings.

> Your analysis suggests a bias towards a psychological explanation. While I reject any suggestion that the cause of Tourette's syndrome can be other than organic, I don't deny that for me, a life of social embarrassment and pain caused by the symptoms have had a marked effect on my psyche, which I am now having to come to terms with. This condition has dominated my life in that it has been such a strong force, in a totally unwanted, wasteful, negative sense.

It is a very emotive subject for Mr RW, who has suffered the whole gamut of symptoms, ranging from eye-blinking, head-shaking and movements of the torso and arms to curious vocal sounds 'and the extremely embarrassing utterance of obscenities'. He adds that he has even experienced violent head-banging, self-mutilation and other destructive tendencies.

Writing tends to reflect speech in that when one is clear, so is the other; when one is muddled the other is too. RW confirms that at the time he produced figure 143 his speech was indeed slurred and incoherent. 'No one, except the relatively few of us who are living through this nightmare disorder, and our families, can begin to *feel* and *know* the endless years of misery it causes,' he reflected.

While there is no doubt in my mind that a neurological disorder can affect one's handwriting, this example illustrates the very potent effects of medication on the mind and by association the script of this writer.

A medical view

The ability to pick out disturbances in writing is not confined to graphologists. The medical profession has long been aware of the phenomenon and specialists have made several studies into their cause and effect. I should like to quote from a definitive textbook on speech and writing disorders by Sir Russell Brain, one of the most eminent medical men of his day.[3] It provides a fascinating clinical background and shows the very great difficulty the writer had in controlling his pen, as demonstrated by Sir Russell (see figure 145).

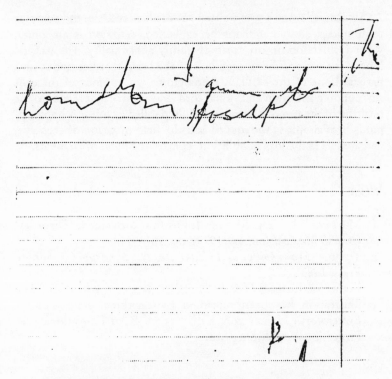

Figure 24. Disturbance of writing associated with a lesion of the right parietal lobe due to an intraventricular meningioma in a right-handed man. The patient had a left homonymous hemianopia, sensory inattention on the left side of the body, a disturbance of the body-image on the left side and apraxia for dressing. The patient was asked to write: 'I am in the London Hospital'. The handwriting shows the characteristics of a constructional apraxia in its disturbed alignment, and its position on the page indicates a neglect of the left half of space

Figure 145

The caption beneath the illustration reads:

Disturbance of writing associated with a lesion of the right parietal lobe due to an intraventricular meningioma in a right-handed man. The patient had a left homonymous hemianopia, sensory inattention on the left side of the body, a disturbance of the body-image on the left side and apraxia for dressing.

The patient was asked to write 'I am in the London Hospital.' The handwriting shows the characteristics of a constructional apraxia in its disturbed alignment and its position on the page indicates a neglect of left half of space.

As Sir Russell's book was written for medical readers, the complex terminology should perhaps be explained. A lesion is an injury, wound, infection or any form of bodily abnormality. The parietal lobe is the major lobe in each half of the brain that lies under each parietal bone of the skull. A meningioma is a tumour of the cells surrounding the brain and spinal cord. Intraventricular relates to the position of the tumour between the fluid-filled cavities. A homonymous hemianopia is the loss of half the field of vision of each eye, and apraxia is the loss of ability to control the hand movements.

Notes:

1 Murray, T.J., 'Dr Samuel Johnson's Movement Disorder' (*British Medical Journal*, 1979), pp. 1610–14.
2 Trimble, M.R., *Gilles de la Tourette, His Syndrome* (Colmore Press, 1983).
3 Brain, Sir Russell, *Speech Disorders* (Butterworth, 1975). The illustration has been reprinted by the kind permission of Butterworth Heinemann, a division of Reed Educational and Professional Publishing Ltd.

Part III
Changes in Writing

11 The Effects of Illness

As we have seen, a person's handwriting might change from time to time simply because of his rather mercurial nature. Adaptability is another reason. Just as we do not wear the same clothes every day, we do not make exactly the same signs and symbols either. While the basic outlines remain constant, our signs and symbols are rarely identical.

Whether our writing is tidy or untidy, formal or informal, because it comes from the depths of our unconscious it can still warn us of weaknesses and deficiencies in the body and provide important clues about what is going on beneath the surface. The main thing for the psycho-graphologist to be aware of is that when a normal script becomes scruffy or wobbly, or changes style, it happens for a reason.

A deteriorating hand

Figures 146, 147 and 148 were all written by my late father.

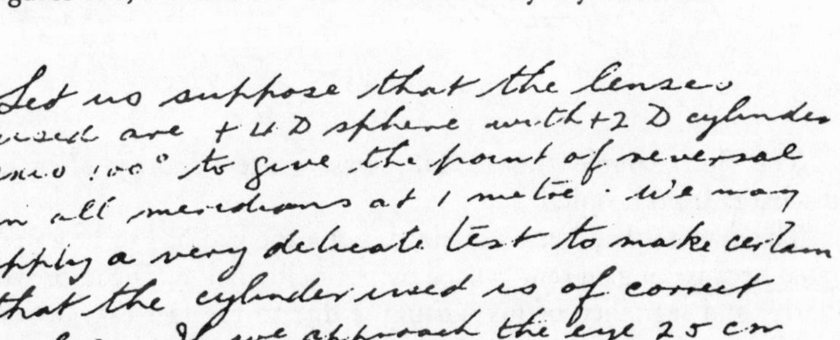
Let us suppose that the lenses used are + 4 D sphere with + 2 D cylinder axis 100° to give the point of reversal in all meridians at 1 metre. We may apply a very delicate test to make certain that the cylinder used is of correct value. If we approach the eye 25 cm

Figure 146 (65%)

Figure 146 dates back to his mid-forties when his only illness was a touch of bronchitis in the winter.

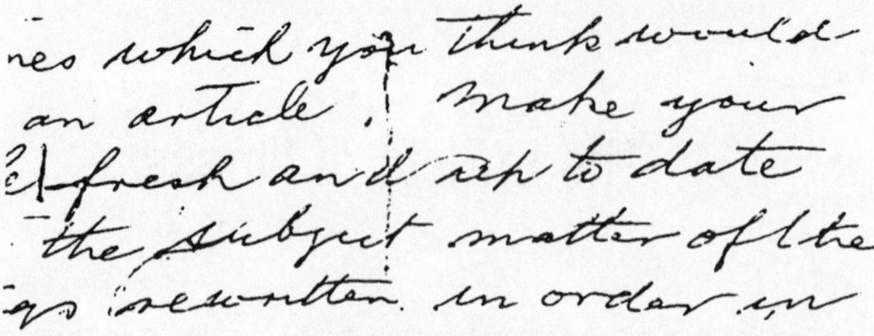
nes which you think would
an article. Make your
fresh and up to date
the subject matter of the
rewritten. In order in

Figure 147 (65%)

Figure 147 was written ten years later, when his health had taken a severe blow on the premature death of my mother. The shock brought on diabetes mellitus in a sudden and severe form, rapidly affecting his heart, eyesight, circulation and virtually his entire system. His condition deteriorated dramatically, all of which is reflected in his writing.

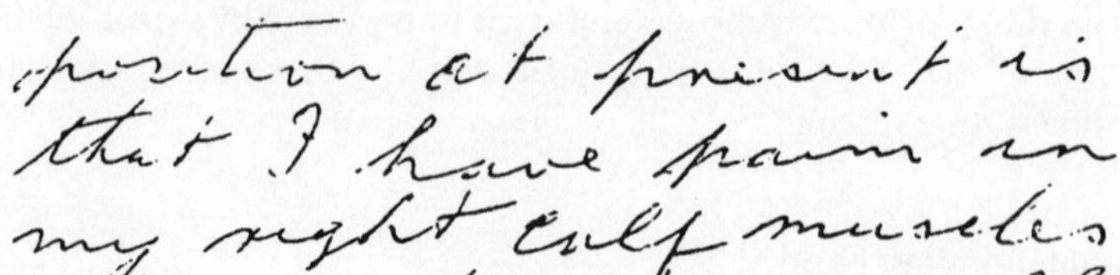
position at present is
that I have pain in
my right calf muscles
when I stand especially
after walking. I have

Figure 148 (65%)

The final sample (figure 148) was written shortly after his discharge from hospital.

The diabetes had been stabilized, but a toe had had to be amputated because of gangrene caused by poor circulation. The improved clarity and legibility of his writing is due to the fact that his eye condition had also recently been attended to. But this is not the writing of a healthy man. Apart from the leg pain referred to in the letter, cardiovascular disease is still very much in evidence.

The same overall weaknesses appear as can be seen in the sample shown in figure 119 (chapter 9). The breaking-up of strokes (particularly the up-strokes) suggests lungs that are crying out for air. This letter disturbed me greatly, for I knew it would probably be one of the last my father would ever write to me. Indeed, three weeks after writing it he had a massive coronary and died very suddenly.

A debilitating disease combined with depression

The following three samples in figures 149, 150 and 151 are very disturbing because while figure 149 shows balance, spontaneity, fluency and vigour, figures 150 and 151 reveal the reverse. It does not take the skills of a professional graphologist to form the opinion that the badly drooping lines indicate depression and that the wavering in size and slant hint at poor neuromuscular co-ordination.

They are confused, uncontrolled and increasingly illegible. Yet all three samples were written by the same woman, with a space of ten years between the first and second, and a month between the second and third (which was penned shortly before the writer's death).

Through these three samples, it is possible to map out the course of a chronic, debilitating disease, allied to classical symptoms of depression and associated behavioural changes.

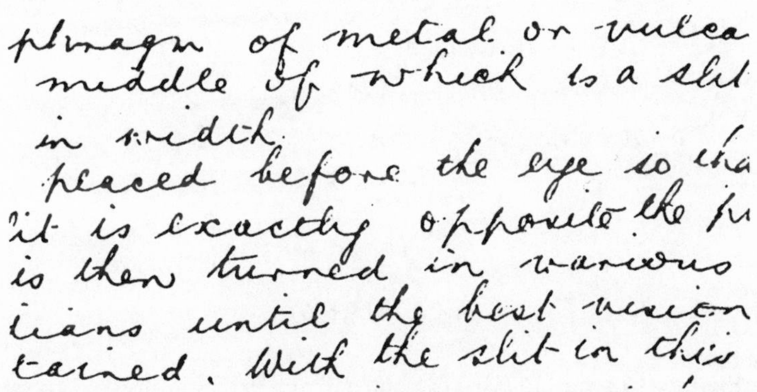
phragm of metal or vulca
middle of which is a slit
in width.
placed before the eye so tha
it is exactly opposite the pu
is then turned in various
tions until the best vision
tained. With the slit in this

Figure 149

At the time of penning the notes from which figure 149 is extracted, the writer was a happy, fulfilled housewife and mother of two relatively young children. Forty years of age with a lively, outgoing personality she was a former schoolteacher, married to a professional man of the same age.

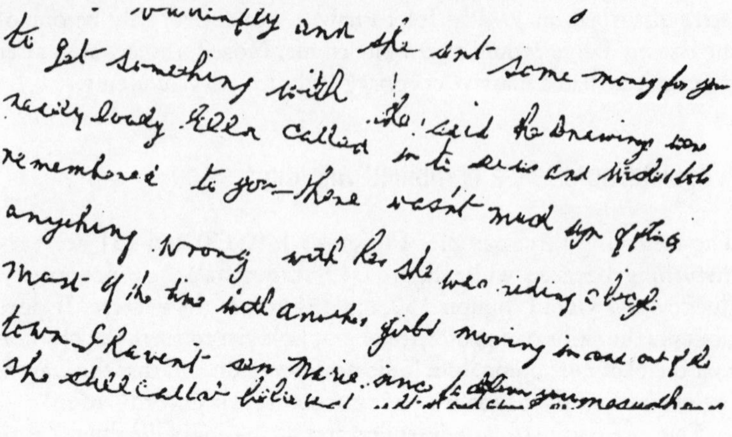

Figure 150 (65%)

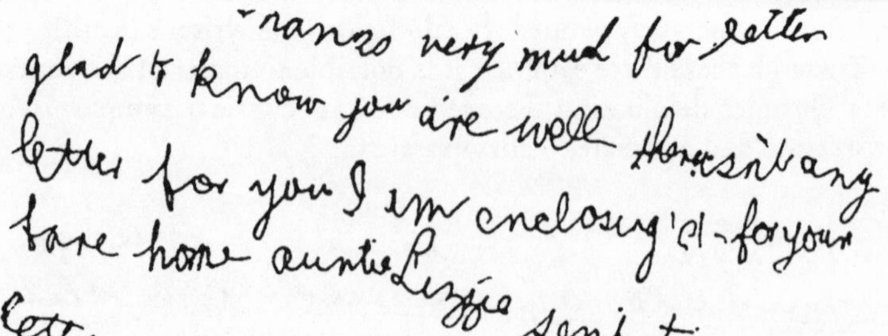

Figure 151 (65%)

Figures 150 and 151 are extracted from letters addressed to her elder daughter, who had recently gone away to boarding school. In the period between writing figures 149 and 150 the mother had developed a degenerative disease of the heart and blood vessels associated with raised blood pressure which was not helped by her severe anxiety state.

144

Whether the arteriosclerosis caused the depression or vice versa is a moot point, for in both the writer and her writing the two are clearly intertwined. As the disease progressed through the cardio-vascular system, its course clearly manifested itself in her writing. A thickening of the body's arteries have caused an increased heaviness in the script. The extra work required by the heart muscles to pump blood through the ever-narrowing vessels shows itself in the strained movement on the paper.

Figure 151 reflects the writer's fatigue and virtual inability to go on. Three weeks after writing that letter she suffered a severe headache with giddiness, resulting in sudden collapse. The rapid loss of consciousness pointed to a massive bleed into the brain and she died next day without regaining consciousness.

The clinical diagnosis of a cerebral haemorrhage caused by hypertension and atheroma (degeneration of the coats of the blood vessels) was confirmed at post mortem.

An analysis of figure 149 shows it to be a mature and sophisti-cated hand – poised, refined, stable. The light pressure and slightly right-slanted script suggests an amiable and gregarious personality. Hers was an outgoing, friendly nature.

Spacing and alignment are good, pressure is even, the writing is that of a charming, intelligent and very feminine person, whose viva-ciousness shows in the high-placed i-dots and t-bars and graceful dashes. The small, well-formed letters confirm her intelligence and grace. Creativity can be seen in the fast-flowing, spontaneous style. It is an attractive script of high form level. On the whole, its neat and regular presentation, good punctuation and legibility show it to be the work of a writer who is orderly, intelligent and (at that stage, before the onset of her illness), mentally well-balanced.

When these notes were penned, the health of the writer was good, apart from mild insomnia and occasional nosebleeds (sometimes an indication of hypertension but as yet discernible only to a diagnos-tician qualified to detect such signs and symptoms and predict their possible outcome).

To determine whether any early warning signs can be detected, we must take a closer look at the letter formations in the housewife's correspondence, at the spacing and general 'feel' of the hand. Sure enough, a few vital clues are present, as follows:

- The baseline is rather uneven.
- Connecting strokes between the letters show a tendency to

droop (the *d*, in line three, *a* in line four, and *p* and *h* in lines five, six, seven, eight).

- One of the connections (*h*, line one) shows a very definite hand-jerk in the sudden, involuntary side movement, although as yet this is an isolated sign.
- The differing sizes of letters (the second *t* in line four is only about half the size of those on the final line).
- Some of the up-strokes are segmented (the *l* in 'slit', in line two, the *f* in 'before' and the *h* in 'that' in line four). Segmentation is a serious graphological sign, being an early indication of illness.

Although the signs were present at this point, they were not yet cause for concern. If one overlooks the insomnia and the nose-bleeds, the discrepancies in the hand could be described as 'presymptomatic' changes, possibly hinting at some disturbance in the central nervous system. The writer's blood pressure may already have been too high, but who could anticipate what was to follow?

Figure 150 is very disturbing indeed. With its vacillating slant and pressure, the writing now shows the severe degeneration which has taken place in nerve–muscle co-ordination and is reminiscent of the writing of the man with the brain tumour featured in figure 145. The generally healthy script of figure 149 has given way to an increasingly irregular style. The grace and refinement are still there, but knocked sideways, so to speak, by forces beyond the writer's control. Unconscious mechanisms have made the letters stiff and angular. There are many graphological pointers to indicate the serious nature of the writer's illness. Notice the hesitancy and the ever-descending baseline.

The words have begun to wander off in various directions – mostly downwards – showing the writer's deeply depressed state of mind. By now, her confusion was such that psychiatric treatment was called for.

The poor alignment indicates her anxiety, irritability, memory disturbances and despondency – all mental symptoms associated with vascular disease. The graphological signs mirror the clinical picture: lack of fluency, tense and rigid strokes, cramped letters. The words do not move forward easily; they are stilted, being held back by the writer's inability to control her pen movements. Muscular spasm has also caused blurred vision and disorientation. As the disease advances, it becomes apparent that the writer has difficulty focusing. Now we can detect the unmistakeable signs of brain involvement.

- pen trails
- dotting
- sudden, involuntary upshoots (seen only once in the previous illustration but repeated regularly here).

Notice the words 'and' (which shows very definite hand-jerk) in line one, 'with' (full of fragmented strokes) in line two, the space between the words 'she' and 'said', also on line two, the g in 'girls' in line six and the final four words on the same line. After that, neuro-muscular and therefore pen control becomes serious impaired.

The dots make spasmodic appearances; they can be seen between the n and t in the word 'wasn't' (line four) and between 'Marie' and 'since' (line seven). As we have seen pen or ink trails and dotting both indicate severe mental exhaustion.

The degeneration in the writer's muscle co-ordination, which began to show in figure 150 leaves no doubt in the mind when it comes to studying figure 151. This letter is ill formed, smudgy and almost indecipherable. The anxiety-ridden, dejected, miserable state of the writer is only too painfully obvious.

Muscular control is now virtually nil. Irreparable damage throughout the system has resulted in a script which is swaying, formless and very difficult to read. Scattered across the page, it changes size and direction, showing the very disturbed state of the writer, both psychologically and physiologically.

Further abnormal signs can be seen as follows:

- mistakes, corrections and regression to childish letter structures
- mirror formation of '10/–'
- the now very obvious contraction and expansion of the letters
- ink smears, which have occurred spontaneously, again because of the severe loss of pen pressure

Note too how the strokes waver and are jerky, with random directional impulses in the words 'well' (line two), 'letter' (line three), and 'in my' (line four). The sudden upshoot – as in the word 'am' (line three) – confirms the jerky and uncontrolled movement. Constant breaks in the loops indicate the writer's chronic heart condition.

Among other corroborating signs, many concealing strokes can be seen. These strokes (which rise and descend without forming loops, but simply overlap each other) tell us that the writer still valued her privacy. Despite her very great difficulty in communicating, this is the one point which emerges more clearly than any other. The most poignant aspect of this sad little extract is that the writer did not wish others to know about her condition, or wish others to intrude into her private thoughts and feelings.

I find that particularly moving because in every other respect the words on the page are as indistinct as those in the increasingly slurred speech which by now would surely have been part of this unfortunate woman's condition. Difficulty in communicating is seen to have become a major obstacle in both the written and spoken word.

The childish letter structures are apparent in the words 'are' (line two) and 'for' (the end of line three). Uncontrolled and exaggerated pen movements are responsible for distortion in individual letters. Note the *s* in 'doughnuts' (lines six), 'to' (line two), and the *h* in 'home' (line four). At this late stage of her illness, the writer was heavily sedated and the confusion manifest in her writing and indeed in her entire waking state might have been at least partially due to the effects of her medication.

Notice also the variation in letter sizes. Some are large, others very small. Compare the tiny black *c* in 'much' (line one) with the huge *c* in 'change' (line five). Being an operative word, 'change' assumes considerable importance in the writer's mind. The *m*s are all large, showing how the writer was still able to attach considerable importance to the state of motherhood; and also the high esteem in which she held her daughter.

The *y* loops are shaky, showing fear and anxiety over 'you' (her addressee) and concern about how the child would cope when the inevitable happened. This was, after all, an intelligent woman who in her moments of rationality must have been aware of the prognosis of her condition.

Terminally ill though she was, her intelligence was not impaired, as can be seen in the still refined albeit wobbly word formation. The trembling execution of some of the letters makes them difficult to read. With her physical condition in such a sorry state, the mechanical disturbances of movement are reflected in the writing. These disturbances can be seen in broken letters and loops, size changes, heavy pressure in certain areas, a jerky baseline and ragged letters, many of which are cramped, compressed and indistinct.

What we have here, therefore, is what the doctor who invited me to study the samples has described as true psycho-neurotic depression. Note the laborious writing and the duplication of letters. See how the words all run into each other, showing the writer to be extremely fearful, anxiety-ridden and dejected. How much of this was due to the effects of tranquillizers is difficult to say. Nor is it easy to establish whether the memory impairment and generalized confusion was an integral part of her illness or the result of the electro-convulsive therapy which formed part of the treatment.

While it is accepted that anti-depressants can have a destructive effect on the ability to write clear, steady letters, here we have something much more dramatic. This is a progressive deterioration of the entire personality. I am reliably informed by the doctor whose patient this was that further attempts on the part of the woman to continue writing to her daughter had to be abandoned because her trembling hands could no longer produce a legible script.

These three samples, then, demonstrate increasing illegibility, varying pen pressure from fine to muddy, alternating slant and size and a baseline which progresses from being mildly off course to being positively disturbed. Together, they indicate with remarkable clarity how changes in the woman's penmanship have echoed the pathological changes in her system and prove quite conclusively how mental and physical signs can manifest themselves in the writing. Graphology therefore has the potential to become a valuable tool for exploring not only behaviour patterns, but also organic disease.

Mental deterioration

The curiously named Alzheimer's disease[1] is named after Alois Alzheimer (1864–1915), the German neurologist who identified it in 1907. A common cause of death in men (and less frequently women) over the age of sixty, the disease is progressive and invariably fatal. The condition is characterized by confusion and forgetfulness in the early stages, dementia and total disintegration of personality towards the end. Medical experts believe it to be associated with nerve cell damage in the brain, but as yet have been able to offer no reasonable explanation as to its cause.

Classical symptoms can include personality changes, irritability, mood swings, depression, progressive loss of memory and other mental faculties. It is an extremely complex condition which ultimately results in shrinkage of the brain. As yet, the disease's trigger mechanism is unknown. Most researchers agree that changes in the brain occur long before the actual onset and progress of the disease and the changes seen in the following three samples of handwriting (figures 152, 153 and 154) do seem to concur with this theory. They were written by Mr H.S., who was, coincidentally, born in the year of Dr Alzheimer's death.

Mr S., was a marketing director and the samples of his handwriting reproduced hereunder were written at the ages respectively, of forty-five, forty-eight and seventy-one. Mr S. died of Alzheimer's disease in 1998 at the age of 83. Unfortunately, no samples of his script are available from the final decade of his life although I am reliably informed that his condition had been deteriorating gradually over many, many years.

If one takes a general view of these samples covering the twenty-six years in question, the overall impression is one of a kind and generous man, who shows little sign of being anything but very well balanced and mentally alert.

Any dramatic deterioration in the script at these three points in his life is minimal. Changes, when they occur, are so subtle as to be almost imperceptible which may well be a feature of the illness itself, until it is much further advanced than it was for Mr S. even in the final extracts reproduced hereunder.

This very high quality writing, based on the copperplate style (see page 20), is the work of a cultured, refined and gently bred individual. The writer is intelligent, shy, sensitive but with a very practical nature. He is heavily influenced by tradition and upbringing. Discretion and a sense of propriety dominate.

The script has a lovely, rhythmical flow. It is the product of a gregarious personality with a razor-sharp mind. Its small size speaks of applied intelligence, the meticulously dotted *i*s and crossed *t*s show thoroughness and a great attention to detail. Here we have a man of dignity, integrity and compassion. Affectionate and caring, his slight forward slant indicates his enjoyment of company, albeit in small doses. The even movement of the script points to honesty, kindness and moderation. The flowing style with its linked t-bars, reflects how, at this stage, the writer's brain is running well ahead of his actions in a series of flowing thoughts.

There *are* some signs and symbols in this extract which tell us

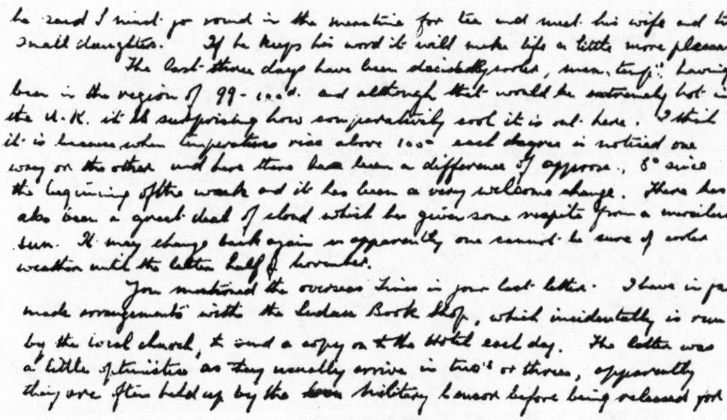

he said I must go round in the meantime for tea and meet his wife and two
small daughters. If he keeps his word it will make life a little more pleasant.
The last three days have been decidedly cooler, max. temp. having
been in the region of 99-100°. and although that would be extremely hot in
the U.K. it is surprising how comparatively cool it is out here. I think
it is because when temperatures rise above 100° each degree is noticed one
way or the other and here there has been a difference of approx. 8° since
the beginning of the week and it has been a very welcome change. There has
also been a great deal of cloud which has given some respite from a merciless
sun. It may change back again as apparently one cannot be sure of cooler
weather until the latter half of November.
You mentioned the overseas Times in your last letter. I have in fact
made arrangements with the Sudan Book Shop, which incidentally is run
by the local church, to send a copy on to the Hotel each day. The letter was
a little optimistic as they usually arrive in two's or threes, apparently
they are often held up by the Military Censor before being released for

Figure 152 (50%)

that all is not as well as it seems. Whether these signs and symbols bear any relationship to the condition which ultimately claimed his life, only a doctor could tell.

As I see it, the indications are mainly of stress. They include over-writing, stumbling and changes of pen pressure. The over-writing can be seen in the upper loops of several letters. Evidence of stumbling appears in the word 'decidedly' (line three), 'it is' (line five) and in several letter structures on line seven. On the final line we see the scored-through word preceding 'Military' and much stumbling over the word 'Military' itself. Changes of pen pressure are evident throughout.

Quite apart from the signs of stress, there would appear to have been some sort of physical problem in relation to one of his feet and/or legs, the pain or discomfort of which might well have affected Mr S.'s writing, at least in 1960, when he penned this note.

Figure 153, written three years later (i.e. thirty-five years before his death) is much more disturbing. Signs of stress and anxiety are even stronger here; much of it now in relation to his personal perception of self. Note the various forms of the personal pronoun and how each is invariably blacked out. What we have here is a very private person, who is generally friendly, but would be the last person to discuss his private life outside his own four walls.

Stumbling over words is now commonplace. Manual dexterity and ability for close concentration do not appear to be top line. The flow from brain to pen to paper is less meticulously executed than in the earlier sample. This is an agitated hand and while there is some

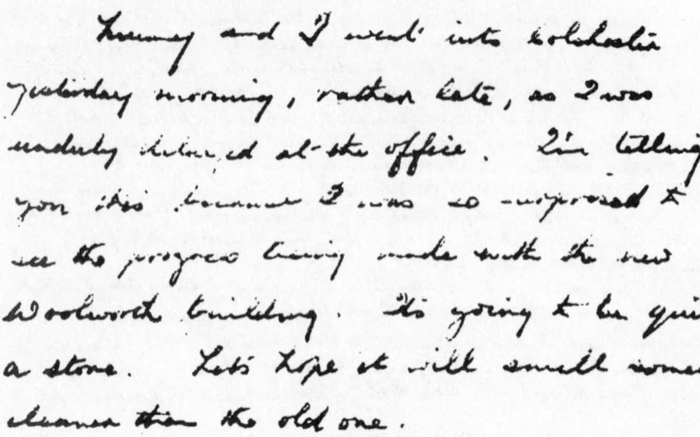

[illegible] and I went into [illegible]
yesterday morning, rather late, as I was
unduly delayed at the office. I'm telling
you this because I was so surprised to
see the progress being made with the new
Woolworth building. It's going to be quite
a stone. Let's hope it will smell somewhat
cleaner than the old one.

Figure 153 (65%)

evidence of restlessness (a slight wobble in the script detectable on the original under strong light and magnification), the writer is still perfectly capable of logical thought.

Negative signs are hardly more than an undercurrent. If Mr S. was suffering from confusion or absent-mindedness at this stage, there is little evidence of it yet. Stress and anxiety yes, reduced mental capacity, no. However, the generalized alterations in pen pressure do indicate some physiological condition beginning to affect his entire body. Again, because Alzheimer's disease is such an enigmatic condition and not understood by many doctors – much less by lay graphologists like myself – it is hardly for me to say whether this writer's weakened physical state was related to his mental condition. This was, after all, thirty-five years before his demise and also some years before his illness was definitively diagnosed.

The two extracts featured in figure 154 show a couple of unusual changes. The first is that pen pressure is considerably lighter than in the earlier samples. The second is that an element of shakiness has been introduced. The third difference is a change in some of the individual letter structures.

The weaker pen pressure simply indicates a reduction in physical energy, which is hardly surprising in view of the writer's advancing years but the shakiness – which is quite a different phenomenon to that of *tremor* seen in some of the other samples featured in this book – hints at a growing sense of agitation. For a writer who

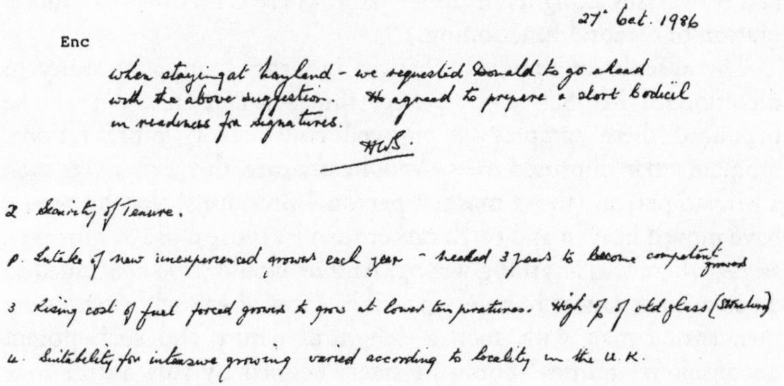

27ᵗ Oct. 1986

Enc

when staying at Hayland - we requested Donald to go ahead with the above suggestion. He agreed to prepare a short Codicil in readiness for signatures.

HWS.

2 *Security of Tenure.*

p. *Intake of new inexperienced growers each year - needed 3 years to become competent growers*

3 *Rising cost of fuel forced growers to grow at lower temperatures. High % of old glass (Stirling)*

4. *Suitability for intensive growing varied according to locality in the U.K.*

Figure 154 (50%)

always attached such importance to producing a neat and correct script (precise, almost to the point of pedantry), it must have been very distressing to have to struggle to keep it flowing. Hence the changes in some of those letters.

The capital 'I' has taken on a different shape . . . whereas before, it appeared as $\mathcal{I}$ and occasionally $\mathcal{I}$ now it is $\mathcal{I}$. Lower case *es* have flattened out a little on top; gs have changed from the literary-type structure ($\mathcal{g}$) and tail-less variety ($\mathcal{g}$) to the more conventional variety. T-bars are shorter, weaker and no longer attach themselves to the following word.

Capital T has changed from the scripted version ($\mathcal{T}$) to the printed ($\mathcal{T}$) as if the writer were making an unconscious plea for continued understanding. Changes in writing reflect corresponding changes in character and personality. One wonders if Mr S. was beginning to experience and mentally question some of the changes taking place in his personality and behaviour patterns. This was, remember, a highly intelligent and perceptive man, whose underlying illness may well have been gnawing away inside his head far longer than anyone suspected.

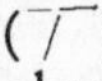

The forward flow and general upward pull show his attempts to keep as cheerful as possible but the signs that all is not well are evident in his hand. They are manifest in breaks, omissions, lack of continuity and degeneration of some strokes into bare threads. But it has to be said that these signs and symbols are so minute as to only be picked up after very close scrutiny and considerable 'rooting out'. They are subtle, ill-defined and virtually undetectable, which may well be the case with the condition itself before it takes hold

153

and progresses along its insidious path. There is no obvious disintegration of cerebral functioning.

The absence of dramatic changes in either form, continuity or direction of Mr S.'s script reflect the fact that in the years he produced these samples he enjoyed considerably more rational moments than confused ones. And, in any case, this writer was such a private person (those masked personal pronouns) that he would have moved heaven and earth rather than let those close to him even *suspect* there was anything wrong. And he would have continued to do so as long as was humanly possible. How absolutely devastating then that a man with such a delightful nature and such potent unconscious abilities should be overwhelmed by this horrendous disease.

Incidentally, the reason why there are no samples of Mr S.'s writing from the final years of his life is because, being the perfectionist that he was, he no longer felt able to produce the neat and tidy script of which he was so proud. He therefore placed all his financial and administrative affairs into the capable hands of his wife.

On Mr S.'s death, his widow and family bequeathed his brain to Cambridge University for the purpose of research.

Note

1 Further information and help can be obtained from the Alzheimer's Disease Society, Gordon House, 10 Greencoat Place, London SW1P 1PH. Telephone number: 020 7306 0606. Helpline: 0845 300 03336. The society is a registered charity (No. 296645).

12   Writing with the Mouth or Foot

The Mouth and Foot Painting Association (MFPA) is a group of professional artists who, because of their disability (either at birth or following illness or injury) cannot use their hands and have learned to paint by holding the brush in the mouth, or with the toes. On my suggestion that any of their members who cared to have their writings and sketches analysed would be welcome to send in samples, several volunteers came forward.

It must be stressed that MFPA members are disabled physically, but not mentally. It is their active minds that enable them to adapt their bodies to cope with their changed circumstances.

Having established that heavy (or pasty) writing is usually associated with deep emotions and artistic mentalities, I half expected that the writings and sketches from my volunteers would be full of heavy strokes. But on the contrary, writings and sketches I received were made up almost entirely of strokes which were light and sensitive, reflecting the sensitive natures of the individuals behind them.

Paul Driver

Paul Driver was born in South London in 1926. During the war, he was directed into the coal-mining industry and worked underground for three years. He later trained as a quantity surveyor but in 1955, while working in Leeds, he contracted polio.

His first year was spent in an iron lung and although he is able to sit in a wheelchair, both arms are completely paralysed and he still relies on a respirator at night (although I was unaware of this fact at the time I conducted the analysis on the various samples featured in this chapter).

After having spent many years in a Cheshire Foundation home, he at the time of writing lives with his wife and two sons in a South London apartment designed to be accessible for wheelchairs and also to be near the respiratory unit of St Thomas's hospital.

For several years after the onset of his illness, Mr Driver's form of transport was a foot-steered invalid tricycle, which he used on a regular basis until it became too tiring. In recent years, he has found the effort involved in using the tricycle too much for him; it began to strain the muscles involving his breathing.

Mr Driver is a very talented artist and over the years he has painted many scenes for reproduction on the cards and calendars of the Mouth and Foot Painting Association. Holding the brush between his toes, he works mainly in oils, painting marine subjects, landscapes and flowers.

Two samples of his writing are reproduced in figures 155 and 156. The first is a copy of two pages torn from an old address book and predates his illness. The second was done afterwards with his foot.

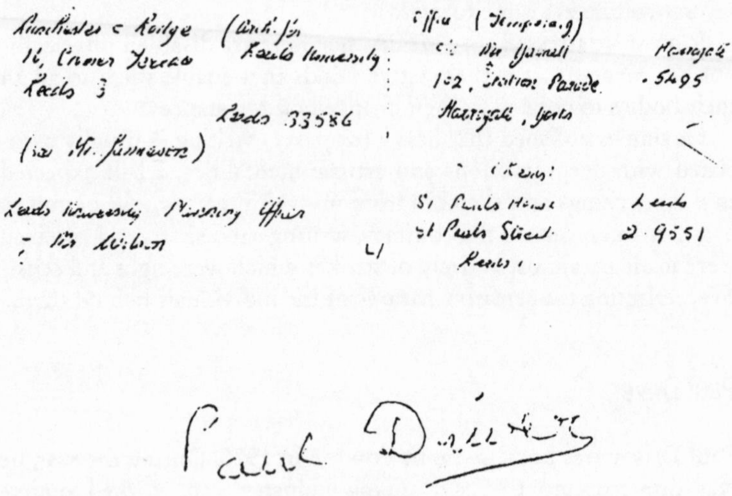

Figure 155 (65%)

While foot-writing is less flexible than handwriting, certain general observations can still be made, particularly when comparing the two, as we shall see. Strong determination is the key factor in figure 156.

His disability is also manifest. Spasmodic looping on some of the

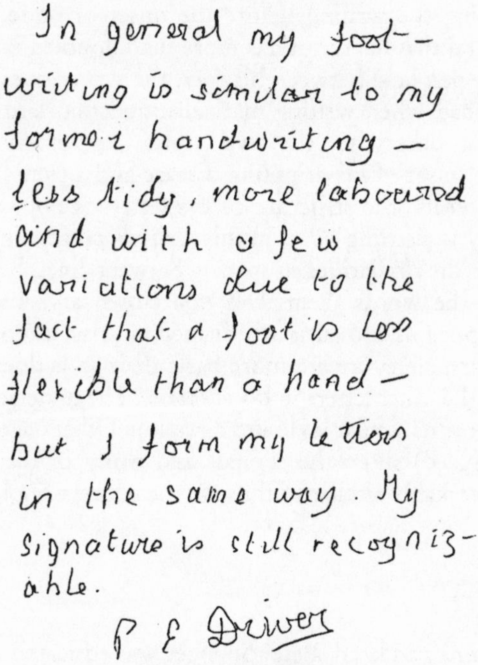

In general my foot-
writing is similar to my
former handwriting —
less tidy, more laboured
and with a few
variations due to the
fact that a foot is less
flexible than a hand —
but I form my letters
in the same way. My
signature is still recognizable.

P F Driver

Figure 156 (50%)

upper zones points to some sort of lung malfunction; laboured breathing is a feature of his condition. As I have said, I did not know that he suffered from respiratory paralysis and needed a respirator at night until the analysis had been completed.

An overall study of this script shows the writer's upstrokes to be considerably lighter than the downstrokes and Mr Driver's wife confirms that due to his breathing difficulties, this has long been a feature of her husband's writing.

Turning to the small letters, we see that the os and as are all closed, reflecting his ability to keep secrets; but the bs are open at the bottom. In a moment of inspiration I asked if he was in the habit of going barefoot – which, on the face of it, seemed a silly question, considering his method of writing. But yes, he said, he was. Just as most of us only wear gloves for special occasions, he regarded shoes in the same light. However, he offered an explanation of his own for the unusual formation of the bs. It was, he believed, due to the difficulty he experienced in completing the letter.

Comparing the writing before the onset of polio with that of today we find that his script has more than doubled in size.

With the pen held between his toes, the writer does not have the control he had when writing manually, and the slant has changed slightly. But otherwise, the two styles are remarkably similar. Despite the onset of his crippling disease and a time lapse of more than thirty years, the structure of the letters is not very different. Consistency is a strong point in this writer's personality.

Note too the similarities in spacing between lines, between words and within the words themselves; the closed and knotted *o*s, the rounded-topped *n*s and curiously shaped *r*s. Also, although the capitals in the first signature are more basic their style does not change. Neither do the other letters in his surname. The underscore is almost identical. Note its similar style and direction. Other pages of the letter (not reproduced) show the capitals and many of the small letters looking remarkably similar to those in the address-book entries.

Peter Spencer

Cheshire born and bred, Peter Spencer was educated at Pembroke College, Cambridge. In March 1945, while serving as an RAF pilot, he was involved in an accident which resulted in the loss of his right arm and the paralysis of his left. Unable to return to university, he began to paint by holding the brush in his mouth. With a scholarship from the MFPA, he attended Wallasey College of Art.

In 1951, he married and had two children. In 1960 he was elected as a local councillor and, as president of the Merseyside branch of the British Limbless Ex-Servicemen's Association (BLESMA) worked tirelessly for the disabled. He also served as a Deputy Lieutenant of the County of Merseyside.

Despite the volume of letters he received, Mr Spencer dealt with all his own correspondence by typing with his feet. A talented and prolific artist, he exhibited his paintings on a regular basis in London, Edinburgh and Paris. He was also very active in the community and in his specially converted foot-controlled car was a familiar figure as he drove around the leafy lanes of Wirral.

Mr Spencer's remarkable achievements were featured extensively in the media and in two books produced by the MFPA. In 1980 his services to his country and to charity received official recognition when he was awarded the MBE in the Queen's Birthday Honours.

My initial approach to him was in the early 1980s when I was researching for a series of features on disability for the paper on which I was then employed as health/medical correspondent. A few years later he co-operated again by searching for the sort of background information I needed for graphological purposes and managed to locate his wartime log book. It dated back to 1944 when he was nineteen years old and training to be a pilot. A page from that log is reproduced in figure 157.

Year 1944.		Aircraft		Pilot, or 1st Pilot	2nd Pilot, Pupil or Passenger	Duty (Including Results and Remarks)
Month	Days	Type	No.			
		—	—	—	—	Totals Brought Forward
Jan	3	A.T.b.A	232	Self.		Formation, 3.
Jan	3	A.T.b.A	262	Self.		Gunnery
						Formation 3.
Jan	4	A.Tb.A	215	Glasgow GG½	Self.	I/E 21,23,25,27,29.
						Hard surface landings
Jan	4	A.Tb.A	215	Glasgow GG½	Self	8 Stalling.
						14 Spinning.
						22 Steep turns
						26 Precautionary landing
						28 Forced landing
						35 Aerobatics.
						I/E 21,23,25,27
Jan	4	A.Tb.C	258	Self.		29 Low level tactical cross county
Jan	5	A.Tb.C	269	Self.		8. Stalling.
						14. Spinning.
						22. Steep turns.
						26. Precautionary landing
						28. Forced landing
						35. Aerobatics.
Jan	5	Link.	8.	Birch ½.	Self.	23
Jan	6	A.Tb.A.	210	Glasgow GG½	Self.	T/E Melbourne Range
						West Palm Beach King
Jan	7	Link.	8.	Dwyer C ½	Self.	24

Grand Total [Cols. (1) to (10)]
163 Hrs. 08 Mins.   Totals Carried Forward

Figure 157 (50%)

The style of writing shows the character behind it to have been an upstanding and independent young man of high principles and morals. Upper zone dominance suggests far more interest in intellectual and academic pursuits than sporting activities (something which was to prove a distinct advantage later on). The script also hints at musical and artistic talent.

Most of the letter structures are arcade, suggesting a 'lid on the emotions', 'grin and bear it' attitude to life. His powers of concentration are good, attention to detail first rate. The pastiness of the writing indicates a degree of sensuousness. Yet beneath the air of confidence is a suggestion that at the age of nineteen, he was not quite as sure of himself as he would have had others believe.

The modern samples in Figure 158 demonstrate the versatility of this talented man in maturity.

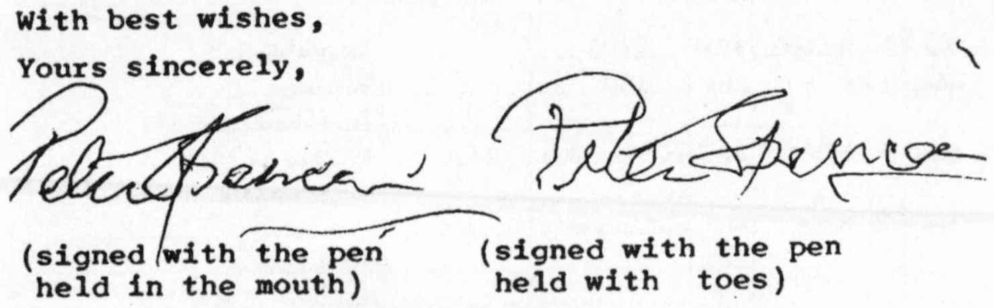

With best wishes,
Yours sincerely,

(signed with the pen held in the mouth)

(signed with the pen held with toes)

Figure 158 (65%)

He showed remarkable versatility in being able to write with both his mouth and his feet and still produce a signature which was poised, elegant, stylish and full of action. The overall impression was that the man himself was full of enthusiasm, determination and tenacity.

Irrespective of where he held the writing instrument, this later writing displays the same basic letter structures. With maturity, it now flows in a much more self-assured manner, and amazingly, it is also faster and more rhythmic. This is very high-quality writing.

When comparing the early and mature samples, we see that the later style is more flamboyant and self-assured, befitting the transition from serviceman to artist, youth to maturity. The keen, offbeat sense of humour that was a feature of Mr Spencer's personality came through strongly in everything he wrote and however he wrote it. He was certainly a remarkable man.

Derrick Vandek

Derrick Vandek was born in Scotland in 1935. From childhood he was a keen sportsman and became a talented gymnast, later joining the armed forces, where he served five years as a physical training instructor.

On leaving the services, he went into show business and became one of the country's top balancing acts. Then one evening in 1961, when rehearsing in Manchester, he fell and broke his neck. He was 26 years old.

The tragic result of this accident was permanent paralysis. Confined to a wheelchair and unable to pursue his original career, he switched to art and became a talented painter, with the brush held in his mouth. He was completely self-taught and painted mainly in oils, his favourite subjects being landscapes and trees.

Mr Vandek could find no samples of his writing which predated his accident, but thought it might be interesting to compare his penmanship in written, printed and sketched samples.

His script contained many flat-topped letters in the middle zone (*h*s, *n*s, *m*s and *r*s) a phenomenon often seen in the writing of people who are paralysed. But his upper and lower loops were nicely filled out, indicating normal imaginative processes. His powers of observation and concentration appeared to be first-rate.

Figure 159 shows a sample of his script, and figure 160 a sample of the printed form of his writing.

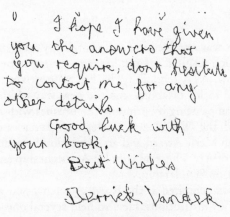

Figure 159 (50%)

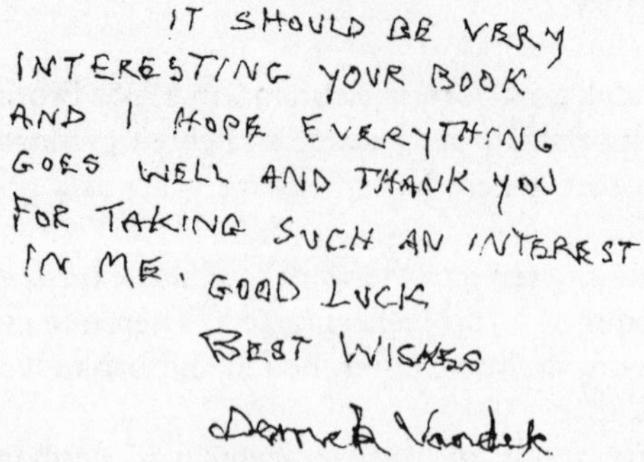

IT SHOULD BE VERY
INTERESTING YOUR BOOK
AND I HOPE EVERYTHING
GOES WELL AND THANK YOU
FOR TAKING SUCH AN INTEREST
IN ME. GOOD LUCK
BEST WISHES

Derrek Vandek

Figure 160 (50%)

Both samples are well placed on the page. Each is attractively spaced out with light pen pressure, indicating the writer's sensitive nature. The slant in the scripted version is generally upright, although it does waver somewhat – hardly surprising in the circumstances. It is evenly balanced between the three zones. The writing is connected and co-ordinated, showing the writer's thoughts to be the same and demonstrating a strong sense of purpose.

The printed version is more controlled, showing Mr Vandek's love of order and method. Intelligent and lucid, both scripted and printed versions show individuality. There is an air of openness and sociability about them, with no evidence of unhealthy inhibitions.

Charles Fowler

Charles Fowler was involved in a serious railway accident at the age of eighteen which resulted in both his arms having to be amputated above the elbow. As a schoolboy, he had won prizes for art, and having adjusted to his disability and the new way of life that went with it, he began painting by gripping the brushes with his teeth.

He attended the Wimbledon College of Art in London and gained the High Merit Award and an Exhibition Scholarship to the Royal College of Art. There he won his Associateship and a fourth-year Continuation Scholarship.

His work was exhibited at the Royal Academy and many other leading British art institutions. He also held several one-man shows and taught painting at the Farnham School of Art, later becoming Head of the Art Department at Richmond Adult College. He worked mainly in watercolours, his favourite subjects being landscapes and woodland scenes.

Another aspect of his work was to give regular illustrated talks to groups of enthusiasts all over Greater London and the Home Counties on the aims and achievements of the MFPA. There was, he told me, nothing he enjoyed more than showing films about his work and that of his fellow artists.

Like Mr Vandek, Mr Fowler could find no samples of writing from his teens. His school books had long since vanished and he was not in the habit of keeping old correspondence, so in this case it is only possible to reproduce a post-accident sample (figure 161).

His script is the most aesthetic of all. Upright, fast-flowing and eminently legible, it shows determination, tenacity, persistence and a liberal sprinkling of panache. It also points to a cool, unruffled approach to his problems.

The structure of his letters suggests that he was blessed with a keen, enquiring mind. His offbeat sense of humour came through in every single letter he wrote to me.

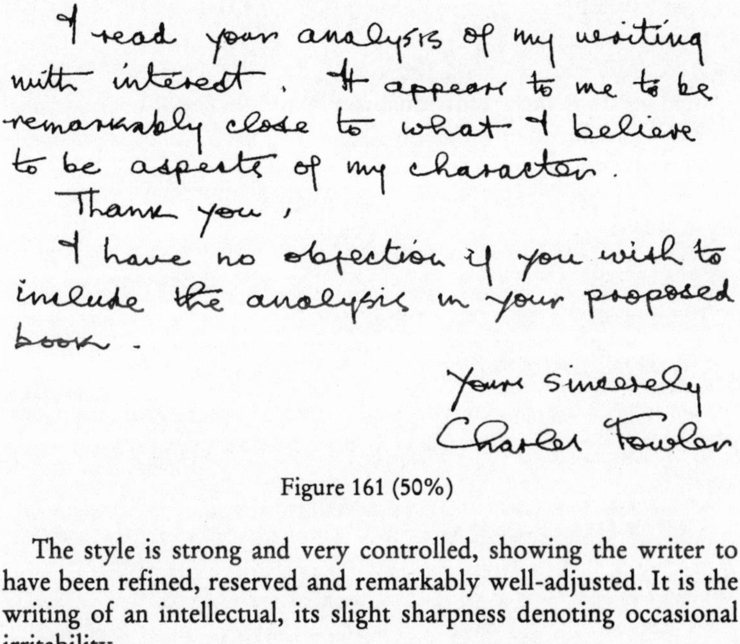

I read your analysis of my writing with interest. It appears to me to be remarkably close to what I believe to be aspects of my character.

Thank you,

I have no objection if you wish to include the analysis in your proposed book.

Yours sincerely
Charles Fowler

Figure 161 (50%)

The style is strong and very controlled, showing the writer to have been refined, reserved and remarkably well-adjusted. It is the writing of an intellectual, its slight sharpness denoting occasional irritability.

The alignment, spacing and lucidity are first rate. The structure of the *m*s shows determination and a stubborn streak. Mr Fowler agreed that he was indeed intuitive, free of inhibitions and something of a perfectionist.

Printed capitals show his abilities as a communicator. Orators and public speakers often resort to this practice.

The signature itself is the same size and shape as the text, showing that he was exactly the same person in public as in private. Some of his t-bars are bowed, which is usually the sign of a writer who is able to keep basic urges under control.

His ability to handle money is shown in the shape of his *g*s (like the figure nine) and the personal pronoun I, which resembles a figure four. The *F* in his surname stretches out protectively and the surname itself is underlined: both of which add up to family (rather than personal) pride.

13   The Effects of Multiple Injuries

Swasie Turner

One dark, wet winter evening in 1987, Police Sergeant Swasie Turner and a colleague were walking in New Brighton, Merseyside. Suddenly there was the roar of a powerful motor cycle approaching at speed. Fearing for the safety of other road-users and confident that he would be seen in the glare of the bright street lights, Sergeant Turner stepped out and signalled its rider to stop. It slowed down and steered towards the kerb, but instead of stopping its rider gave his machine full throttle and hurled headlong into the officer.

Swasie Turner suffered multiple injuries, and underwent fourteen operations to try and save his shattered leg before the surgeon ultimately decided to amputate it above the knee. In that one insane act of violence, the unknown motor cyclist (who was never caught or identified) began a chain of events which ended his victim's career and altered his entire life.

He had enjoyed every minute of his career and was distraught by the idea of having to give it up at the relatively young age of 50. But worse was to follow. As if his physical pain and the trauma of everything he had already been through were not enough, his wife died from cancer eleven months after the amputation of his injured leg.

However he has not allowed his injuries and the desolation of his wife's death to destroy him. He has used it as a catalyst, and now devotes all his time and energies into raising funds for research into the cancer which claimed his beloved wife.

His aim is to tackle as many groundbreaking events as possible to raise funds for the Cancer Gene Appeal at Clatterbridge Hospital in Wirral. In the two years following his amputation, he has propelled himself in his standard-issue National Health Service wheelchair through the Mersey Tunnel, along the coastal roads of Anglesey, and around the TT course on the Isle of Man. With the lumbering chair tied to one of his big sturdy arms, wrapped around his waist or just dragged along behind him, he has also scaled three lighthouses on the Wirral and one in North Wales. More remarkable still, he has

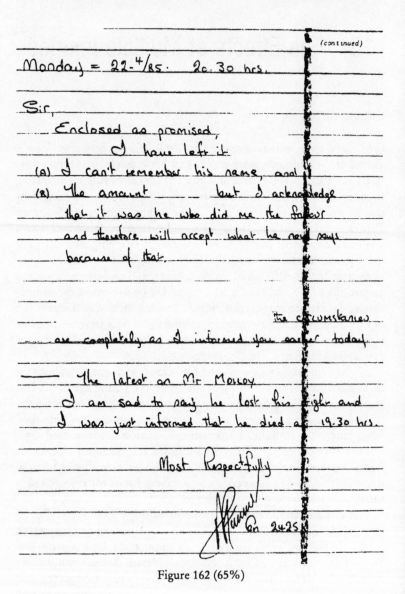

(continued)

Monday = 22-4/85. 2c.30 hrs.

Sir,
    Enclosed as promised,
         I have left it
(a) I can't remember his name, and
(B) The amount ____ but I acknowledge
that it was he who did me the favour
and therefore will accept what he now says
because of that.

           the circumstances
are completely as I informed you earlier today.

——— The latest on Mr Molloy
I am sad to say he lost his fight and
I was just informed that he died at 19.30 hrs.

        Most Respectfully

          Cn 2425

Figure 162 (65%)

166

climbed Blackpool Tower's spiral staircase, right up to the base of the flagpole.

That, then, is this man's remarkable background. So what aspects of his personality are revealed in his handwriting? And how does his script as a disabled writer compare with that produced when he was able-bodied?

Irreparable nerve damage and loss of muscle control in his right hand means that Mr Turner's right wrist is permanently encased in a metal brace. Also, the loss of two fingers – leaving him only with a thumb and index and middle fingers – means that while he can still write with that hand, he is now ambidextrous.

Intrigued by the concept of graphological analysis, Mr Turner very kindly provided me with three samples of his writing for purposes of comparison. Figure 162 is extracted from a police report dated 22 April 1985. Figures 163 and 164 were written some thirteen years later, on New Year's Eve, 1998.

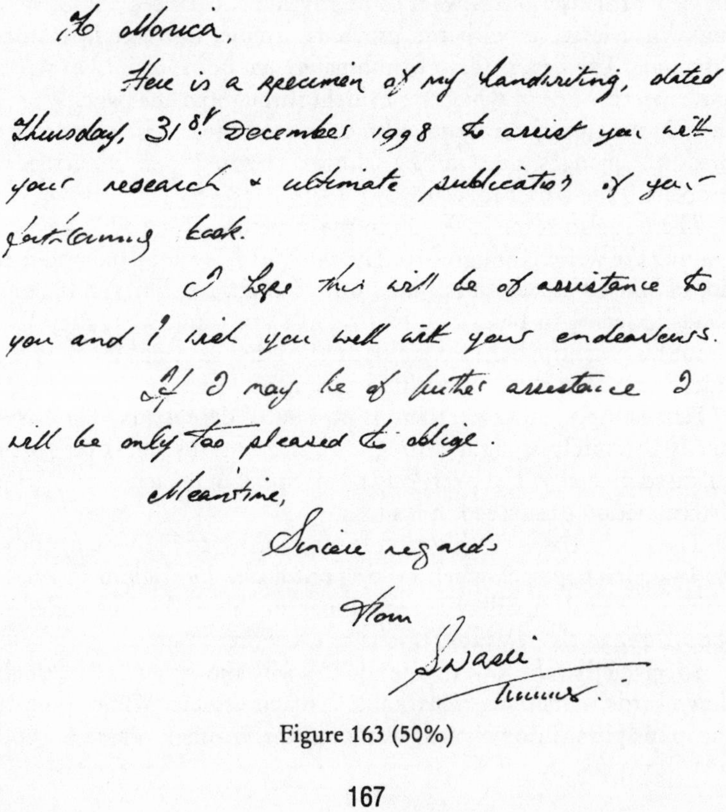
To Monica,

Here is a specimen of my handwriting, dated Thursday, 31st December 1998 to assist you with your research & ultimate publication of your forthcoming book.

I hope this will be of assistance to you and I wish you well with your endeavours.

If I may be of further assistance I will be only too pleased to oblige.

Meantime,

Sincere regards

from

Turner.

Figure 163 (50%)

Before comparing the 1985 sample with the more recent ones, let us take an overall look at each one individually.

The first impressions of figure 162 are of its upright stand and independent letter structures. This is a positive, balanced script, assertive, dominant and well laid out on the page.

The arcade (lid-on-the-emotions) form of lettering combined with tightly closed *a*s and *o*s demonstrate the writer's ability to keep confidences. Printed capitals tell of the importance he attaches to clarity: the two versions of *M* suggest versatility, while the epsilon *E* shows culture. Literary abilities are seen in the structure of the lower-case *g*s. Musical appreciation is indicated in the shape of the lower-case *b*s.

All told, the hand of the then 45-year-old police constable is strong, authoritative and energetic. Respect for his peers is also much in evidence – note the huge *r* in the word 'respectfully'. A versatile and fast-flowing script, it is surprisingly unaggressive.

As I have said, figure 163 postdates Mr Turner's trauma. An overall view of the script shows it to be rhythmic, balanced and of very high form-level, as with the previous sample, but certain factors dominate. The first is that of sublimated emotions, mainly of stress and anxiety, signs of which are evident throughout the page. We see them in the taut upper loops, with their blackened tops, in the many pressure changes and in the almost frenzied pen movements propelling the writer forward.

There is also some variation in the structure of the PPI suggesting that the writer, though strongly motivated, is a little uncertain, if not of himself at least about how others might see him. On the one hand he seems to be saying that people can think what they like about his eccentric behaviour, but on the other he needs them on his side if he is to succeed in his fund-raising activities.

Refreshingly, however, there is no hint of depression. The baseline is absolutely straight throughout, showing that he is very well balanced mentally. The over-long t-bars speak of tenacity and a grim determination to succeed in his task.

The lower zones of this sample are worthy of individual study. As I said in chapter 9, when seeking out health indications in handwriting, an analyst will relate the upper, middle and lower zones of the writing to the relevant regions of the writer's body.

So, given that the lower zone equates with the area from the thigh downwards, something remarkable is manifest here. While some of the loops plunge downwards in the normal manner, others do not.

Note, for example, the normality of the *f* in 'of' and the *y* in 'my' (line two), the *f* in 'of' (line six), the *y* in 'may' and the *f* in 'of' and 'further' (line eight), and the g in 'regards' as he signs off. Compare those with the much shorter *f* in 'of' and *y* in 'your' (line four), the g in 'forthcoming' (line five), the *y* in 'you' and 'your' (line seven), and the g in oblige' (line nine). Signs and symbols shaped thus invariably point to the loss or paralysis of a lower limb. If *all* the descenders were shaped in this way, the interpretation would be that the writer was a double amputee.

We also see how generalized changes of pressure point to generalized physiological changes. Nevertheless, it has to be said that despite – or possibly because of – his broken body, this man's spirit is mighty strong. However great his mental suffering, the forward thrust of his script shows the lengths to which he will go to achieve his aim. He is blessed with an abundance of mental stamina.

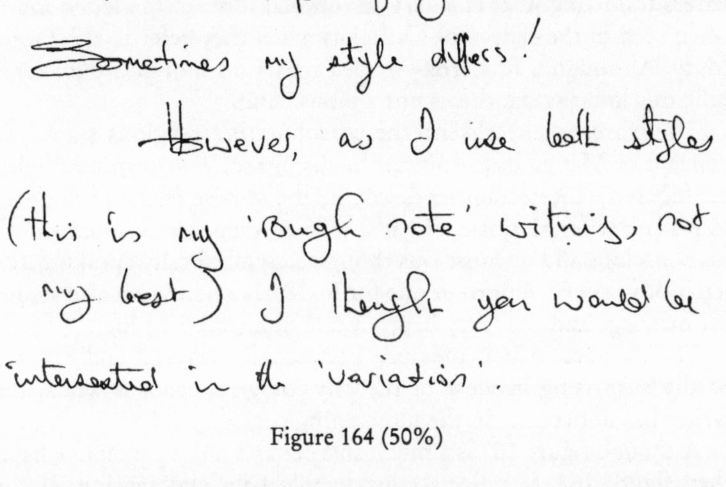

Figure 164 (50%)

The sample depicted in figure 164, which the writer refers to as his 'variation', is pleasant, relaxed and informal.

Now let us make the necessary comparisons. In comparing figures 162 and 163, we find various differences. While most of the letter structures are basically the same, there are some interesting changes. The first is in the PPI. You will recall that the PPI's three sections – top, stem and base – represent the writer's relationship with his mother (or mother substitute), the base his relation with his father (or father substitute), and the stem indicates how the writer feels about himself.

With that in mind, the large rounded curve at the base of the PPI in figure 162 suggests that the writer greatly admired and respected his father and generally felt very close to him. The sharper and more restricted upper segment indicates that maternal influence was less strong.

In figure 163 the symbol has changed somewhat; it has softened a little in attitude to the mother, making the whole more rounded, the implication being that thirteen years on, the writer himself was a more rounded and balanced individual.

The second change to have occurred can be seen in the capital *T*, which has moved on from being shaped like a figure seven (suggesting money worries?) to a more mature and artistic form with the odd swirl here and there.

The capital *M* also has a new form. Instead of being a straightforward printed version, it begins with a little curl, sweeps up and down twice, to end back on the baseline, quite detached from the letters following it. It is a very devotional form of the letter and is often seen in the scripts of Catholics when they refer to the Virgin Mary. Although a few cross-shaped t-bars do hint at a traditional religious upbringing, this is not a pious hand.

Therefore, in the absence of corroborating religious signs, the concept of Marian devotion can be dismissed. This man's thoughts are focused in quite another direction: the *M* here relates exclusively to his late wife, Marjorie. She it is who continues to dominate both his conscious and unconscious thoughts. Symbolically speaking, the letter *M* is a very important one for Mr Turner because it also stands for marriage and the forty happy years of his married life.

The changes in pen pressure between figures 162 and 163 are hardly surprising in view of the physiological changes which the writer has undergone in the intervening period.

Although figure 163 is a much sharper and more perceptive hand than figure 162, it reflects considerable pain and tension. If the change in slant seems initially surprising, it does make sense. As a young able-bodied officer, the writer could be as independent as he wished, but his present lifestyle means that he is obliged to mix with and rely on others – at least, as far as his fund-raising is concerned.

On the whole the contemporary style is the more classy, but then his lifestyle is more cultured today. He is the author of several books about the police force, he paints and sketches, and he is in constant demand for his lively and enthusiastic after-dinner presentations.

The t-bar covering his surname has grown out of all proportion to become one of the most determined and tenacious a graphologist is likely to encounter. In this hand, it is a very positive sign. So too is the final *r*, as it sweeps optimistically forward to end on an upbeat note.

Figure 164 differs from the others, in that it is by far the most relaxed. Enthusiastically inflated loops indicate a fertile imagination (upper zone) and physical stamina (lower zone), both of which can be called upon whenever the writer pleases.

The script is back to its upright stand, and the letters in it are larger, although their basic structures remain unchanged. Notice the top of the capital *F*. It is not very different from the top of the capital *T* in figure 163. The t-bars still pull to the right and the i-dots are to the right of the letter as before. And apart from one little blip on figure 163 (in the second paragraph) the personal pronouns are also much the same.

The importance of symbolism in graphology should never be overlooked. Look carefully at the big balloons in the words 'rough' and 'thought'. They conjure up images of a wheelchair. The swirling capital *S* in 'sometimes' is an obsessive letter structure, but in it too we can readily detect the wheels of the chair.

Simon Weston

Simon Weston was a bright, energetic young Welsh Guardsman serving in the South Atlantic when the Argentines bombed his troop carrier *Sir Galahad*. The ensuing inferno killed several of his friends outright and caused Simon to suffer extensive burns to his face, head, hands, legs and body. Forty-seven per cent of his body was burnt, more than 80 per cent scarred by surgery.

The incident occurred just two months before his twenty-first birthday. The injuries he received were so horrendous they would have killed most people and he admits that there were times when he did indeed wish himself dead. He also confessed to having experienced pangs of guilt at his own survival when so many of his friends were dead.

Two years later, at the age of twenty-three, Simon was discharged from the Army. Although he was initially overwhelmed by depression, he fought back, determined to turn adversity to advantage. He conquered agonizing pain, not all of which was physical. In addition to the more than seventy skin grafts needed to rebuild his shattered face and body, in those early days he had to put up with a variety of reactions from the general public, including stares, whispers and undisguised curiosity.

On holiday in Tenerife he was attacked by a group of Spanish youths who, on learning the cause of his injuries, subjected him to further torture by beating him up. On top of all that, he was being suffocated by love and kindness in his South Wales village home. Although motivated by the very best of reasons, the villagers could not see that their attitude was threatening to stifle him. 'Being Welsh certainly helped me through the really bad patches,' he told me shortly after the incident. 'The closeness and strength of my people means that they rally around anyone in trouble, but it means too that they make it difficult for someone like me to be independent.'

Six years after the event, he moved to Liverpool where he felt he could be his own man and perhaps help other people at the same time, and in 1989 he set up the Weston Spirit with Paul Oginsky and Ben Harrison under the umbrella of Merseyside Council for Voluntary Services.

The purpose of the project was to help young unemployed people to remotivate themselves and to run residential courses where teenagers could learn leadership skills. He is totally committed to the project. 'The idea behind it is to change attitudes,' he told me. 'Weston Spirit provides a sense of purpose.' Shortly after founding it, he organized a sponsored walk for the elderly by ten young people.

His grit and determination showed in other ways too. He won a place on a Douglas Bader flying scholarship, and has also cycled across America for the Royal Star and Garter Home, done a tandem parachute jump, taken part in the New York marathon and walked across Finland.

A tireless worker for the Royal British Legion and the Royal Star and Garter Home, his charitable work earned him a richly deserved OBE in the 1992 Queen's Birthday Honours.

When the opportunity arose for him to be a regular broadcaster for BBC Radio Wales, he jumped at the chance. 'Well,' he quipped, showing that his sense of humour is still very much intact: 'Why not? after all, I'm never going to be a film star or a sex symbol.'

Simon invariably focuses on the positive. His family, marriage and children have all helped him understand and face up to life's difficulties. 'I am very very lucky,' he says.

In 1992, he visited Buenos Aires, where he met Carlos Cachon, the fighter pilot responsible for the carnage. The atmosphere was strained but Simon bore no grudges. They shook hands and he told the Argentinian: 'What you did was professional, not personal.' When the two men met again in London six years later, the relationship was much less tense, the handshakes and embraces genuinely warm. The soldiers once sworn to kill were joined in friendship.

I first met Simon in 1988 to interview him for the *Liverpool Echo*. He was attending the opening of a Lifestyles Fair organized by Mersey Regional Health Authority. Despite the fact that he knew I was about to 'graphologize' him, he bravely autographed my programme (figure 165)!

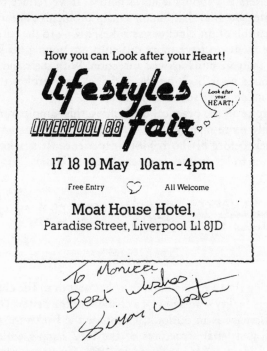

Figure 165 (65%)

The signature shows him to be still very much his own man. Note the determined crossing of the *t* for instance. Indeed, in the entire sample, it is through the lower-case *t* that Simon's personality emerges most strongly. The looped stem shows his sensitive nature; his emotional hurt is hidden deep beneath the surface. Note too how the stem progresses below the baseline (as it has in the word 'best' above), revealing stubbornness and a determination to press on despite the difficulties.

The long cross-bar of the *t* in his surname, points to his tenacity, endurance and unwillingness to let go. It also provides clues about the protective side of his nature, the symbolic reaching out of an arm to help anyone who might need it. This is very significant in view of his concern for disadvantaged young people.

The speed of his writing reflects the speed of his thoughts, but the physical difficulties can also be seen, noticeably in the *n, c* and *a* of 'Monica', the two *ss* in 'wishes', and the *m* and *n* in 'Simon'. None of these letters is a spontaneous structure. If we retrace their individual routes, we find that Simon's main problems appear to occur in the execution of the clockwise strokes; owing to the nature of his injuries he seems to have more difficulty in moving his hand in a clockwise than an anticlockwise direction. With the *c* and the *a* for instance, once he is back on the anticlockwise strokes the movements are much more spontaneous.

Yet, despite all the practical difficulties, this sample from 1988 is considerably more mature than figure 166, which was written just over a week before his horrendous experience. It is taken from a letter written to his mother from the South Atlantic.

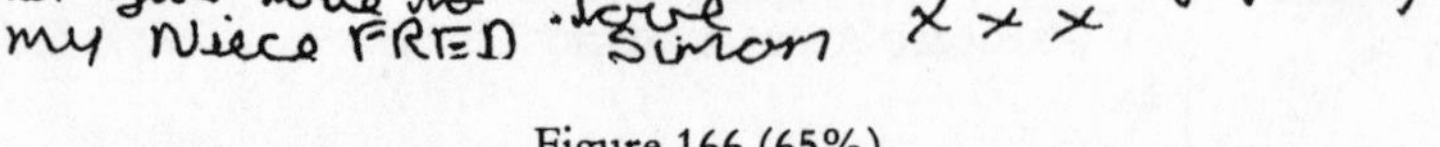

Figure 166 (65%)

Examining the two, one finds that the most dramatic change is in Simon's personality – amazingly, a change for the better. The fundamental difference is in outlook. Compare the backward slant and unsophisticated letter structures of the 1982 sample with the big, strong, confident tones produced in 1988. Six years, even at that stage in a young man's life, should not account for such a difference.

In 1982, Simon was rather unsure of himself; happy enough with his friends or as 'one of the boys', but lacking the confidence and self-assurance that were to become integral parts of his personality in later years. In the later sample he shows himself to be very much

174

his own man. Essentially, it is the difference between immaturity and maturity; more interestingly, figure 165 shows a leaning away from self and self-interest. One cannot help wondering how his style might have developed had the circumstances been different. As it is, he is one of the most well-adjusted people I have ever met.

His writing has no overt signs of lasting psychological hurt, or of hidden resentment resulting from his appalling physical injuries and the nightmare years that followed. One might expect mental scarring of equal magnitude to the physical, but it is not indicated.

Ten years on, I invited Simon to supply me with another sample of his writing to determine whether any further graphological changes had taken place. After all, his life had moved on in the intervening period. He had married, returned to his native Wales, fathered two sons and a daughter, written his autobiography,[1] returned to the Falklands to test and write about his reactions in the aftermath of the war,[2] received numerous awards for his charitable works (including that OBE) and launched himself as a writer of crime fiction.[3] He was living life to the full.

Once more, he happily complied with my request, and the result is shown in figure 167.

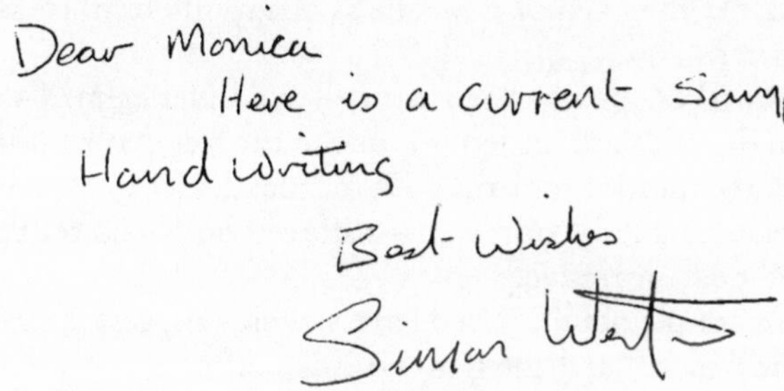
Dear Monica
Here is a current sample of my Hand writing
Best Wishes
Simon Weston

Figure 167 (50%)

The script is even bigger, bolder, more confident and more self-assured than before. It is also faster, more free-flowing and more optimistic. And it also shows something else: just enough healthy assertiveness to provide balance in what might otherwise be quite an emotional style.

Legible and consistent, it is a natural hand, reflecting clarity of judgement and of thought. Its speed demonstrates adaptability and enthusiasm.

It is refreshingly free of ornamentation and neurotic overwriting, and its full round letters indicate generosity and warmth of feeling. Whereas in figures 165 and 166 the script was connected, figure 167 shows it to have developed into an interesting mix of connected and disconnected letters.

Such a combination is the work of a writer with good powers of intuition and reasoning and a liberal sprinkling of creative ability. What we have here is a man of ideas, blessed with acute mental processes yet innate shyness and reticence, although well below the surface, are still likely to manifest themselves, albeit rarely.

The complete lack of ostentatious embellishments in all three samples of this writer's script tell us that he is someone who works hard, plays hard and expects the same standards from others.

The latest version however, is not without its quirky signs. One is the way certain letters plunge dramatically below the baseline (the final stroke of the *m* in 'sample', the *y* in 'my' and again that *t* in his surname, which also figures in the earlier sample). The stubbornness is still there and now also a touch of frustration.

This plunging sign is sometimes seen in the scripts of people who feel they have much to offer, but for one reason or another are prevented from reaching their full potential. It does seem a shade surprising to find it in the hand of someone as manifestly fulfilled as this particular writer.

The printed capital *H*s point to self-control and inner calm. The slight variation in the width of the letter is due to the fact that he still appears to have some minor problems with manual dexterity, which is perfectly understandable in view of his stiffness, both as a result of his injuries and post-operatively.

There are also a couple of unfinished letters, which suggest impatience, such as the *f* in 'of' and the *g* in 'writing'. After all, this is a real man of action, whose speedy and uplifting script suggests a mind full of ideas and an enthusiasm to put them into effect. I must emphasize that they are not negative signs, because the general tone of the script is positive as befits a writer with such a generous, easy-going nature.

Angular i-dots show him to be astute and perceptive. Rounded letter tops suggest that although deeply sensitive, he is not one to wear his emotions on his sleeve.

Versatility is seen in the varying structure of the t-bars. The flicked bar on the one in 'current' shows a sense of humour and a real ability to work with the general public. The one in the word 'writing' is a copybook structure, suggesting that the writer will comply with convention whenever he feels it necessary to do so.

The huge, outstretched bar running the length of his surname indicates an even greater level of protectiveness than that demonstrated in figure 165. This one moves dramatically backwards and forwards in a symbolic gesture of reaching out to protect all around him. Protectiveness is a dominant aspect of Simon's script, reflecting as it does the caring aspects of his personality. This applies both personally and professionally: personally, in relation to his wife and three small children; professionally in his commitment to young people. It is significant that this symbol manifests itself more strongly now than a decade ago, before he had met his wife and fathered three children.

Another point worth mentioning about the big, decisive t-bar is that it is invariably the work of an honest man who is under no illusions, one who accepts life as it is. This is a leader, not a follower. Another clue is that the *S* in his signature is larger than the *W* which indicates that he prefers to be addressed as Simon rather than Mr Weston. Generally speaking, he prefers the informal approach.

The level baseline, which tells us that he keeps his feet firmly on the ground, only alters by rising slightly as he signs off, reflecting healthy optimism.

All told, the level of manual dexterity is much higher here than it was in figure 165. This is most clearly seen by comparing the way he has structured the name 'Monica'. The sharp edginess of the earlier sample and the difficulties encountered in penning the letters *n* and *c* have now vanished. There are still some slight changes of pen pressure, similar to those seen in the script of Swasie Turner, but they are considerably fewer than in figure 165.

Notice too how the fractured *S* in 'Simon' has now completely repaired itself. Consistency is a dominant factor of his personality. This is most clearly manifest in the uniformity of the greeting 'Best wishes'.

Case III

If success is the keynote to Simon Weston's script, the story is sadly very different for the writer in the next example. It features a seaman who suffered an accident aboard ship in the early days of the twentieth century. It is a well-documented case and the following account has been reproduced with the kind permission of the editor of the *British Medical Journal*.

It was published in the *BMJ* on 30 September 1911, under the title 'The Relation of Head Injury to Nervous and Mental Disease'.[4] Written by F.W. Mott, MD, FRS, FRCP, Physician to Charing Cross Hospital and Pathologist to the London County Asylums, it demonstrates how the relationship between head injury, nervous mental disease and handwriting had been established even then. The patient is identified simply as Case III. Dr Mott writes:

Male, aged 35. Was admitted to Bexley Asylum, October 18th, 1903; died April 20th, 1907. The patient had been an engineer's artificer in the Royal Navy. He was on the *RENOWN*, stationed in the Mediterranean.

He wrote frequently to his wife and those letters were very affectionately worded and denoted love for his home, his wife and children: they showed no sign of failing intelligence or loss of the auto-critical faculty.

In August he met with an accident, which is described in a portion of a letter to his wife, here reproduced [figure 168].

A month later he wrote, addressing his wife as Lady R., and in October – two months after the accident, as the letter [figure 169] shows – there are marked grandiose delusions of wealth, and the handwriting has markedly deteriorated.

The comparison of these two letters shows that immediately following the accident the degenerative process, if it were present, did not manifest itself in his letter to his wife describing the accident: within two months there were very marked signs of dementia, indicative of a degenerative process . . .

It may be reasonably asserted that if this man had not met with the accident he would not have suffered from general paralysis: or, at least, the chances were 50 to one against it occurring . . .

There are several facts in this case which support this contention.

First, the man was in good health, employed as a skilled artisan: secondly, the injury was the result of an accident in no way dependent upon the man's actions or state of consciousness: thirdly, letters prior to and immediately after the accident were not indicative of any mental decay; fourthly, there was a definite correlation of the accident with the onset shortly after of mania; fifthly, the patient lived for more than three years after the onset.

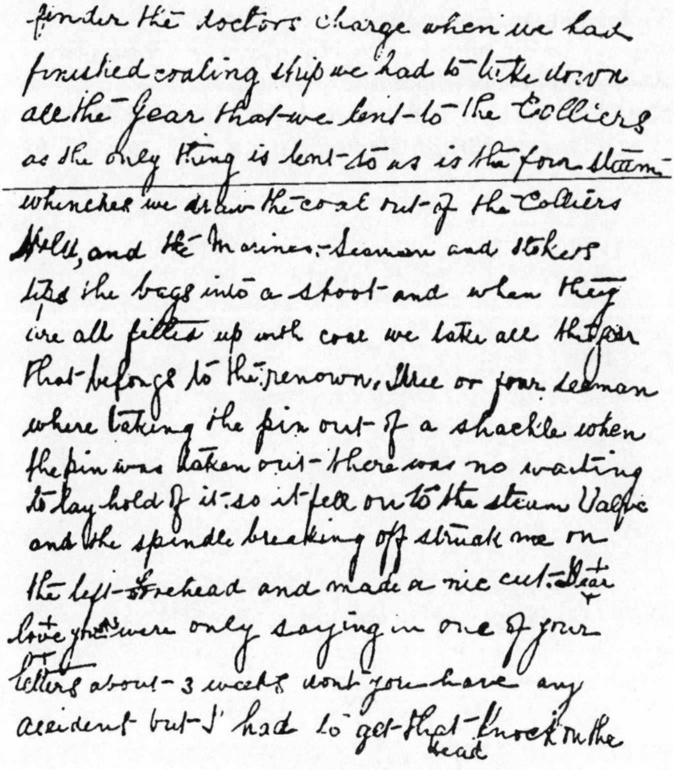
-finder the doctors charge when we had
finished coaling ship we had to take down
all the Gear that we lent to the Colliers
as the only thing is lent to us is the four steam
whinches we draw the coal out of the Colliers
Hold, and the Marines Seaman and Stokers
fills the bags into a stool and when they
are all filled up with coal we take all the gear
that belongs to the renown, three or four seaman
where taking the pin out of a shackle when
the pin was taken out there was no waiting
to lay hold of it so it fell on to the steam Valve
and the spindle breaking off struck me on
the left forehead and made a nic cut. Dear
love you were only saying in one of your
letters about 3 weeks dont you have any
accident but I had to get that knock on the head

Figure 168

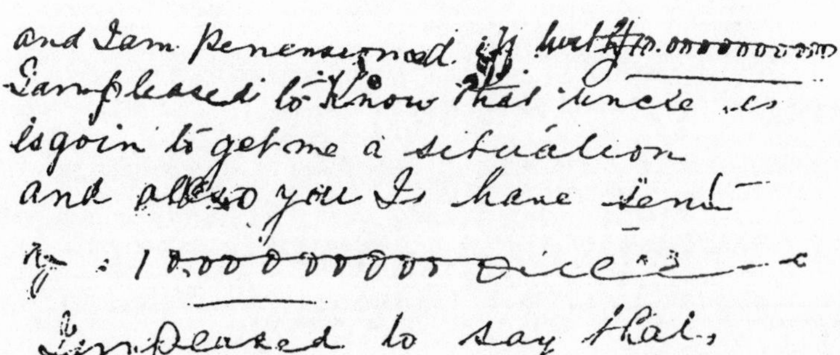
and I am Renenaeyned.
I am pleased to know that uncle
is goin to get me a situation
and also you Is have sent
: 10,000000000
I am pleased to say that,

Figure 169 (65%)

Notes

1 Weston, Simon, *Walking Tall* (Bloomsbury, 1989).
2 Weston, Simon, *Going Back* (Bloomsbury, 1992).
3 Weston, Simon, with Patrick Hill, *Cause of Death* (Two-Four, 1994) and Phoenix (Bloomsbury, 1996).
4 Mott, F.W. et al., 'The Relation of Head Injury to Nervous and Mental Disease' (*British Medical Journal*, 1911), pp. 735–6).

14   The Effects of Defeat

In this chapter I would like to look at the effect that military defeat
(and the collapse of all their ambitions) had on the writing of certain
leaders.

Napoleon Bonaparte (1769–1821)

Napoleon Bonaparte had a different signature for every day of the
week and many more besides. My own collection includes facsimi-
les of at least twenty and I feel sure there are many more in existence. The man was so mercurial, he may well have had one for
every day of the year. Sometimes he signed himself 'Napoleon'
(figure 170), or sometimes 'Buonaparte' (figure 171)

Figure 170

Figure 171

Verified versions also appear as just a scrawly N, but whatever signature he used he never failed to finish off with a heavy underscore to assert his authority. These underscores are so heavily executed that they speak not only of self-importance, but of arrogance, ruthlessness and bad temper. The Emperor was autocratic in the extreme, and for a graphologist studying his many signatures, it is not surprising to find that they rose or fell according to his fortunes. A further selection of these signatures is reproduced in figures 172 to 176.

Figure 172

Figure 172 was written in 1804 shortly after he had declared himself Emperor and set out to conquer the world. It shows him to be unscrupulous, arrogant and ruthless. Of all the underscores to be found accompanying his signature, this one is worthy of particular mention.

It is one of the most unpleasant any graphologist is likely to encounter. I find it positively sinister because of its symbolic resemblance to a sword, and a heavy iron one at that, complete with handle and all ready for sharpening. It speaks of innate brutality and a temper threatening to explode beyond control.

Figure 173

Figure 173 is taken from a document signed a year later, when he had won the battle of Austerlitz and was off to conquer more of Europe. The signature itself is still scrawly and shows little emotional control, but note the ambitious uplift. The underscore is nothing like as heavy. In the flush of success, it does not need to be.

The sword has been sharpened and is ready to strike again in the next stage of his career.

Figure 174

Figure 174 was written on the retreat from Moscow and is rather hasty. There is no time for a full signature, just a speedy initial. But two vital clues manifest themselves. The first is the full stop *before* the initial, suggestive of a brief pause to work out his next plan of action. The underscore has taken on yet another form. Angular now, it is still very aggressive, but here we only see the point of the sword as the writer unconsciously prepares to plunge it into his next adversary.

Napoleon's signatures before and after the Battle of Waterloo are very similar in shape and form and differ only in two respects. The first is that before the historic battle, it takes on its usual large, confident style; afterwards, it is reduced to less than half its size. The second is in the underscore. Before the battle it doubles back on itself in the usual manner; afterwards it takes on the form of a single thick and heavy line. That line denotes the anger and defiance associated with defeat, in further confirmation of which he extends it far beyond the signature at both ends.

Figure 175

Moving on two years, in figure 175 we have another version of the initial, only this time the full stop comes after the letter rather than before it. The point of the sword is still there, but now lying horizontally, and the writer finishes off, for the first time, with a downward turn. Like any other descending stroke, this one speaks multitudes about the writer's thoughts and his general state of mind.

Figure 176

The signature on St Helena (figure 176) is one of abject despair. Defeated in battle and broken in spirit, his career as a military leader is over. Now it is not just the underscore than points downwards, the whole signature has taken a tumble. Yet the addition of his underscore hints at continued defiance. Does Napoleon really believe he is finished? Note the quaint chicken-wishbone shape of that underscore!

Adolf Hitler (1889–1945)

Now let us see how Hitler's signature and mental processes also changed in defeat. The first sample of his signature (figure 177) is dated 1933, before his rise to power.

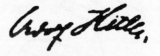

Figure 177

Dark, heavy and depressive, it speaks of obsession and brutality. Obsession is seen in the swing of the *H*, brutality in the heavy execution of the letters. No surprises there. But one aspect of this signature that *is* surprising is the very weak i-dot, which speaks of physical weakness. Hitler *weak?*

Figure 178

The second sample (figure 178) still has the brutal touch, now with arrogance (indicated by the vertical stroke at the curve of the *H*). There is undisputed criminality, sadism and manic depression in this hand. Criminality shows itself in its unnatural non-spontaneous execution, which is an unconscious pull against the natural flow of the hand. Sadism can be detected by the sharp edginess of its execution. The sadist often writes with a pasty script, the brush-like strokes of which tend to become heavier as they progress (instead of remaining constant or growing lighter as in a non-criminal hand). The manic depressive's script is full of huge, distorted letters (particularly in the upper zone), again its flow is interrupted and it is also likely to feature the falling baseline common to most depressives.

This signature, dated 1936, shows the dictator at the height of his power; the second was written eight years later.

Figure 179

The name Adolf is deliberately thready, because that is clearly not how the signator wished to be known. Informality formed no part of Hitler's public image. Note the scoring through of the *f* and the small size of the forename compared with that of the surname. Note, too, how that one brief symbol is made up entirely of hard lines and angles.

There is not a single curve of warmth or affection in this hand. See how the *f* thickens as it progresses on its downward path, providing us with a real clue to the man's brutality. A few more strokes on that forename would turn it into his dreaded Swastika.

The acute angle running into the *H* of his surname is an aggres-

185

sive sign, showing the world he means business. The *Sacré Coeur* swirl of the *H*, combined with the cross sign inside it hint at his religious background and the fanaticism with which he rejected that background. The downward pull is surprising in a man who believed he had the world at his fingertips. It suggests that beneath all the aggression he was deeply unhappy.

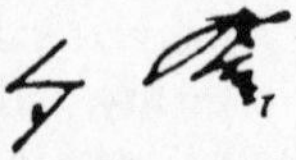

Figure 180

In defeat, Hitler's signature (dated December 1944) shrinks to a fraction of its previous size. The black blobs and general disintegration are further evidence of his severely disturbed state of mind and body. Injured following an assassination attempt, he was to commit suicide four months later.

Hermann Goering (1893–1946)

Goering was the man responsible for founding the Gestapo and setting up Nazi concentration camps. After the war, he managed to escape from Germany but was captured by US troops.

Principal defendant at the Nuremberg War Crimes Trial, Goering was condemned to death, but poisoned himself before the execution could be carried out. Sample one (figure 181) was written during his period as Reichmarshal of the Luftwaffe. Sample two was written when in his prison cell at Nuremberg and is extracted from a letter to his wife.

Figure 181

This signature is fast and stylish, its cocky swing giving the impression of confidence and self-assurance. But the confidence is a mask. Beneath the surface, this writing is shaky and fragmented, almost as if he suspects trouble on the way.

Figure 182

The second sample, is blacker and has become disjointed. With its heavy pen strokes and virtual illegibility, it is nasty in the extreme. What is one to make of that pair of triangles? Prison cell windows from which there is no escape? The final *g*, tumbling down and ending so abruptly suggests the writer is only too well aware of his fate.

Richard Nixon (1913–1994)

Richard Nixon, thirty-seventh President of the US, was involved in a series of illegal acts leading to the Watergate affair as a result of which he resigned from office in 1974. The first of these three samples is dated 1955, the second, 1973 and the third, 1974.

Figure 183

Here is a man of ambition and determination. Written during his term as vice-president, his style is sharp and shows very great mental acuity. Aggression is seen too in that *N* of the surname, which is not unlike the *N* of Napoleon (figure 174). But already, the negative side of his personality can be detected. Note the sharp stroke of the *x* running down to create a superficial lower zone, reflecting the superficial side of his character. Note, too, the general threadiness of the surname, as it trails off into illegibility. It is an unconscious message for others to keep their distance and not probe his personality.

The second signature is strong. Now, he is very sure of himself and his position of power. What we have here is a huge, protective cover running over his name. Self-protection and preservation have become the key issues.

Figure 184

Just one year later, as a result of Watergate, Nixon has been stripped of his power and facing impeachment, resigns. The disproportionate stroke of the x is still there, but now it pulls in the opposite direction. Its backward slant reflects the enforced backward route of the man who wrote it.

Figure 185

15 Altered States

Sleep-writing

The connection between an individual's state of mind and the workings of his body has already been firmly established. We have also seen how stress and tiredness can bring about quite noticeable changes in the hand. But what about when it goes beyond tiredness and into sleep itself? In this chapter, we will be looking at the scripts of writers who were fast asleep at the time they wrote. Both writers are known to me personally and I can vouch for their integrity.

The writer of the first two extracts was completely confused by her outpourings. A psychiatric nurse, she is well used to patients presenting her with unusual and offbeat situations. But when something completely inexplicable and bizarre comes from within herself, it is a different matter!

Figure 186 is taken from a postcard sent to my husband and myself when she was holidaying in Canada. Figure 187 is an extract from notes written at her home while sleepwalking. This was the first – and to our knowledge the only – time she had ever sleepwalked.

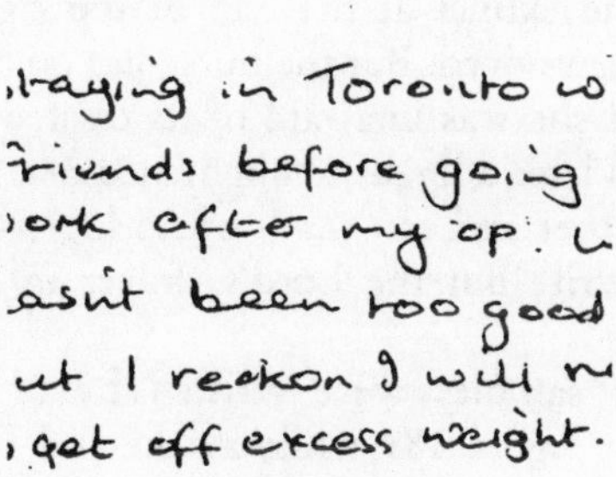
staying in Toronto w
friends before going
work after my op. u
asnt been too good
ut I reckon I will n
get off excess weight.

Figure 186

The sleep-writing is very much larger than that seen in the waking sample. Yet, apart from the size and the fact that the nurse's natural style is a connected form of script whereas that written in sleep is mainly disconnected, it is again obvious that one individual has written both.

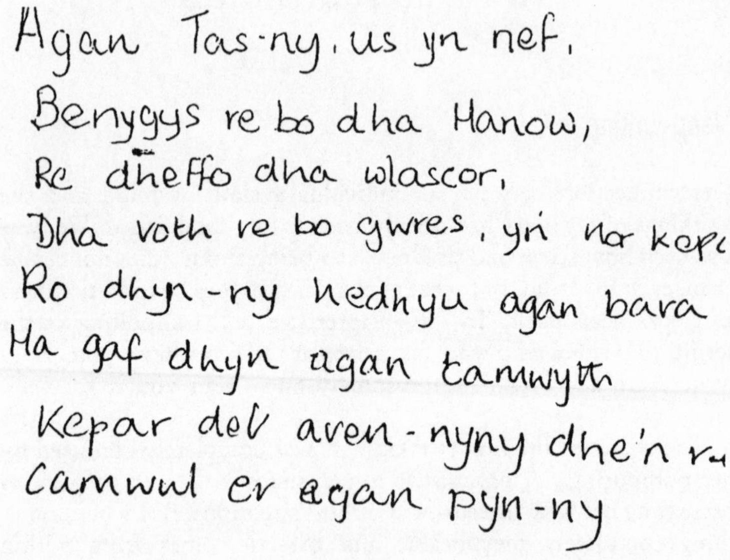

Agan Tas-ny, us yn nef,

Benyggys re bo dha Hanow,

Re dheffo dha wlascor,

Dha voth re bo gwres, yn nor kepe

Ro dhyn-ny hedhyu agan bara

Ha gaf dhyn agan camwyth

Kepar del aven-nyny dhe'n ru

Camwul er agan pyn-ny

Figure 187

The most amazing aspect of Figure 187, however, is that it is part of the Lord's Prayer in 'revived' Cornish. Yet the writer lives on Merseyside and at the time of this incident had never been to Cornwall and had no friends or relatives living there.

Cornish became extinct at the end of the eighteenth century, although it is being revived. But the nurse has no conscious knowledge of it. Indeed she was unaware of its existence until her own sleeping mind and later a linguist enlightened her. She is not particularly religious either and can think of no logical reason why she should want to write out the Lord's Prayer in her sleep in *any* language.

The next two samples were written by a former editorial colleague of mine: figure 189 while awake and figure 188 during sleep.

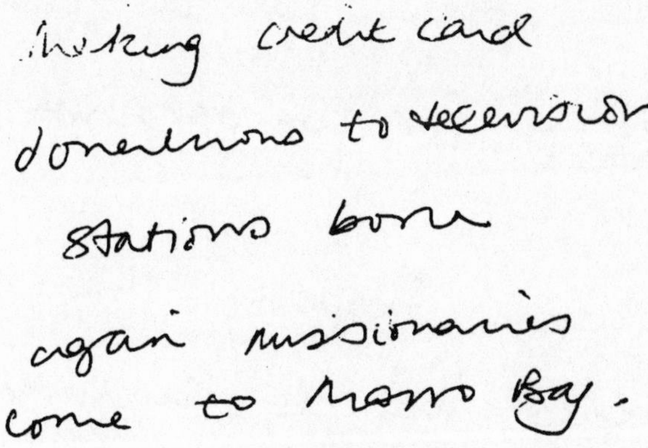

...hoking credit card donations to television stations born again missionaries come to Morro Bay.

Figure 188 (65%)

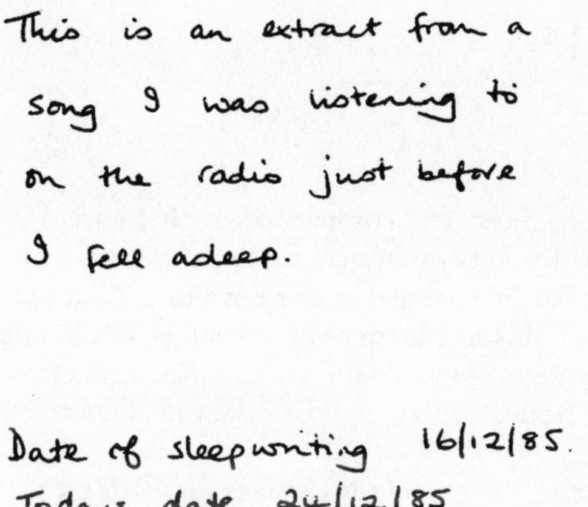

This is an extract from a song I was listening to on the radio just before I fell asleep.

Date of sleepwriting 16/12/85.
Todays date 24/12/85.

Figure 189 (65%)

Apart from the variation in some words and the fact that some wander around the paper, and one *t* is without its cross-bar ('donations' in line two) there are no great surprises here. In her own distinct, lucid and highly intelligent style, the writer herself explains what motivated her action. She was repeating the words of a song she was listening to just before she fell asleep.

Here (figure 190) is a sample of her current script.

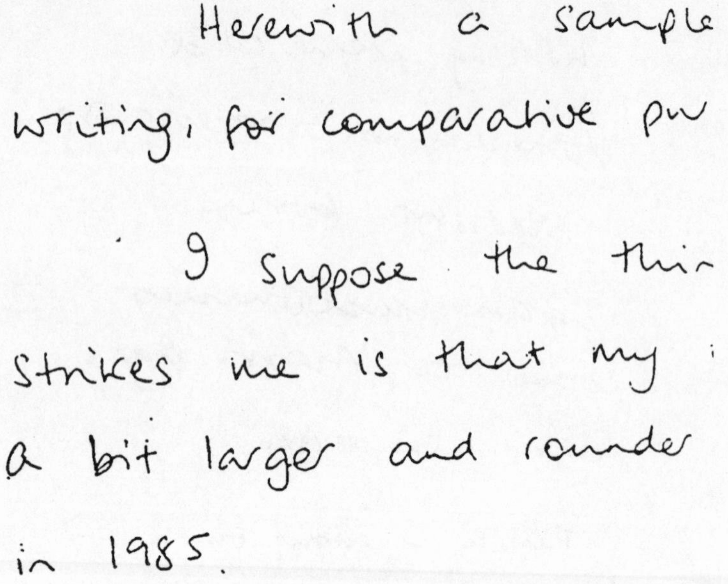

Herewith a sample

writing, for comparative pu

I suppose the thir

Strikes me is that my

a bit larger and rounder

in 1985.

Figure 190

It is reproduced for comparison with figure 189 and, as the writer herself points out, apart from its size and apparent 'round-ness', it has hardly changed in thirteen years. Nor, in the absence of illness, injury or some form of deep trauma would one expect it to. It is still a very independent style, lucid, articulate and of high form-level. Both samples are well balanced and attractively laid out on the page.

Nevertheless, a few minor changes do manifest themselves. The later sample is faster than its predecessor and shows subtle little nuances such as the occasional upward-curling t-bar, denoting a more developed sense of humour. Also, whereas the earlier sample contains a few blacked-out es, there are none in the later sample. The blacking-out hints at some secret occupying the writer's waking (though not her sleeping) mind in 1985. The nature of that secret cannot have been very serious because it no longer features in her hand.

Also, whereas the script in figure 189 is almost entirely connected, that in figure 190 is a mixture of connected and disconnected, showing a recently developed ability to take intuitive jumps.

And in the 1985 version, almost all the *s*s are submissive, whereas in the 1998 version, nine of the twelve are dominant, showing that the writer is self-assured.

However, the most obvious difference between the two is in the pen pressure, which in the earlier sample, is disturbingly variable. Magnification shows weakness in several of the pen strokes, some of which can be seen with the naked eye. Notice the breaks in the *r* of 'radio', the *j* in 'just', the *l* and *t* in 'listening', the *o* and *g* in 'song' and the *a* in 'asleep'. The pen pressure in the later sample shows none of these weaknesses. Its consistency points to a much healthier state of mind and body.

Could this bear any relationship to the fact that the writer has 'found herself' professionally and is therefore more mentally fulfilled? In the period between the two samples her career has come on in the proverbial leaps and bounds.

Hypnotherapy

Many disorders of mind and body can be explored and treated by hypnosis and hypnotherapy has proved remarkably successful in their treatment.

Valerie, a housewife, has kindly permitted me to reproduce three samples of her signature to illustrate how her writing changed over a matter of weeks, reflecting how she herself also changed in that time as a result of having learned the technique of autohypnosis.

In the days before I knew her, Valerie had been in almost constant pain from arthritis. She also suffered from insomnia and tension. She therefore tried deep hypnosis. She responded to the induction and under hypnosis was taught the technique of self-treatment to offset further troubles.

A quiet, self-effacing woman, she found that learning to control her mind in this way had beneficial side-effects with long-lasting results. Timid as a child, Valerie had always been reserved and chose not to mix in strange company if it could be avoided.

Having been taught to relax, she found she could cope with virtually any situation. No longer handicapped by pain, insomnia and tension, she became confident and assertive, and began to enjoy life.

Figure 191

The three versions of her signature in figure 191 are: one taken from her first letter asking if my husband and I would help, one written shortly after her first meeting with us and one produced when she had been taught the technique of self-treatment. They show that her progress was quite marked.

In the first, the V is closed and wrapped protectively around itself. It is an inhibited signature, with great rigidity of movement. In the second the letter is not so rigid or so taut, although it does still look more like an O than a V, but the third is a much more confident letter structure.

Nor is the capital the only letter to have opened up. Note how the *l* has advanced from being a stick-formation to a loop (which is still somewhat congested) to one filling our nicely. The final signature is also much less inhibited, reflecting the writer's improved state of health and general progress.

16   Sex Change

There are two types of gender deviation, transsexual and transvestite, and it is important to differentiate between the two. A transsexual longs to be a member of the opposite sex. A transvestite does not want to join the opposite sex, but simply wants to cross-dress. It is more common for males to be transsexuals or transvestites than females.

Sex and gender have different meanings too. Sex refers to the anatomy and physiology of the individual, while gender refers to a person's masculine or feminine behaviour and belief in his or her nature.

Gender identity and social gender role are both very important. Most transsexuals trace their conviction of having the 'wrong' body back to early childhood, while transvestites think of their personality as altering between masculine and feminine or being a mixture of both. Transsexuals are disturbed by their body's form and function and seek to change it, while transvestites are not and do not.

Transvestites frequently cross-dress as a relief from tension and anxiety. (The term is normally applied only to men since the complimentary state of women has few social stigmas attached.) Some people gain contentment and emotional relief from smoking, others overeat, or bite their nails. By the same token, cross-dressing enables the transvestite to return to his normal masculine role, refreshed.

A typical case I have been studying is that of an eminent medical man who 'becomes' his cousin Rose when off duty, but only after he has driven many miles from the hospital where he is well-known. For most of his life he is a normal man, heterosexual, married with children and a responsible position. He does not crave to be a woman. By reflecting his feminine aspect he releases the tensions arising from the pressure of what he sees as his masculine role.

Michelle

Michelle is a transsexual who became a woman at the age of thirty-four, after a two-year transition period which involved several operations as well as the inevitable physiological and psychological adjustment.

Fortunately there were no problems with the employers for whom she had worked for almost twenty years, first as a locomotive cleaner then as a fireman. At the time of writing, she is based in a busy north-western office, where she finds her colleagues (who know exactly what she has been through) both understanding and sympathetic.

Reproduced below are three samples of her writing. The first was penned many years before her sex change; the others were written a few months and one year afterwards respectively. They clearly demonstrate how the dramatic change in her life has affected her writing.

In all three samples, the form-level is good and the words are clear and legible, with no attempt to deceive or delude. Nor are there any signs of irrational fears or phobias in either male or female specimens.

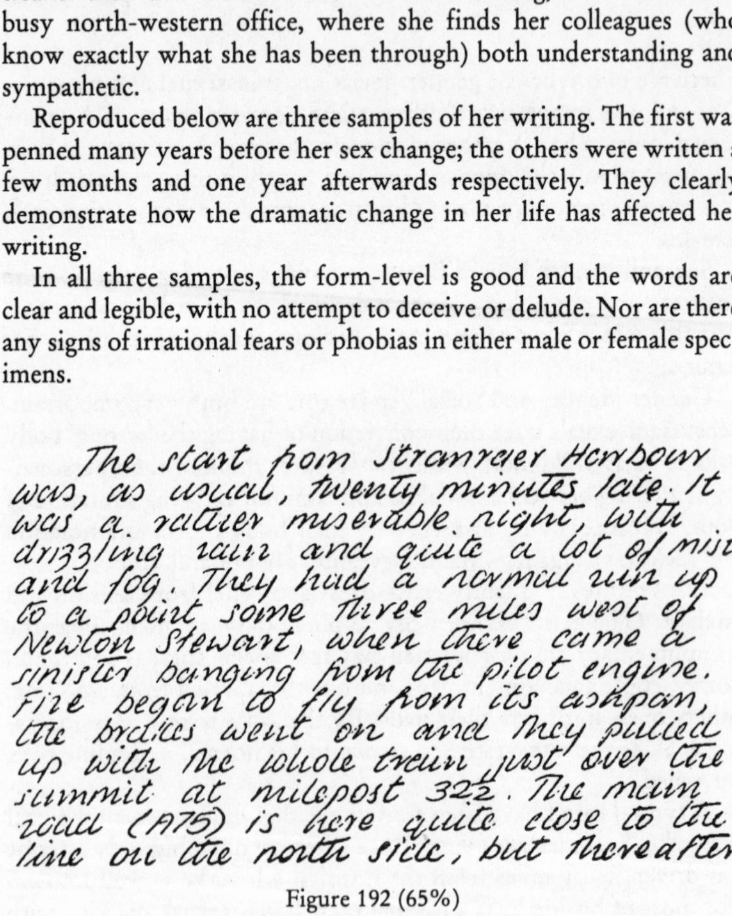
The start from Stranraer Harbour
was, as usual, twenty minutes late. It
was a rather miserable night, with
drizzling rain and quite a lot of mist
and fog. They had a normal run up
to a point some three miles west of
Newton Stewart, when there came a
sinister banging from the pilot engine.
Fire began to fly from its ashpan,
the brakes went on and they pulled
up with the whole train just over the
summit at milepost 32½. The main
road (A75) is here quite close to the
line on the north side, but thereafter

Figure 192 (65%)

Figure 192 is a strong, bold style with good inter-word and inter-linear spacing. The angularity and heavy pressure suggest strength and masculine fitness, and the rightward slant indicates an outgoing nature. This, therefore, is someone who enjoys company and is intuitive (denoted by gaps within some of the words), perceptive (angular i-dots) and able to keep confidences (the *o*s are all tightly closed, as are most of the *a*s).

It is an artistic hand. Low-crossed t-bars and low-placed i-dots represent good powers of concentration. The writer is versatile and adaptable.

There is also an element of compassion; the hand shows none of the aggressive traits one might expect. While the pressure denotes strong energy drives, descenders into the lower zone are short and light, suggesting only moderate interest in sex, which is hardly surprising in the circumstances.

Dash-type i-dots show occasional irritability and a general mood of anxiety, neither of which is surprising when one remembers that this first sample dates from a period when the writer was uncomfortable with her situation, but had as yet given no thoughts to gender reassignment and the opportunity such a change might afford for releasing pent-up feelings. The small *r*s are slightly repressed and the lower loops occasionally entwine themselves among the strokes of the line below.

In the original though not in the copy, a strange psychological quirk appears in the formation of the letter *t*, in that it stands out over all the other letters. Symbolically, if we assume that in the case of this specific writer *t* stands for 'transsex', it seems apparent that although she might not have been consciously thinking along these lines at the time, her unconscious was churning over the possibilities.

Indeed, Michelle herself agreed on that point: 'I knew from the age of about three that I wanted to be a girl,' she told me. 'My mind was totally obsessed with the idea. Superficially, I was quite content but I was, as you suggest, desperately unhappy.'

Figures 193 and 194, written very soon after the operation, show a script that is much more controlled and although graphologists can not as a rule describe any one specimen of writing as being essentially male or essentially female, these samples can be seen, even by an untrained eye, to have a round, feminine softness – apart from one very important clue. Note that the personal pronoun has adopted a sharp, edgy shape and decreased somewhat. Its small size reflects the writer's lack of self-confidence.

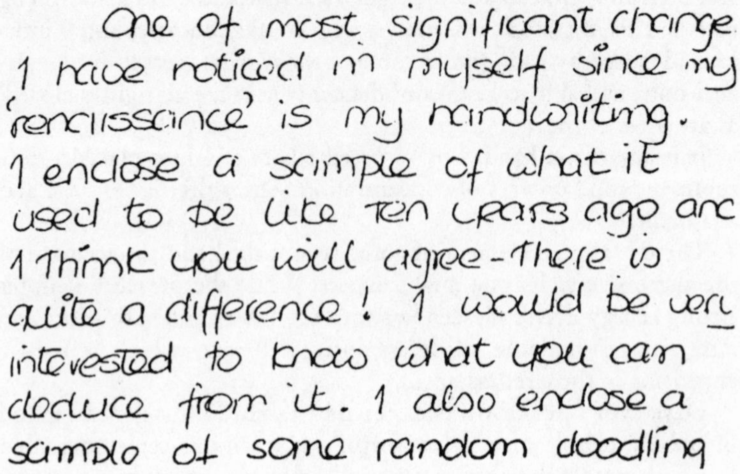

One of most significant change
1 have noticed in myself since my
'renaissance' is my handwriting.
1 enclose a sample of what it
used to be like ten years ago and
1 think you will agree - There is
quite a difference! 1 would be very
interested to know what you can
deduce from it. 1 also enclose a
sample of some random doodling

Figure 193 (65%)

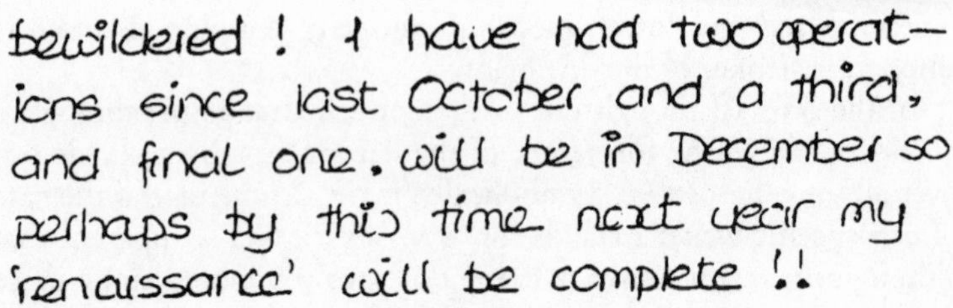

bewildered! 1 have had two operations since last October and a third,
and final one, will be in December so
perhaps by this time next year my
'renaissance' will be complete!!

Figure 194 (65%)

On the whole, though, the general roundness of Michelle's writing in this second sample and also in the third indicates her newly acquired femininity and reflects her more gentle and compassionate approach to life.

Studying figure 193 more closely, it might be pertinent to point out that the overlapping letters suggest a flow of writing which has been held back with great self-control. It is as if the writer were battling within herself to re-establish self-esteem. There does now seem a certain hesitancy to allow others to invade her very private space.

On the other hand, the overriding signs of tension and anxiety so obvious in the male writing have completely vanished. The female hand shows Michelle to be more at peace with herself and with the world in general.

The tiny lower loops suggest a continuing lack of sex drive and the speed of writing has slowed down considerably, in line with the writer's functioning. Nevertheless, both male and female styles are regular and both are disconnected, reflecting unchanged intuition and self-reliance.

While the writing in figure 192 is more arcade than angular, it still has some angular characteristics, whereas that in figure 193 is all arcade apart from the persona personal pronoun, as I have said. The male writing is narrow, while the female is wide, and although at first glance they might seem totally different, a close examination of the letter structures does prove that they have come from the same hand.

In figures 193 and 194 we have a choice of i-dots. We see a predominance of the circular type so popular with artists, models and young women concerned about their personal appearance. These reflect the importance Michelle attaches to her personal appearance and her desire to make the best of herself.

Her os are more closed and the entire structure of her letters is clearer and more precise, as if there were suddenly a need to prove that, despite appearances, Michelle is still intelligent and articulate. She agreed with this observation, pointing out in one of her many letters to me: 'In my first days as a woman, I found that I was auto-matically treated as if my capabilities were less than those of a man. That is why I found – and still find – myself trying to impress.'

Returning briefly to the personal pronoun, note that in the male style we see a stick-like formation, whereas in the female style it resembles a continental figure one, suggesting familiarity with figures (the main figure being her own?). On a more practical level, it could also be due to the fact that Michelle's treatment took place abroad and that now her writing was reflecting the European influ-ence.

The fact that that same letter has become small and sharp could be because at the time of writing those two letters, Michelle admit-ted that she occasionally felt self-conscious about her change of lifestyle.

Therefore, the male writing, although giving the impression of being cheery and outgoing, is actually far more tense and inhibited than the female style. In her feminine persona, the letters have opened up to reveal a more relaxed outlook on life and a new-found confidence.

The only overt problem (revealed by a lack of margins in all her letters) is a hint of uncertainty, a finding with which Michelle fully agreed. Her response was: 'I sometimes wonder what people really think of me as a transsexual and what they might be saying behind my back. The uncertainty is not and never has been related to myself. As I have already mentioned, I have known from the time I was a very small child that all I ever wanted to be was a girl.'

A consultant psychiatrist

Let us now look at another script.

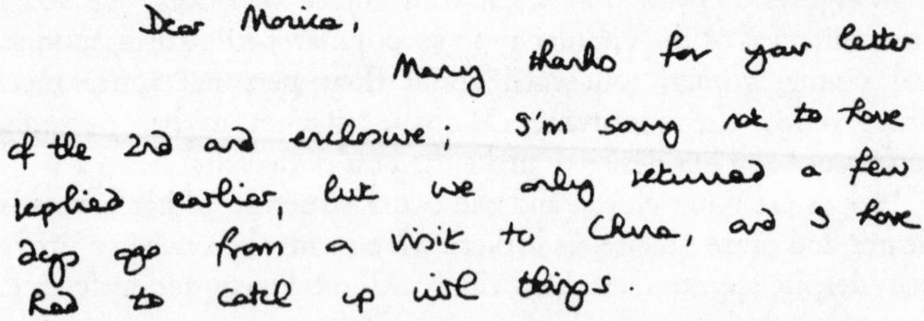

Figure 195 (65%)

Figure 195 is a very balanced, rhythmical and intellectual hand. It is also very literary. Its legibility shows the importance the writer attaches to lucidity of thought and speech, while its small size indicates an ability to assess and analyse.

Delta *d*s denote culture, *g*s written like the figure eight emphasize a literary bent, and bowed t-strokes show an ability to curb basic desires.

The tailing-off of the final letters in many of the words indicates diplomacy. These letters do occasionally extend beyond the norm, showing tenacity, but on the whole it is a round, warmhearted, generous and kind hand, with not an aggressive streak in sight.

Moving beyond the generalities, we can get a good clue to the writer's personality, from the structure of the lower-case *g*s. Note the curious way he wraps these letters around themselves until they are almost foetal-shaped. In chapter 5, it was shown how writers sometimes construct their PPI thus, but this is the only script in which I have ever found a foetal-shaped lower-case g. To complicate the issue further, the movement of the g alters so that sometimes it is written in a clockwise direction, sometimes anticlockwise. This seems to suggest a connection with gender and gender identification, however tenuous.

In fact, the script is from a leading consultant psychiatrist, a man who had treated many patients with gender problems, although I did not know about his speciality when I was analysing his hand. He has considerable knowledge of the subject, so much so that it figures prominently in his mind and by association in his writing.

How very significant that the clockwise/anticlockwise movements only happen in the g 'gender' and nowhere else. And whichever way they turn they are foetal-shaped, making one wonder if in the deep recesses of the psychiatrist's mind is the belief that his patients' problems are related to very early trauma – possibly experienced in infancy or early childhood.

There is another interesting pointer. His personal pronouns could be mistaken for capital Gs, an important corroborative sign. The emphasis on g (for whatever reason) is a dominant factor in the doctor's hand.

17   A Thalidomide Survivor

The drug Thalidomide had an earth-shattering effect on a great many families in the late 1950s and early 1960s. This supposedly safe sleeping pill which was prescribed to cure morning sickness was responsible for 10,000 birth deformities in Western Germany alone.[1]

Exposure of a foetus to the drug had devastating effects. Its widespread use was responsible for more than 8,000 surviving children with severe birth deformities.[2] The story went down in history as one of the worst medical tragedies of all time.

Phocomelia was the medical term used to describe the most severely malformed infants. The word is derived from the Latin *phoca*, meaning seal, because children in that category had been born without arms or legs and the hands and feet of some resembled flippers.

Thalidomide had been issued without any control or warnings about its side-effects. In Britain, an estimated 450 mothers were prescribed the drug in early pregnancy. The effect on their unborn babies was catastrophic; they gave birth to infants with missing limbs or with sight or hearing difficulties.

In my capacity as a medical writer, I followed the progress of the twenty-two Thalidomide children born on Merseyside from their early schooldays to adulthood. With the blessing of their head teachers and college principals, I sat in on classes with most of these young people for a month at their school and then for a week at the college of commerce most went on to attend. The children and their parents welcomed me to their homes and introduced me to their families, friends, teachers, educational psychologists and paediatricians.

Integrated education proved very successful for this group

although it has to be said that many would not have been able to be there unless they had first attended schools for children with special needs. These schools played an important role in that their teachers were able to advise others on the practicalities and individual needs of the physically disabled. And the children turned out to be remarkably well adjusted.

Kevin Donnellon was one of that group, born without limbs or hips and with severe internal damage. By a cruel and ironic twist of fate his date of birth was 28 November 1961, the very day the manufacturers withdrew the drug because of its dangerous side-effects.

Much credit is due to his mother Agnes, his late father John and his five brothers and sisters for the fact that Kevin grew up to be such a well-balanced man, whose main aim in life is to fight for the rights of the disabled. Having worked for some time in public relations[3] he is well equipped to handle the media and any thorny issue which might arise in relation to the interests of the disabled.

He has always coped well with his disabilities. Although he was singled out by press, radio and TV reporters for most of his life and forced on the attention of the public from a very early age, he has never shown any indication of psychological problems. Nor have I ever found any such signs in his writing.

This writing makes a fascinating study and I am indebted to him for his co-operation in what has turned out to be a rather intensive exercise. Reproduced in the following pages are samples of his writing from the ages of twelve to thirty-seven, from which we shall be able to follow the development of his mind, see his changing views and interests and detect those personality strengths which have turned him into the bright, lively and gregarious man he is today.

However, I feel it is important to point out that his writing hand (his right) has only two fingers (index and middle) and a thumb. The act of writing, therefore, involves holding the pen between those two fingers in a way that the rest of us might find extremely difficult.

Aged twelve

Figures 196 and 197 are taken from mathematics and French exercise books dating back to 1974, when he was twelve.

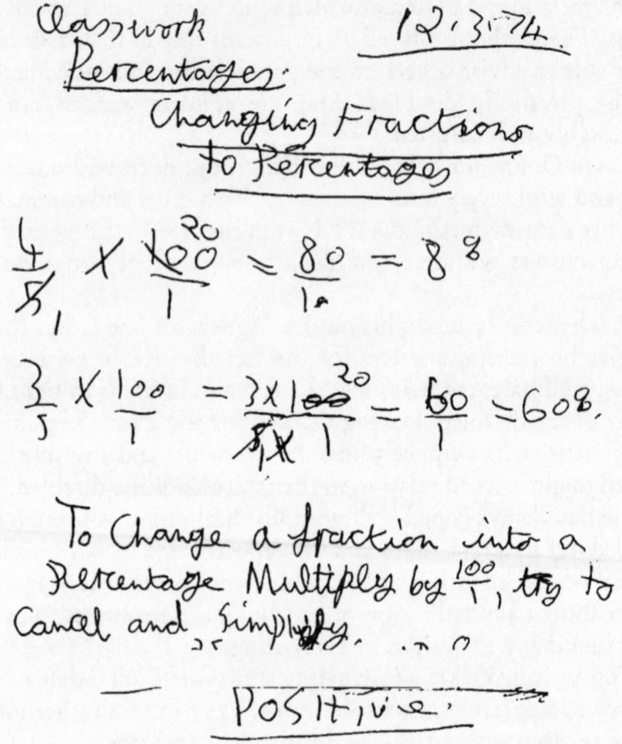

Classwork   12.3.74.

Percentages:
        Changing Fractions
            to Percentages

$$\frac{4}{\cancel{5}_1} \times \frac{\overset{20}{\cancel{100}}}{1} = \frac{80}{1\diamond} = 8\%$$

$$\frac{3}{5} \times \frac{100}{1} = \frac{3 \times \overset{20}{\cancel{100}}}{\cancel{5} \times 1} = \frac{60}{1} = 60\%.$$

To change a fraction into a
Percentage Multiply by $\frac{100}{1}$, try to
Cancel and, simplify.

POSITIVE.

Je suis fatigué
Je vais au cinéma
    il fait beau
J'ai un vélo

So it can be seen
cases. the Ne come
the verb, and pas

Figure 196 (65%)

204

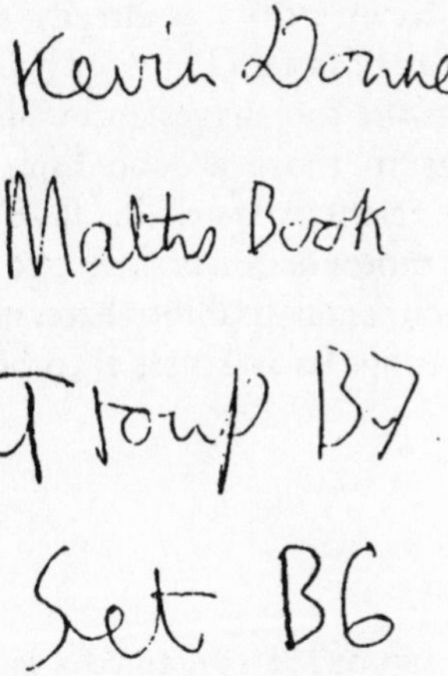

Kevin Donnellan

Maths Book

Group B7

Set B6

Figure 197

Overlooking the various corrections, crossings out and general untidiness which is typical of the work of many schoolchildren, disabled or not, the first unusual sign is that the lower loops hardly venture into the lower zone. Note the gs in the words 'percentages' and 'fatigué'. Nor is it only the g. Other letters also fail to descend in the conventional manner, such as the ys in 'multiply', 'by' and 'try'.

In an adult hand, this phenomenon can have both physiological and psychological implications. But in the hand of a child there is normally only one interpretation, particularly if the script is otherwise balanced and rhythmical as is Kevin's. It is that the writer is physically disabled.

Corroborative signs include a weakness of pressure and stiffness of style throughout the script and the occasional appearance of curves where there should be straight lines – for example, in the downstrokes of the capitals such as the D in 'Donnellon', the P in 'percentage' and the F in 'fraction' and the T in 'to'. Yet, despite all this, it is a stylish hand.

Kevin's sense of humour already shows in the 'smile-shaped' top to the capital T and the i-dot on the word 'simplify'. Another positive sign is the manner in which the capital G has been structured. Great care and attention have been given to this letter, showing the writer's desire to complete his practical tasks as well as the next person.

At the age of twelve, Kevin's drive is already strong. The little loop at the bottom left of the capital *D* hints at his stubborn persistence, the inward curve at the top suggests unwillingness to reveal too much of his feelings to those around him. Otherwise, the printed capitals show his aesthetic tastes, his love of literature, art and music. On the whole, motor action is slow, but the problems are purely physical; there is no mental disability here, nothing disturbed or distorted about the writing. Its jerkiness is to be expected in the circumstances.

Aged fourteen

The envelope featured in figure 198 contained a letter Kevin wrote to me when he was fourteen years old. The signature in figure 199 comes from that letter.

Figure 198 (65%)

First, the envelope. At this stage, his writing is very stiff and heavy, although its strong pressure also reflects his developing confidence and self-assurance. Its very angular structure suggests persistence and an aggressive will to succeed.

Kevin is already showing himself to have a tougher nature than many of his friends and relatives might have suspected. These words

206

have been written slowly and with very great effort. The angles change slightly, but the form-level is generally good.

It has its own jagged sort of rhythm, reflecting Kevin's bumpy ride through life. But the pressure is regular. Considering his disability, the writing is remarkably well co-ordinated and has been created with a determined effort, although the style was one he soon abandoned. Having been taught to write in that style of semi-print, he was now finding it too forced and unnatural for his taste.

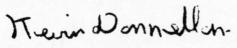

Figure 199

His signature at this age is more relaxed than the writing seen on the envelope. It is very similar to that in figure 197, which was written two years earlier, but magnification shows rather more changes of pen pressure here than in the earlier signature. Some strain and fatigue are indicated, and on reflection Kevin recalled that school-work was probably responsible for his state of mind. A bright academic student, he was determined to give of his best, whatever the difficulties, but sometimes, the practical challenges were very great. Because of his disabilities, Kevin needed to exert more effort than most of his classmates, as a result of which tiredness and mental exhaustion were factors with which he frequently had to cope.

Despite its easier style, the writing of the signature is less regular than that on the envelope. Note the weakening of intensity and the sudden lurches when writing the double *l*, suggesting an occasional loss of muscle control, which I would attribute to physical strain. The compressed loops are further evidence of this. Nevertheless, it is obvious that he is not one to give in. Persistence has always been a dominant factor in his hand.

Aged twenty-three

In the next signature, written nine years later when he was twenty-three (figure 200), we still have evidence of strain and fatigue, still the weakening of intensity on the double *l*s and their continued compression.

An examination of the downstrokes of both the *K* and the *D* shows that they are bent forward even, as Kevin himself must have bent forward to write them. The *K* is knotted, showing that he is capable and thorough, a stickler for detail. The writing is more connected here than in the earlier sample. The *D* is more closed, the letter endings more discreet. He might not be as talkative as he used to be, but he is much more perceptive, as proved by the now angular i-dot.

In adulthood, the signature is larger, stronger, more confident, and expressive. It has also matured considerably.

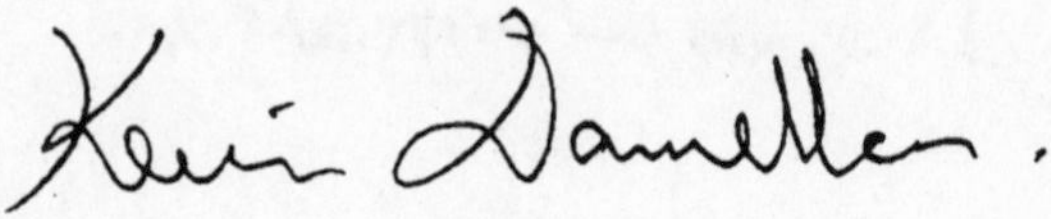

Figure 200

Aged thirty-seven

Kevin has featured in many TV programmes over the years, and in late 1998 he appeared in a networked documentary,[4] denouncing the drug which damaged him and so many others so severely. The reason for his appearance was that the medical profession had suddenly begun to see Thalidomide in a positive light again. 'I'm living proof of what that drug can do,' he said.

In the spring of 1999, I invited Kevin to produce an updated sample of his writing. With ten O Levels, four A Levels and a degree in hypnotherapy to his credit he had, since our last meeting, gone on to study art, had exhibited a selection of his animations at the Tate Gallery in Liverpool and was now halfway through a university course in Applied Social Sciences. He was also busy preparing for a student-exchange visit to Massachusetts.

During the previous decade or so Kevin had gone through a period of what he described as an attempt to find himself, which involved immersing himself in a variety of revolutionary politics and obscure religious practices. The political activities had resulted in his being arrested on a couple of occasions because of his participation in some very public demonstrations, while his religion had taken him to a world Congress of the Baha'i in Manhattan.

He objects to the emotive terms 'victim' and 'sufferer', describing himself as a Thalidomide survivor. As such he lives life to the full and one tends to overlook his disability in favour of his dynamic personality and offbeat sense of humour. Having gone through what he described as a period of denial of his disability when he refused to face up to it, he is now totally committed to an organization called Disabled People's Direct Action Network (DAN) and has only recently stood down as elected organizer in order to concentrate on his university studies.

A real force to be reckoned with, he is also seriously considering standing for the local council. That way, he believes, he can fight for the rights not just of the disabled, but also of other minority groups. He feels strongly on the issue of raising such people's self-esteem and making them feel more like the rest of the population.

'Thalidomide is my impairment,' he pointed out. 'What disables me, and others like me, is society's attitudes and prejudices.' DAN's aim is to arouse people's awareness, he added. Its motto is: 'Rights, not charity . . . Respect, not pity.'

I could not help wondering how much of Kevin's militancy and implied aggression might show up in his writing. On a more fundamental level, I wondered how his writing might have changed since earlier analyses. His latest sample is shown in figure 201.

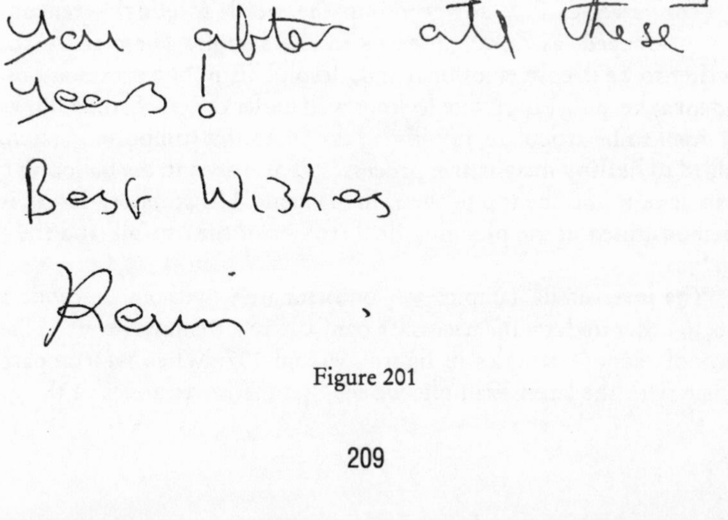
Dear Monica,

It was lovely meeting you after all these years!

Best Wishes

Kevin.

Figure 201

This writing is fast, its touch light, its message clear and positive. The speed of the script (despite the practical difficulties) indicates the speed of the writer's thoughts. The light touch reflects his sensitive nature and the whole impression is one of a healthy, robust person with an ability to survive, despite the odds.

Although the writing is fast, the speed has no detrimental effect on clarity and lucidity. The generous spacing between words shows discrimination and good taste, and the lack of cramping reflects an organized mind. Individual letter variations do manifest themselves, but in the case of this writer, I would attribute these to practical difficulties.

Kevin described himself as egocentric, yet there is no evidence of this in his script. Egocentric writers have huge, flashy signatures, totally at variance with their text. Kevin's signature and text are the same size, shape and structure, showing him to be honest, true to himself and sincere in his dealings with others.

In the absence of a personal pronoun, we are left with the lower-case *e*, the secondary ego-sign. Self-important writers often give themselves away with this letter. In Kevin's case, it has a perfectly normal structure, with no sinister connotations. This confirms what I felt about his signature.

An examination of individual letters shows that the capital *D* has hardly changed since he last penned it for me. A capital *D* shaped thus is the work of a writer whose strong feelings are linked to practical issues. The capital *M* has sharpened itself into what is now a printed version of the letter. Such a structure is invariably the work of an articulate writer who believes in the importance of making himself understood.

The lower-case *m* however – in the word 'meeting' – remains arcade-shaped, as do all three *n*s in the sample. These show the writer to be deeply emotional and, despite his public protestations, adept at keeping his private feelings well under cover. He thus shows himself to be articulate, intuitive, passionate and stubborn. Passion, allied to healthy imaginative processes, is also seen in the ballooning *l* in 'lovely' and the top of the *K* in his name. His stubborn streak is demonstrated in the plunging final strokes of the *l* in 'all' and the *e* in 'years'.

The intervening samples are, unfortunately, without descenders so, in order to draw the necessary comparisons we must revert to the school exercise samples in figure 196 and 197. When we compare them with the latest example, we see that the lower zones of the *gs* and *ys* have become more angular, showing self-assertion to be an important aspect of Kevin's personality. Such jarred understrokes are frequently (but not exclusively) seen in the scripts of writers who are physically disabled. They point to frustration and irritation.

This leaves the emphasis in Kevin's contemporary writing focused on upper and middle zones. The even balance of these two zones shows the writer's energies to be evenly channelled into thought and action. In other words, he places equal emphasis on intellectual pursuits and practical activities.

The jerkiness of Kevin's writing should not be confused with shakiness (tremor). It appears spasmodically and in Kevin's case is due to the way he holds his pen and the fact that he wrote this note on a rather wobbly table. Tremor is an entirely different phenomenon and if it is present, it is seen throughout a writer's script.

Under strong magnification, some slight pressure changes can be seen at the base of the letters in figure 201, indicating a weakness or physiological problem in that region. This, explained Kevin, would be due to the presence of kidney stones, which were not currently bothering him but had caused considerable pain in the not-too-distant past.

Notes

1 Porter, Dr Mark, in *Radio Times*, 24–30 October 1998.
2 Figures quoted are from *Horizon*, a BBC TV documentary screened on 29 October 1998.
3 Kevin Donnellon was employed as Information Officer for the Disabled for Sefton Social Services on Merseyside from 1980 to 1990.
4 *Horizon* showed how Thalidomide could once again find favour with the medical community in the treatment of AIDS and other conditions relating to immunological deficiency. More disturbingly, the programme also showed how, after being prescribed this terrible drug, a whole new generation of mothers in the Third World had given birth to babies with similarly deformed bodies to those of their predecessors.

18   Other Reasons for Changes in Writing

Trauma

Most people are familiar with the story of the sinking of the *Titanic* with the loss of more than 1,500 lives. One of the people concerned in that tragedy was Captain Stanley Lord of the SS *Californian*, who had been the subject of much controversy. Some people believe that he was guilty of neglecting his duties on that momentous night, others that he was totally innocent of any crime and that he was made a scapegoat to cover the misdeeds of others.

His opponents claim that the SS *Californian* was within sight of *Titanic* but that her captain did nothing to help the sinking liner. They further claim that had Captain Lord acted responsibly the number of casualties would have been considerably reduced. His supporters maintain that the ship seen by *Titanic* was not *Californian*, which was miles away and that Captain Lord was utterly blameless. They reject the accusations out of hand.

Stanley Lord himself insisted over and over again that his ship was never close enough to the stricken vessel to render assistance to her passengers before the sinking. He was nevertheless charged in 1912 with being responsible for the massive loss of life. He was never given a chance to defend himself against the accusations and went to his grave protesting his innocence. A later inquiry partially cleared him, but Leslie Harrison, Captain Lord's biographer, described the original findings as 'the grossest miscarriage of justice in the history of British inquiries'.

Knowing my interest in the case, Mr Harrison presented me with two samples of Captain Lord's handwriting. One was written in 1912, shortly after the sinking, when he was thirty-five years old; the other, in 1957, when he had just turned eighty. With the permission of the late Mr Harrison, they are reproduced in figures 202 and 203.

When I first studied them, I focused on forensic aspects and when the results were published the findings attracted considerable media attention because I was able to state categorically that there was no evidence whatever of criminal tendencies in that hand.

Now I intend to concentrate on the health aspects of Stanley Lord's writing.

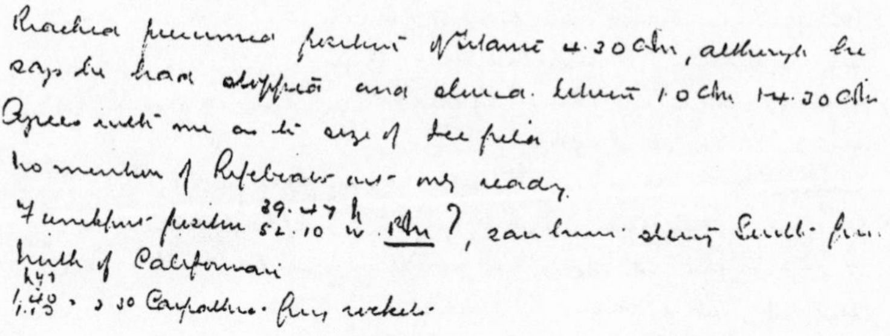

Figure 202 (50%)

The overall impression is that both samples are smooth, flowing and somewhat narrow. Some repression and inhibitions are suggested, which is perfectly natural for a man of his time and upbringing. The fast, high form-level of the 1912 sample (figure 202) denotes the writer's intelligence and ability, and its rhythmic balance tells us that he is unlikely to crack under pressure.

In confirmation of this we have a remarkably level baseline. The upright stand and widely spaced words and lines are the work of a man who stands tall and believes in keeping himself to himself.

Tall, thin and upright, the writing speaks of a natural reserve and an unwillingness to give in to his feelings. In other words, it is tense but controlled. It does, however show considerable evidence of pressure weakness and the type of fragmentation one associates with sudden shock or trauma. None of this is surprising in view of what the writer was experiencing at the time he produced this sample.

But of course his health had suffered as a result of what he had been through, and the clue lies in the way he has written the name of his ship, *Californian*. If we compare its size with that of the words *Carpathia* immediately below it and *Titanic* on line one, we find that the capital *C* in '*Californian*' is noticeably larger than that of '*Carpathia*' and considerably larger than the *T* in '*Titanic*'.

This provides a hint of how proud the captain was of his vessel

213

but how disappointed too that events should have turned out as they did. Note how it drops from the baseline until the end of the final *n* in as far down as the tip of the lower loop of the *f*.

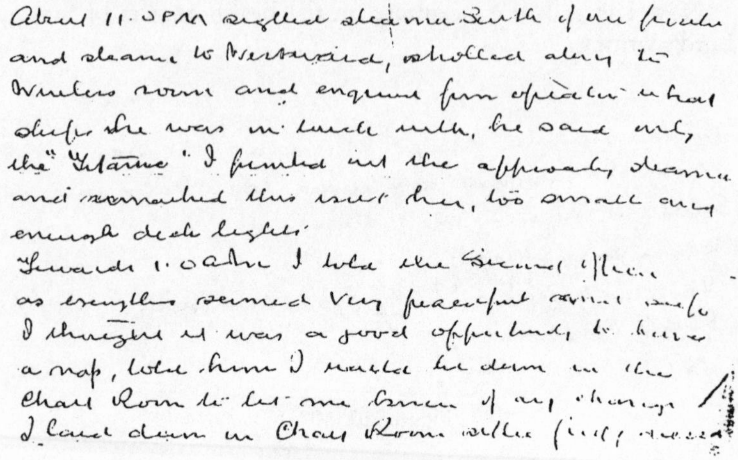

[handwritten facsimile]

Figure 203 (50%)

In the later sample (figure 203) various signs and symbols which are missing in the earlier sample begin to manifest themselves. Now we see that many of the letters have looped stems, showing how deeply he has been wounded by the slur on both his personal character and his professional judgement. All those years later the scars still stung but his ability to remain calm and not give in to pressure is still very much in evidence.

One strange sign, absent in the earlier sample, manifests itself in the second. It is a double looping at the top of the capital *T*, a dominant feature in this later sample, although absent in the earlier one. What do those double loops signify? In simple terms, they show that the writer stumbles when he begins to write the word '*Titanic*' and, for that matter, most other words commencing with capital *T*. This is a typical stumbling block and shows how very deeply Captain Lord was affected by the circumstances surrounding the disaster.

The 1957 sample contains many changes of pressure, indicating the increasing frailty of his body, although his mind is still very alert. He appears to be suffering from failing eyesight (the increasingly large letter structures) and to be a trifle hard of hearing; as I explained in chapter 5, ear-shaped personal pronouns indicate hearing loss.

214

I never knew Captain Lord personally, but I did meet his son, also named Stanley Lord, and got to know him quite well in the last few years of his life. He told me: 'My father always maintained that the light seen from the *Titanic* approaching and then receding into the distance could not have been from the *Californian* as she was stationary from approximately 10.00 p.m. until 6.00 a.m., when she set off on the two-and-a-half-hour journey through massive ice-fields, to where *Titanic* went down.'

On the graphological reading, he observed: 'In your analysis of father's handwriting, you suggest that it shows deep, psychological trauma, loss of self-esteem and depression. You must remember that he was over eighty years of age when that letter was written and with a cataract forming on one eye and a somewhat shaky hand, I feel he did very well. As for self-esteem, while he was always a very retiring and unflamboyant person he most certainly never lost his self-esteem.'

Mr Lord also explained that at the time his father wrote this second sample, his mother had been dead only a matter of months after a very long illness, during which his father had cared for her with great love and attention. Her death had left him utterly shattered. 'I attribute the depression you have detected to that and that alone,' he insisted.

Emotional shock

The next two samples were given to me by a 47-year-old engineer, married with a teenaged son and daughter. Some twelve months separate the writing of the two samples.

Figure 204 was written at a happy, carefree time of his life, figure 205 after the writer had suffered what he described as 'some heavy emotional shocks'. He wondered if there was any noticeable difference between them.

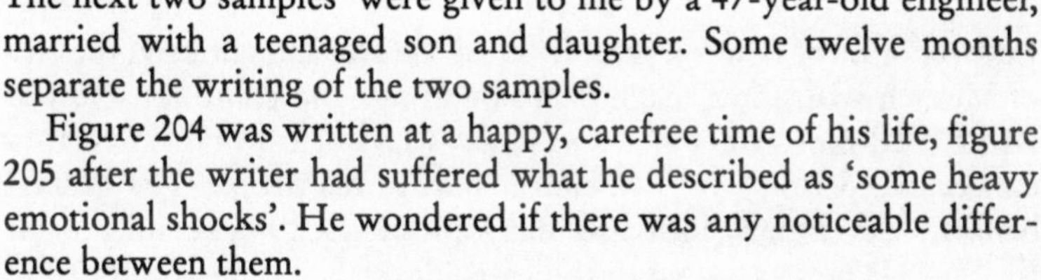
Input normalizers are used for checking or adjusting the input capacitance of oscilloscopes where high-impedance attenuator probes may be used. – In a sense they are dummy-probes.

Input capacitance should be adjusted for each setting of the input attenuator switch, so that you will not need to readjust an input probe each time the attenuator setting is changed.

Figure 204 (50%)

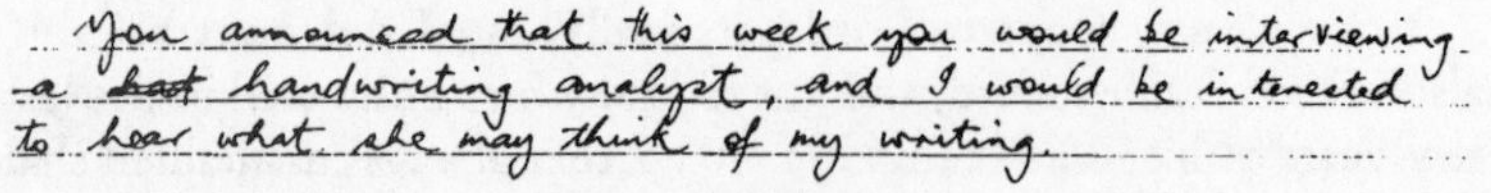

You announced that this week you would be interviewing a best handwriting analyst, and I would be interested to hear what she may think of my writing.

Figure 205 (50%)

The answer is yes, there are a few minor changes. The first and most obvious signs manifest in figure 205 (the 'unhappy' sample) are the neurotic overwriting in the word 'announced' and the scoring through of the three letters on line two. The earlier sample shows no such signs. The second factor to emerge is that the script in figure 205 is slightly larger than its predecessor. Pen pressure is less regular in the second sample and one of the letters, the *l* in 'would' (line two), shows a break in its loop.

Although the style is still rhythmic, balanced and of high form-level, letter sizes in the 'unhappy' sample are more variable than in the 'happy' one. Notice the middle zone section of the *g* in 'handwriting' (line two) and that of 'writing' (line three).

And finally, whereas the letters of figure 204 mostly end on an upward curve – note, particularly, the *es* – those of figure 205 either stay on the baseline or pull downward, as in 'be' (lines one and two). These little signs more than any other denote the writer's state of mind.

Madness

Ludwig of Bavaria was a great lover of the arts and enriched the city of Munich with some magnificent buildings and paintings. He was also a total eccentric and the vast sums lavished on his mistress (a dancer called Lola) did not endear him to his people. His general behaviour eventually raised so many questions about his judgement that in 1848 he was forced to abdicate. Nevertheless, he continued to support the arts and was a great patron of the composer Richard Wagner, for whom he built the magnificent Bayreuth Festival Theatre, which opened in 1876.

Sadly, Ludwig's rational moments decreased as his psychotic episodes increased and fears were voiced about his state of mind. Eventually, his mental health declined so dramatically that in 1886 he was declared insane. He drowned himself shortly afterwards.

The four signatures in figure 206 show his descent to madness.

The first sample of his signature is legible, albeit with a flamboyant underlining. Nothing unusual about that. Many kings and queens in history used such underscores. Elizabeth I's was probably the most flashy of all. The second sample is a poor representation and few people would recognize the name for what it was. The letters all show signs of disintegration. The underline is larger and more flam-

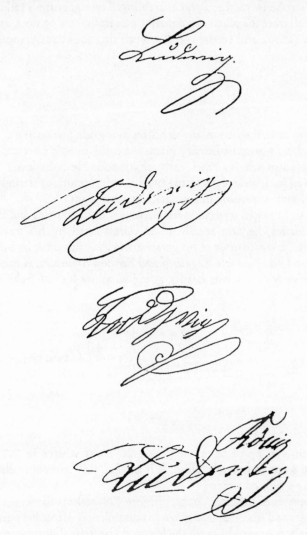

Figure 206

boyant, showing him to be much more fanciful (particularly in his sexual activities). In the third signature his thoughts are as fanciful and off-course as his sexual activities. But in terms of his actual name, his 'stamp of self' (middle-zone), he has, to quote a modern idiom 'lost it'. In the final sample, although we can just about decipher his name, we also see even without magnification that virtually every pen stroke is fractured and crumbling. The signature is falling apart. It is all over the place and contains pen trails, resting dots, and poignantly (above and to the right) a word that looks suspiciously like 'adieu'.

Blindness

John Milton is ranked by many scholars alongside Shakespeare as one of England's greatest literary giants – a brilliant epic poet and a Greek and Latin scholar from early childhood. He is believed to have suffered with weak eyes virtually all his life; historians attribute this to his habit of reading in the dark until midnight.

His eyesight began to deteriorate seriously in his thirties and by his early forties, he was totally blind. Undaunted by his visual impairment, he wrote most of his greatest works at this time, including *Paradise Lost, Paradise Regained* and *Samson Agonistes*. A mind as brilliant as Milton's was hardly going to allow loss of sight to handicap him.

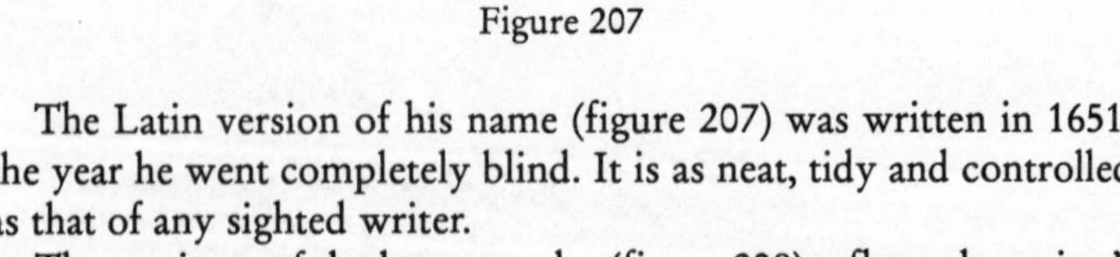

Figure 207

The Latin version of his name (figure 207) was written in 1651, the year he went completely blind. It is as neat, tidy and controlled as that of any sighted writer.

The pastiness of the later samples (figure 208) reflects the writer's sensuousness and his refusal to allow his disability to affect his writing. Strangely enough, although the letters do become slightly larger with time, his writing never loses its style.

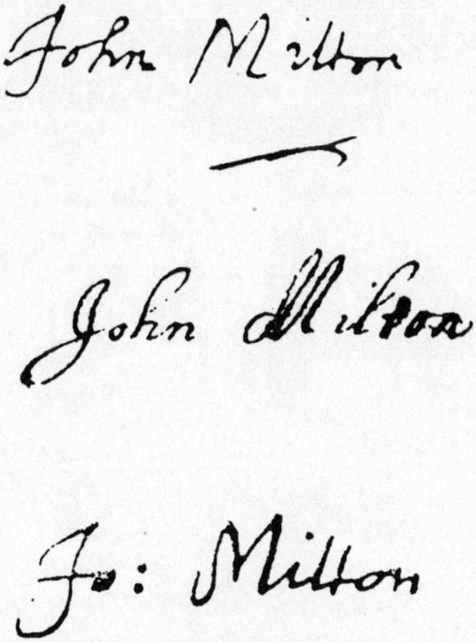

Figure 208

Part IV
Pictorial Images

19   Doodles

A key can lock or unlock a door. A wall can shut someone into or out of an enclosure. So it is with writing or drawing. Tell-tale indications that a writer has locked away his thoughts include very narrowed upper loops and taut personal pronouns. Spontaneous drawings, on the other hand, can provide valuable keys to *unconscious* mental activity.

When writing, we commit our conscious thoughts to paper. When doodling, however, our conscious thoughts are usually elsewhere; we may be chatting on the telephone, working out how much we can afford to spend at the January sales or wondering what to give the dog for his tea. A doodle is more than an abstract drawing, it is an ambiguous one, because it has many possible meanings. The doodler might say his scribbles represent a mouse or a duck, but the analyst might see them altogether differently because each person's interpretation is subjective. We each base our interpretation on what we see, then we form our own opinion about its appearance. But the important point to remember is that when studying doodles we are not doing so with a view to awarding prizes for art and design, but trying to determine the mental functioning behind them.

Sacré Coeur

How, for example, does one describe the drawing in figure 209?

Figure 209

This style of swirly penmanship is called *Sacré Coeur* (Sacred Heart) because it is believed to have been introduced in nineteenth-century French convent boarding schools by nuns of the Sacred Heart order, who encouraged it as a writing exercise. The object was to break in their pupils' new pens and enable hand movement to flow in order to acquire a steady style.

Today's interpretation of that swirly style is that individuals who make such pen sketches are aware but frightened of their own sexuality. A repetitive doodle invariably points to an obsessive personality. This one is very interesting because of its many possible interpretations. Some people see it simply as a succession of repeating patterns or overlapping loops. Others describe it as a series of *ss*, and I have also heard it referred to as a rhythmical form with musical and mathematical implications.

My own interpretation is that it is an outward sign of inner conflict. As well as being obsessive, people whose drawings spontaneously take on this shape tend towards compulsiveness. They are also usually inhibited. If the loops contain little dots or are blacked-out as in figures 210 and 211, the interpretation is the same as it would be with similar blacking-out in the script.

Those who doodle thus are likely to repeat themselves, be bored at home and at work and nag their partners. They are on a treadmill and do not know how to get off it. Frustration is the key factor here. These random images provide real clues to the personality traits which motivated them.

Figure 210

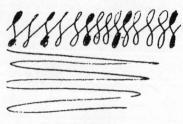

Figure 211

General signs

Drawings which face left, or are placed to the left of the page can (like such writings) be taken to represent past traditions, mother and childhood. Those facing right represent the future and whatever it might hold. An upward-moving drawing symbolizes thought processes rising to an imaginative, intellectual or even spiritual level. A downward movement would represent the doodler's thoughts moving towards the material or sensuous.

Conflict in the drawing indicates conflict in the mind of the artist who sketched it. Cartoon-type sketches indicate a fertile imagination and an off-beat sense of humour. Soft, rounded curves denote warmth, kindness and friendliness, but sharp, pointed sketches hint at aggression, tension and resentment.

A drawing consisting mainly of strong, bold lines suggests strength and energy whereas weak, quivery lines point to the reverse.

Robert

The drawing in figure 212 contains 'locked away' thoughts. It emerged spontaneously from the pen of a newspaper journalist almost every time he spoke on the telephone (in other words, when his conscious mind was otherwise engaged).

Figure 212

Robert (not his real name) worked on a national weekly as its northern editor. He had progressed as far as he could on that newspaper. Being in his mid-forties, he believed the only alternatives were to relocate to the paper's head office in London or apply for a post on another publication nearer his home, neither of which appealed. With a hefty mortgage and constantly rising school fees for his two children, Robert did not relish the idea of domestic disruption any more than he wanted to take what he believed would inevitably be a drop in salary if he took a less senior post on another paper in the locality. And without realizing it, he was making his professional impotence and frustrations abundantly clear through his drawings.

If we accept that the rectangles represent his newspaper and the blobs himself, then his thought processes begin to emerge. We can see Robert's highly placed position in his present office – right up near the ceiling, as it were. The fact that he has placed himself inside a series of rectangles rather than circles or ovals denotes his inner conflict. It will be recalled that curves, arcs and circles indicate soft, warm emotions, whereas sharp lines and angles represent aggression. Robert's desire for change, coupled with apprehension about his future career prospects, was causing him considerable stress. Unhappy in his current post but in early middle age unsure of his future in the cut-throat world of newspaper journalism, he simply did not know which way to turn.

In the event, Robert's problem resolved itself when the proprietors of his newspaper unexpectedly closed down their northern office. No sooner had news of his imminent redundancy broken than the director of a rapidly expanding public relations company offered him a post with a much higher salary, more prestige and ample opportunities for promotion. Not only that, because he would now be working from home, Robert would be able to spend more time with his family, stop worrying about his children's school fees and pay off his mortgage.

A subsequent check revealed that not only had he stopped scribbling rectangles with blobs, he had stopped doodling altogether, showing how much more professionally fulfilled he felt in public relations than in journalism. His tensions, like his doodle pad, had been left behind on the newsdesk.

James

Figures 213 and 214 are the doodles of another journalist, this time a senior editor on a busy evening paper, a man on the fast track and enjoying every minute of it. I shall call him James, but again that is not his real name.

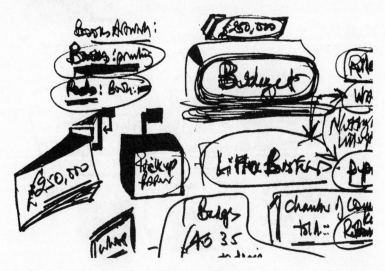

Figure 213 (50%)

Aggressive, dynamic and bursting with nervous energy, James sketched the heavy doodle in figure 213 during a telephone conversation with someone to whom he felt obliged to listen, but he was being driven to distraction by what he considered to be a time-wasting effort – hence the frustrated over-writing. He wanted to get on with his job, and did so the minute his caller replaced the receiver.

This doodler is the type who works best when his back is against a wall. He needs the adrenalin provided by the pressures of daily newspaper journalism. Headlines and deadlines are what keep him going. He loves the buzz of it all and thrives on stress.

James's second doodle (figure 214) was produced while briefing one of his reporters about the day's assignments.

James's desk is always covered with, and his waste paper basket always full of, doodle-covered scraps of paper. He admits to being a constant scribbler and handed me several of his sketches for analysis. All showed the same heavy pen strokes, the same dynamism and assertiveness. Yet each of those drawings also demonstrated that just beneath the hard professional shell was a warm-hearted nature, as

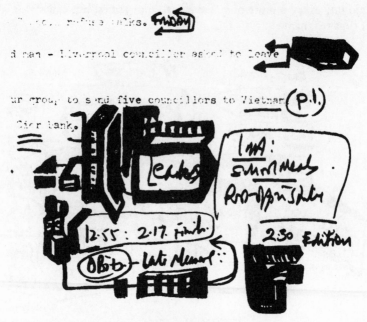

Figure 214 (65%)

indicated by the curvy lines surrounding many of his heavy black outbursts.

In the office, James has a reputation for 'chewing up reporters for breakfast'. At home with his wife and family, he is known as a 'big softie'. Work is left firmly behind so that he can participate in and fully enjoy the comfortable home life that work provides. Caring for his family is the whole purpose of James's life.

While James and Robert are both highly successful (each in his own way) and shine in their respective disciplines, the methods of getting their story are entirely different. In their days as investigative reporters, James's form of interviewing was always aggressive, whereas Robert's was softer, easier on the interviewee and was once colourfully described by a colleague as 'verbal seduction'. The difference in pen pressure between their sketches tells its own story.

A doodle done with the foot

Paul Driver, whose writing was analysed in chapter 12, writes and draws with his foot, since polio paralysed his arms. The two doodles he produced for me are highly unusual. One shows what looks like cloud formations and below it a row of rooftops. Because they were so obviously sketched together, I am featuring them together (figure 215).

Figure 215 (50%)

Given that the mind controls the actual movements as we write it is in its deepest recesses that the unconscious can express itself while the conscious is busy getting on with other matters. By means of these very revealing drawings, the voice of the unconscious tells us much more about ourselves than anyone would ever suspect.

If you turn the picture sideways, the clouds begin to take on another form: that of a tree. With the drawing once more in its upright position we see that the tree has been felled: struck down when it was coming along so nicely. What a remarkable communicator the unconscious mind can be.

The rooftops could be said to represent the peak Mr Driver has reached in his chosen profession. Curly signs are offset by sharp lines and squiggles indicating that while the pinnacles are there, all are firmly placed on horizontal lines. My own conclusion is that he is attempting to show that his feet are firmly placed on the ground and that his head is most definitely not in the clouds. This man is a realist, whose philosophy is to focus attention on what he can do, rather than on what he cannot. Like the writing, the drawing is strong, dominant and positive.

Something else is indicated in this doodle. The squiggles have actually formed themselves into a word (albeit disjointed) 'smile' – reflecting a rather delightful sense of humour. The felled tree is still animated. It is alive and functioning, despite its prone position.

When I included this drawing in a slide-illustrated lecture at a Cheshire arts centre, one member of the audience remarked that the sketch reminded him of the kind of drawing which at first appears to depict one image, then suddenly changes to another.

'If that sketch were mine,' he observed, 'I would frame it and keep it in a room where I could see it constantly because it is the sort of picture which has added attractions at every viewing.'

Thus, spontaneous drawings can echo the writer's attitude to the past, present and future as well as to himself and others. Conflict in the drawing indicates conflict in the mind of the artist who sketched it. Cartoon-type drawings indicate a fertile imagination and off-beat sense of humour. Sharp, pointed sketches hint at aggression, tension and possibly resentment.

A transvestite

The doodles in figure 216 were sketched by a 47-year-old married man. An engineer by profession, he is a transvestite.

It is interesting that he felt the need to do three separate sketches. The square shapes of the first feature the sharp angles and lines of his masculine persona. By switching briefly to the soft, feminine curves of the little flowers, he can enjoy a brief period of relaxation, but not for long. The sharp lines and angles are still there, making the pointed leaves plunge downwards in a symbolic suggestion that as a 'woman' he is going nowhere, hence the darkened arrow pointing to the final drawing.

This one is the sharpest, most aggressive, ambitious sketch of the

Figure 216 (65%)

three. The upward pointing spikes are very definite signs of ambition. The whole structure is the artist's attempt to make a statement about his career prospects. There is no place for soft, warm emotions in his line of work. He knows that he must revert to his male self if he is to achieve his professional ambitions. The heavy shading within this is a clear indicator of his secret thoughts and his wish for them to remain so.

A mother

The doodler who produced figure 217 is also very intelligent, but her anxiety level is high.

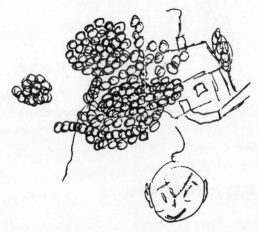

Figure 217

231

Housework is the cause of her depression, as indicated by the dark cloud threatening to overwhelm her home. She has taken the precaution of removing her funny little baby to safety, well away from the path of the menacing cloud.

This doodler's trouble is that her reserved and inhibited nature makes her apprehensive about giving in to the strong emotions associated with motherhood. It is significant that the chimney's smoke and the baby's curl are both shaped like question marks. The implication is that the doodler is not yet sure of her skills as a new mother and homemaker.

The love she feels for her baby is not in question. His placement at the front of her drawing shows his dominance in her mind.

A compulsive doodler

The *Sacré Coeur* doodle and swirling circle in figure 218 add up to compulsiveness bordering on neurosis.

Figure 218

To prove the point, we have two further indicators: the overwriting on the word 'doodles' and the S in 'always', which could almost be part of the repetitive doodle below it.

Signs of happiness, content and activity

By way of contrast, figure 219 shows happiness and contentment.

232

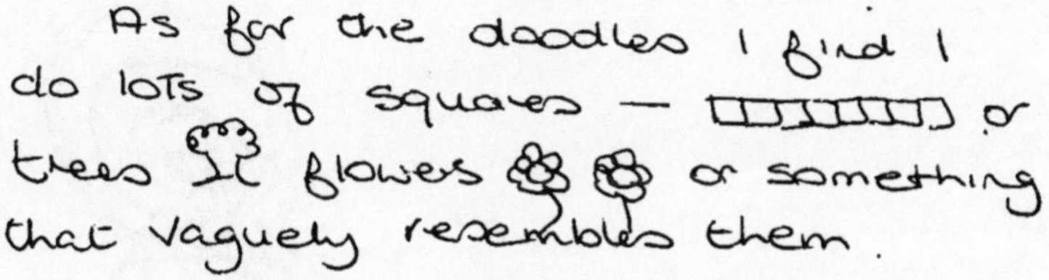

As for the doodles I find I do lots of squares — ⬜⬜⬜ or trees 🌳 flowers 🌸 🌼 or something that vaguely resembles them.

Figure 219

The artist has many interests and hobbies. She takes pride in her appearance, is friendly, flirty and gregarious. She is keenly interested in the welfare of others and will always be willing to help anyone in trouble.

There's not a single negative sign here. The soft round curves indicate warmth, sharp angles equal aggression. There are more rounded curves than sharp angles here, but the fact that both appear tell us that her personality is balanced. The little squares simply indicate that she is always on the go, bustling about with her daily chores.

A friend of mine tells me that the only doodle she ever does is to write the word 'and' over and over. Knowing her, this does not surprise me. She is a very energetic person, always on the go. A wife, mother and grandmother, she is constantly helping members of her extended family.

She also assists her busy executive husband with his accounts, is on the committees of various charities and heavily involved in their fund-raising activities. Small wonder that the word 'and' figures so prominently in her mind.

Signs of tension

Despite the curvaceous swing of the hand-shaped symbol in figure 220 (see overleaf), this whole doodle has a raw starkness to it. The black shading and overwriting introduce a note of tension. The curious hand-shaped illustration pointing forward in an attempt to penetrate the swirly obsessional sign suggests that the doodler would like to explore new fields and consolidate his thoughts. He is, unfortunately, being held back by his own inhibitions.

Figure 220

Disturbing doodles

And finally, a word about the habit some people have of simply writing out a single word and overwriting a letter or letters within that word, or in some cases overwriting the entire word.

These doodlers do not resort to any type of scribble, artistic or otherwise. They just continue to write out an individual word, sometimes repeating that word over and over.

Figure 221 shows such a doodle, and this is a very negative sign; any script accompanying it would also show a host of negative signs. Anxiety and depression are the key factors.

Figure 221

So even without seeing a sample of the doodler's writing, his spontaneous drawings can tell the analyst much about his attitude to the past, present and future as well as to himself and others. Combined with a sample of writing, these random sketches can provide an even more valuable insight into the workings of the unconscious.

20 Tree Drawings

When asked to do an in-depth character analysis by means of graphology, it helps if the script is accompanied by a spontaneous drawing of a tree. I also frequently find myself analysing trees which have been submitted without any script or signature. When I say spontaneous drawings, I mean precisely that. I am not interested in a carefully drawn effort which has taken some time to produce and is possibly the artist's third or fourth attempt in pursuit of perfection.

The drawing in figure 222 was delivered to the BBC television studios in Manchester one Sunday afternoon as I was preparing to be interviewed about graphology. A beautifully drawn tree, it was sketched by an elderly man and shows remarkable artistic talent. But it is precisely the type of drawing I do *not* want for analysis, because it is not spontaneous.

Figure 222

Like writing, tree drawings must have been created without any conscious interference. Only then will the unconscious mental activity filter through, enabling the value of these drawings to be estimated.

Spontaneously drawn trees are generally more reliable than pages and pages of script because, as with doodles, the artist has no idea what the graphologist is looking for. Occasionally the graphologist has no idea either, which adds to the excitement when something significant or dramatic is encountered.

What to look for

In tree drawings as in doodles and indeed writing itself, the graphological study relies heavily on symbolism. The way the artist sketches his tree can give vital clues about his adaptability to the world around him.

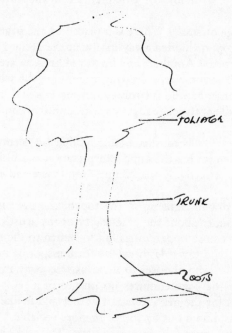

Figure 223

A quickly sketched tree will have three basic areas – roots, trunk and foliage, as shown in figure 223. If roots can be taken to represent home background (family roots), then certain assumptions can be made from their presence, their absence or their scoring through. The trunk represents the artist's growing-up period, and foliage his present circumstances.

An alternative interpretation is to think of the tree trunk as equivalent to the middle zone in a sample of writing, with the foliage and roots representing the upper and lower zones respectively. Looked at in this way, the trunk would then symbolize the rational part of the individual who drew it. The foliage (depending on how far up it soared) would represent the intellect and imagination, while the roots would provide clues about sexuality.

As with writing, it is important first of all to make an overall assessment of the drawing. Is it immediately recognizable as a tree? Is it round and curvy or made up entirely of geometric shapes? Maybe it is a totally abstract creation, completely unrecognizable for what it is. Or perhaps it is a flamboyant effort, big and showy with lots of ornamentation and little 'extras', like figure 224.

Is it large or small? Where is it placed on the page: in the middle, up at the top, or hidden away in one of the corners? How firm are the pen strokes? Are there any fractured lines, or areas of darkness?

As with script, a tree drawing occupying the whole page is the work of someone who is strongly self-motivated. One placed firmly in the middle of the page suggests self-confidence and a love of being centre-stage.

A centrally placed sketch surrounded by plenty of space and without blemish has the same interpretation as a well-formed script that is also attractively spaced out. Good taste and culture are indicated.

A tree drawn right up at the top of the page might make the analyst wonder about the practicality of the artist's thoughts. Like the writer whose upper zones fail to return to the middle, such an artist may tend towards absent-mindedness, or be rather dreamy.

The artist who chooses to tuck his tree away in a corner at the bottom of the page conjures up images of a reluctant party-goer who heads for the nearest vacant corner and is likely to stay there unless he is drawn out by someone more sociable.

An island around the tree, as in figure 224, is like an island around the signature: it equals isolation. An island around a signature, a tree drawing, a doodle, or anything else tells the analyst that the writer/artist wants to be left alone. Self-protection is the name of the game. It is the unconscious equivalent of putting a moat around one's property.

Figure 224

Crossed branches, as in figure 225, equate with a mixed slant in the script. They hint at confusion or moodiness.

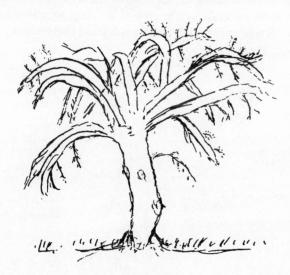

Figure 225

Dark patches along the tree trunk generally indicate trauma. Figure 226 is a typical example.

Figure 226 (50%)

A trunk free of dark areas need not necessarily reflect a happy childhood; it may simply be that none of the events in that period has left an indelible mark on the mind of the artist. I discovered this to my cost when studying the tree of a young woman who has a highly successful career in the legal profession (figure 227).

Figure 227

I drew the conclusion that hers had been a happy, carefree childhood, but she informed me that her father had beaten her regularly. She was not a battered child in the accepted sense of the term, but the daughter of a man who believed implicitly in the Victorian adage of sparing the rod and spoiling the child.

'I *was* a naughty little girl,' she confessed. 'I'm sure I deserved it.' The fact that she believed her thrashings were justified would account for the fact that they left no mental scars. Children do know whether they deserve punishment or not; it is *unearned* punishment that causes the scars.

So the word 'happy' when the trunk of the tree is free of blemish is inappropriate. 'Well-adjusted' is a more apt term.

Remembering that the trunk of the tree represents the artist's years of growing up, it is possible to estimate when any major events in his life might have taken place. First it is necessary to establish (at least roughly) the artist's age. The next step is to measure how high up the tree the blemish appears. For example, if the artist is thirty years old and the blemish appears about halfway up, then the problem could be said to have arisen when he was around fifteen years old. If it appears right at the beginning, then the artist would have been little more than a baby; up near the top would signify very recent trauma. Bumps, bends and any other strange signs in the trunk can be very significant.

A Holocaust survivor

The most unusual tree in figure 228 was sketched for me by a middle-aged woman of whose background I knew nothing.

Figure 228

I had just completed a technical interview with her husband for a feature in a hospital magazine and the subject of our conversation moved on from medical matters to graphology in general and tree analysis in particular.

The way this artist's trunk came to an abrupt halt at what I took to be early childhood suggested trauma very early on in her life. The sketching of a separate tree confirmed my suspicions. If this represented a true picture of her life then whatever it was that occurred in her childhood must have been quite dreadful.

When I asked if her life had taken a totally different path from its original one, I got a reaction I could hardly have anticipated. The unfortunate woman was rendered practically speechless. Her face drained of colour and she immediately left the room to sob her heart out in the privacy of her kitchen.

Completely unaware of what I had done, I apologized profusely for causing such distress, but her husband who was a doctor insisted that no apologies were necessary and proceeded to enlighten me.

His wife was Jewish, born of German parentage, and had witnessed the extermination of her entire family at Auschwitz during the Second World War. My conclusion that her life had followed a whole new course was only too painfully accurate. For half a century, she had blocked off all conscious memories of her trauma but that tree drawing had come direct from her unconscious, bringing the whole appalling episode out into the open. Being faced with that long-suppressed memory had provided the release his wife so desperately needed, the doctor assured me.

In theory of course I was well aware of the potential damage suppressed memories could cause to the system, but I had never had such a reaction to my analysis of a tree drawing. It was an unnerving experience.

A transvestite

Is figure 229 another severed trunk? At first glance, it would appear that the middle-aged professional man who sketched it had also had some sort of major problem in early childhood. But no. This artist claimed that his only childhood problem was 'a sense of disappointment at being male'. He had been drawn towards transvestism at a very early age.

Figure 229

I reproduce it immediately after the 'Auschwitz' tree to draw attention to the danger of jumping to quick conclusions. Apart from its curious 'roots', this is actually a very well-formed tree and clearly recognizable as such. Its small size, firm and unbroken pen strokes and central placement on the scrap of paper on which it was sketched all add up to clear-mindedness and lucidity. It is refreshingly free of any areas of darkness.

A foster parent

The tree featured in figure 230 might resemble a Christmas tree, but as it was drawn in midsummer, Christmas would hardly have been the most dominant thought in the artist's mind.

Figure 230

Its placement firmly in the centre of the page indicates the woman's love of order and method. The angular strokes point to her strong will and ability to cope, whatever the circumstances. The boxed base suggests the emphasis she places on a good, solid, upbringing.

The tree, which was sketched by a woman in her early sixties, gives an impression of someone who is a strict, no-nonsense type of person. That one-line trunk running straight up the middle conjures up images of someone who is ramrod straight, honest and entirely open in her dealings with others; the sort who might attach considerable importance to family life and values.

But what of the nine spiky branches? She did not seem at all 'spiky' by nature. Perhaps she herself had an answer? She certainly had.

I'm a foster parent and your choice of the word spiky couldn't be more appropriate. The nine little imps I've given homes to over the years have all come from deprived backgrounds and most of them took a lot of breaking in because apart from one little girl who came to me when her mum was in hospital, the others had spent most of their lives in care.
  I've taken in skinheads, punk-rockers and some real misfits. I've also had a couple of youngsters with multiple handicaps.

Fallen leaf

This prettily-drawn tree (figure 231) is the work of a 37-year-old housewife and mother of four.

The most obvious difference between figure 231 above and all the other trees featured in these pages is its fallen leaf.

When the sketch was handed to me, I had to confess that I had never previously encountered such a phenomenon. Working on the theory that new leaves indicate new life, and bearing in mind the trauma of the woman who had sketched a little trunk before proceeding with her tree proper (figure 228), I approached this artist as tactfully as possible to ask if she had ever lost a baby. 'Yes,' she responded, with controlled emotion: 'I had a miscarriage before my eldest child was born.'

The siting of the fallen leaf alongside the trunk did indeed suggest that she would have been in her mid-twenties at the time.

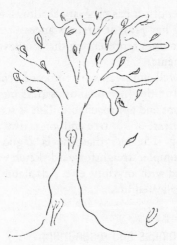

Figure 231 (50%)

Turning to the branches and all those other leaves, we find a few more curious indicators. First of all, the branches total six in number: a significant figure as it happens because, with her husband and four children, her own family numbers six. Not only that, she is one of six children in her parents' family. Nor is there anything haphazard about the 18 leaves. The unconscious motivation behind this number is that our artist has 18 nieces and nephews. None of this, as already explained, was a conscious effort on the part of the artist. Her tree was one of several spontaneous sketches scribbled at the end of a rather lively dinner party.

Signs of openness and warmth

Figure 232 is a simple, straightforward tree sketched by a nurse, whose tree is not unlike that of the lawyer (figure 227).

Figure 232

245

Open and friendly, it has no nasty shadings, no sign of childhood trauma affecting her present circumstances or lifestyle, and lots of warm, rounded curves representing the compassion the artist shows towards her patients.

The nurse is well endowed with common sense and wide open to whatever opportunities (personal or professional) are available. She is relaxed, pleasant and approachable. This is seen in the way we are invited into the heart of her tree and, on arrival there, find no nasty surprises lurking. The fact that she is a good communicator is revealed by the simple, straightforward sketch which is in no danger of being confused with anything else. Adaptable and friendly, hers is a happy, uncomplicated life.

Signs of unhappiness and resentment

By way of contrast, the dark shading all over the trees in figures 233 and 234 shows these middle-aged women to be unhappy, resentful individuals.

The bowed trunks indicate depression, and the nervous over-writing throughout suggests that each one is suffering from some form of obsessional neurosis.

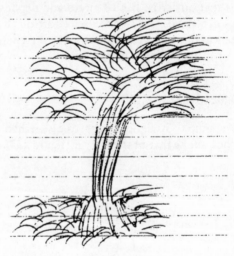

Figure 233

Figure 234

The placement of figure 234 up in the top right hand corner of the paper hints at a possible detachment from reality.

In each case, the roots have been scored through in a most determined way and although the trees themselves are easily recognizable for what they are, the explanatory script accompanying figure 234 is completely illegible.

Signs of edginess and aggression

The tree featured in figure 235 shows extreme edginess, with much bottled-up aggression, as illustrated by the heavy, jagged scribble alongside the base of the tree.

The very angular tree featured in figure 236 is the work of an individual who is reflective, self-contained, narcissistic and totally uninterested in anyone else's point of view.

The lightness of pen pressure, weakness of strokes and nervous overwriting of lines all add up to a state of high anxiety. There is also evidence of some aggression beneath the surface, but nothing as strong as that seen in the previous sample.

Figure 235 (50%)

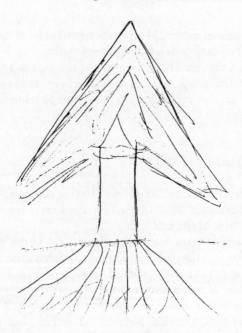

Figure 236 (50%)

Signs of injury

Bearing in mind what I have said about areas of the tree representing areas of the body, one can see that the person who drew the tree featured in figure 237 had a shoulder problem. The area of darkness is in the area of the tree representing neck and shoulders. And, as it does not stretch into the neck area or across both shoulders, it is obviously localized.

The artist, a reluctant gardener, admitted that he had recently pulled a muscle during some overenthusiastic weeding.

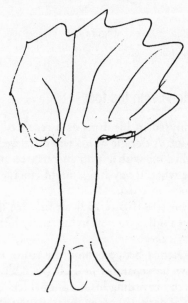

Figure 237

A circus performer

To prove just how symbolic a tree drawing can be and to end this section on a light-hearted note, look at figure 238 (overleaf).

It does not take the skills of a graphologist to work out the nature of this man's line of work.

Figure 238

Yes, he is a juggler!

Tree drawings done with the foot

Paul Driver, paralysed in his arms as a result of polio writes and draws with his foot. A doodle of his was discussed in the last chapter. He also supplied me with a spontaneous tree drawing. It is interesting here to see what, if anything, might emerge from the unconscious mind of such an artist.

In examining his tree (figure 239) we first see the trouble he has taken to sketch an abiding interest in his family history and ancestral roots.

The lightly sketched hedge behind the trunk is an unconscious revelation of how he separates himself (mentally and physically) from others, thereby revealing his occasional feelings of isolation.

The profusion of dark patches in the tree suggests that many tears were shed in his childhood. The arm on the left has a veritable pool beneath, giving the impression that some great tragedy had occurred when he was quite young. To my question whether his parents had been separated, by death or otherwise, when he was little more than an infant, he responded that his mother had died when he was four years old.

The conclusion from the now-blossoming foliage is that his troubles have faded. It is as if, at last, he has emerged from the dark into the daylight.

Derrick Vandek is another artist who paints with his mouth and he gave me two pictures, one formal and the other informal. The first picture, entitled 'mountain stream' (figure 240), is taken from an original painted with the mouth.

Figure 239 (50%)

Figure 240 (50%)

The formal trees are slim, young and springlike, rather as the artist must have seen himself before his accident.

The woodland scene is a sample of the type of painting he produced for MFPA calendars and greetings cards. It is very attractive and shows how much he enjoyed sketching trees and how well he depicted them. But this was a structured scene, a conscious effort, whereas the less formal tree in figure 241 sends out rather different messages.

Figure 241 (65%)

This second tree was one produced specifically for analysis and its message is far more subtle because of the shortcut it takes from deep inside his psyche. It shows that the artist is happy drawing trees. The sketch itself is cursive and free-flowing. Trees meant a lot to this artist; not only did they represent the new life he had made for himself since his accident, but they had taken the place (so to speak) of the tightrope.

The trunk of the tree represents the artist's growing-up period, the foliage where he is today and, as in writing, areas of darkness can be taken to represent trauma. In the case of Mr Vandek's tree, note how it actually depicts his fall from a great height. To the right is a sawn-off branch. Above it (to the right, in the foliage), we see a tent-shaped form, and alongside it the letter *f* (for 'fall'). Also note several arrows pointing downwards.

The black, heavily scribbled patch in the middle of the tree could be taken to represent his trauma, which seemed particularly bad in the period immediately following the accident, although it was not necessarily connected with it.

Samples of Mr Vandek's script (figures 242 and 243) confirm the trauma. Mr Vandek explained that his wife died of cancer three years after his accident.

Taking everything into consideration, this spontaneous tree is a strong, free-standing, upright effort, suggesting that he himself also had those qualities. He did not deny any of these findings. His talents and skills, his own belief in them and his strong will to get on with his life were his prime motivations.

Turning from Mr Vandek's sketches back to his writings, a remarkable factor emerges. It is that, as an artist, he is in complete control. The lines are steady, relaxed and show no signs of the shakiness seen in his script. However, his disability which hardly manifests itself at all in the drawings, is quite obvious in his writing. Apart from the shakiness of the script, note how the tops and bottoms of the loops have been squared off, as they so often are in the writings of people who are physically disabled.

What makes the analysis of trees so exciting is that the artist is less restricted than when he is writing. Handwriting techniques and styles vary from country to country and from generation to generation within the same country, but not so tree drawings. Artists can give vent to their imagination without having to adhere to any standard letter forms which may have been dictated by fashion or culture.

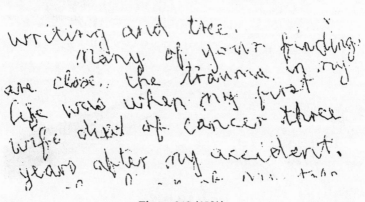

Figure 242 (65%)

253

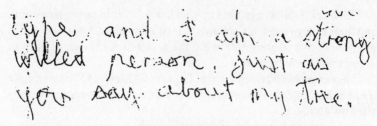

Figure 243 (65%)

A tree is a tree whatever the nationality of the author. The graphologist who is adept at deciphering the thought processes behind such sketches should be able to analyse the pictures of any nation's people without too much difficulty. Indeed, the question of an artist's nationality may never arise. In this particular form of analysis, it is quire irrelevant.

A tree drawing by a thalidomide survivor

Kevin Donnellon, whose writing was analysed in chapter 17, was born without limbs or hips as a result of his mother taking the drug Thalidomide during her pregnancy. I invited him to draw a tree and a typical doodle, and he combined them in one sketch as per figure 244.

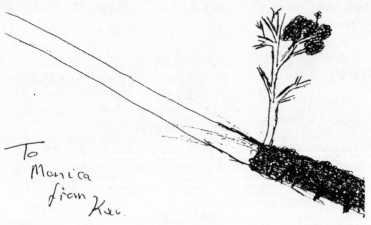

Figure 244 (50%)

He was, he said, constantly drawing hedges and on reflection agreed that it was an unconscious manifestation of his feelings of separation from other people.

If we interpret the left side of Kevin's tree as his past and the right side as his future (primarily relating to his family), then the obvious point of difference is that while those on the left are sharp, disjointed and barren, the upper branches of those on the right are showing healthy new growth. Their lines are round, warm and emotional, and they are filled in and heavily leafed. A significant and rather delightful little quirk here is that tiny branch shooting up at the top. This could be said to represent the very latest branch of the family tree, Kevin's toddler nephew James, to whom he is devoted.

The hedge should not be interpreted as falling with the blackening lines indicating despondency, because the reverse is actually the case. Kevin always draws from right to left. As he explains: 'I hold down the paper with my left hand, so I find it easier to start a drawing on the right.'

The hedge, initially blacked in and heavily thicketed soon opens up, rises and eventually tails off altogether. Far from being depressed, he is a very happy, humorous, optimistic person with a most positive outlook on life. I find it quite remarkable that Kevin, like many severely disabled people never misses an opportunity to help others whom he considers less fortunate than himself. Even as a very young schoolboy he frequently involved himself in sponsored swims and other fund-raising events.

21 House Drawings

Spontaneously drawn houses can also provide the graphologist with valuable clues about the functioning of the artist's unconscious. In their own way they are as symbolic as doodles and tree drawings, and they can tell the analyst whether the artist is confident and self-assured or timid and withdrawn.

Apart from any artistic abilities which might be manifest the shape, form and pen pressure of a quickly drawn house can reveal many aspects of the artist's personality, including aggression, ambition, humour, contentment, defensiveness, depression, frustration, imagination, insecurity, loneliness, self-importance, snobbishness, sociability, and versatility.

A house drawing by a librarian

Figure 245 (65%)

Figure 245 is very complex, its dominant themes being inhibition and feelings of isolation. The tension of the artist comes through in every stroke, but notice five specific clues:

- scribbled horizontal lines representing a road or pathway in the foreground and in the background a hedge
- a firmly closed gate defended by 'sentinels'
- a long pathway leading to the door which is shut, as are all the windows
- the lack of a chimney or any other entry
- unyielding trees

The house was drawn by a 30-year-old librarian who shall be called Anne, an academic who admits to having difficulty forming social relationships, although once having found them she does usually manage to retain them.

This last point is confirmed by other little clues in her drawing. While she has closed her gate, she makes a point of providing access to the lawns and, almost as an afterthought, has scribbled through the hedges as if she did not really intend them to be there.

The final clue to Anne's personality comes in the general presentation of her offering. The entire sketch is neat, precise and as organized as the books on her library shelves. With everything in its proper place, what we have here is a neat and tidy drawing from a neat and tidy mind.

A house drawing by a grandmother

Figure 246 is the house of a proud grandmother who enjoys nothing better than to be surrounded by her family.

It is a much less complicated and more friendly sketch than figure 245. Bright and cheery, its path leads direct to a door on which the artist has troubled to write the number, so that her visitors can find her easily. Flowers are springing up all over her lawns and the windows are clear, with curtains (if there are any) firmly drawn back.

She is obviously a modern grandmother, because her house has no chimney, but she still cannot resist drawing in the smoke suggesting the presence of a friendly fire inside.

Figure 246

What I also like about this sketch is the slight forward slant of her house, showing her to be a gregarious personality. Another lovely touch is the framed picture of her children, who have now left home, making a happy little nest for themselves not too far away from the one in which they grew up. An alternative interpretation of the smaller drawing is that it is a framed picture of two grandchildren.

Signs of contentment

Contentment is the dominant theme of figure 247.

This artist is also middle-aged and also friendly, but not quite as outgoing as the previous one and rather more fond of her privacy.

While the tree and chimney smoke are soft and curvy (indicating her sociability), the roof comes to a sharp point and the fence surrounding the property keeps her family apart from her neighbours. The implication is that friendship is strictly on her own terms, and not generalized.

The fact that the tree is actually beyond the bounds of her property suggests her awareness of neighbours, intimating that she will help if necessary, but prefers to keep herself to herself. In

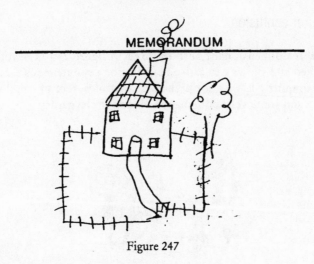

Figure 247

confirmation of this, we have lawns which are stark and without any form of vegetation, and a firmly closed front gate.

Signs of warmth and love

The house featured in figure 248 has a lovely wide flower-bedecked approach. The knocker on the door is an open invitation to test the hospitality of the occupier. The huge upstairs window, allowing the maximum amount of light to enter the house shows it to be a home full of warmth and sunshine.

The round top on the door and the general welcoming approach suggests that the artist has a sunny disposition, is healthy, happy and easy-going, and has a non-aggressive personality.

Figure 248

Signs of confusion

The three-dimensional house featured in figure 249 is beautifully sketched and shows real artistic talent. For a spontaneous sketch, it takes in quite a lot: a door with some sort of porch, six windows, a garage and some very odd-shaped objects in the garden.

Figure 249

She is certainly a very lively personality, but she is also very confused. On the one hand, the trees, bushes and friendly smoke suggest that what we have here is someone who is warm, welcoming and hospitable; she has even drawn a candle to light the way. But on the other hand, the overwritten areas of darkness (on the shrub in front of the house and the tree behind it) tell us that she is a nervy, anxious sort of person, not always sure about the reactions of others.

To confirm that confusion, we have one tree which is sharp and tending towards angularity and another which is soft and curvaceous.

The areas of darkness are spasmodic and do not appear on the house itself, which suggests that her home life is happy and contented. The hedge in front tells us that, in it, she also feels secure.

Her problems are all to do with external relationships, which would appear to be rooted in her past. The clue lies in the positioning of the 'fir' tree to the left of the house and slightly behind it. The round curviness of the tree on the right (representing future hopes and plans) is a much more friendly effort, despite its dark trunk.

What we have here, therefore, is someone who believes in old-fashioned values and morals.

Because she considers it such bad form to show her irritation, she bottles up her feelings and broods, resulting in the anxiety manifested by the dark shading.

A tree house

Figure 250 is the house of a rising young executive, with lofty ideals and great hopes for the future.

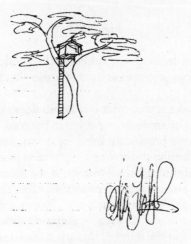

Figure 250 (50%)

He is a slightly enigmatic character too, as indicated by the signature below the tree. Note how similar the tree and signature are in style. This young man is well on his way to a highly successful career. From such a lofty perch he should have no trouble keeping tabs on competitors or anyone involved in shady practices. Try forging that signature!

A hypnotherapist

The most intriguing drawing in this short selection is that sketched by my husband (figure 251).

Figure 251

What sets it apart from all the others is the window in the roof, a feature which does not appear in any other sample in my entire collection.

And let me make it clear that our house does not have a dormer window, skylight or any other opening in the roof. Nor have any of the houses we have previously lived in, or my husband before we met. So we can dismiss the obvious practical explanation.

Taking the graphological viewpoint, if we equate the top of the house with the artist's mental processes, then the extra window depicts a keenly perceptive 'mind's eye'. In other words, the ability to perceive rather more of what is going on around him is more acutely developed in the mind of this artist than it may be in the rest of us. In view of his profession as a hypnotherapist whose philosophy is to get straight to the root of his patients' problems, that perceptiveness is obviously a very great advantage.

The house itself is a basic, no-nonsense, no-frills sort of structure. It stands proud and is free of any form of neurotic overwriting or sinister areas of darkness to hint at subconscious fears. The windows are not exactly symmetrical and the roof is slightly off-centre. That, too, is symptomatic of my husband's thinking. He is the first to admit that he never has been the sort of person to conform to expectations.

It is nevertheless a very open, friendly sort of house, with its doorknob all ready for turning and its assorted windows providing visitors to the property with alternative view of life outside.

On a deeper level, the house as a whole reflects the artist's qualities of decisiveness, determination and self-discipline. The upward-curling tops on the door and the upstairs window to its left denote a highly developed sense of humour.

The house is the sort to emerge from the type of personality who makes a decision, sticks with it and is true to himself. It shows the artist to be a healthy, relaxed, home-loving character refreshingly free of negative fears or phobias.

22   Children's Drawings

Some graphologists claim that the scribbles of pre-school children are very revealing because the thinking processes behind them have not yet been directed onto the tramtracks of conventional writing and thinking.

I do not altogether agree. In my opinion, the mind of a toddler is far too immature to give any significant graphological clues. As a general rule, I hesitate to work on samples produced by a child below the age of seven, although bright five- and six-year-olds have occasionally had something worthwhile to offer.

The drawings of young children, however, are very revealing and the observation and interpretation of children's drawings is a particularly fascinating aspect of a graphologist's work. Although it is not something on which I work professionally, I do enjoy taking a peek at any such sketches that come my way.

What I find particularly enchanting is the way three- to four-year-old children's attempts to draw members of their family invariably end up with head and body combined. These sketches are generally referred to as 'tadpole people' because of their stick-type arms and legs. When they realize we have hands and feet these are sketched in to resemble the prongs of a garden fork.

As a developmental pattern emerges and the little artists become more observant, they elaborate on their drawings and stop sketching abstract symbols. In the words of an educational psychologist: 'Their visual language advances as an integral part of their mental development.'

In passing, I would like to mention something which came to light when I was interviewing the head-teacher of a school for deaf and hearing-impaired children whose ages ran the whole gamut from three to eighteen.

The teacher who was very keen on encouraging any latent artistic abilities in his pupils told me that he had found a common factor running throughout their drawings. It was that when asked to sketch faces, profoundly deaf children below the age of seven invariably omitted to add on any ears but made the mouths much larger than life.

The reasoning behind this strange phenomenon, he explained, was that as these children could not hear, ears were irrelevant, but their reliance on lip-reading made the mouths of those around them assume major importance. As they matured so did their drawings and ears began to make their appearance.

By observing and interpreting children's drawings, we see various similarities and variations emerge and can apply the same basic principles to children's drawings as we do to those of adults.

Five-year-olds

Here are three drawings from 5-year-olds. Figures 252 and 253 by a girl, figure 254 by a boy.

The girl was preparing for her first day at school when she sketched her figure.

Figure 252

Note the happy smile and general perkiness of the picture. The character is almost 'jumping for joy'. She was obviously very much looking forward to the event.

Now look at figure 253. This drawing features her arrival back home, being greeted by the dog next door.

Figure 253 (65%)

Her mother tells me she is never far from colouring pencils or crayons and is forever sketching. She loves dogs – a fact confirmed by her drawing – although she does not have one of her own.

The boy's sketch reflects his interest in ice-skating. Note the emphasis placed on the feet of his character.

Figure 254 (65%)

Ten years on, ice-skating is still his major interest and activity.

Teenagers

Figures 255 and 256 were drawn by two very different boys, both aged fourteen. Their sketches will show the marked contrast in their personalities.

Figure 255 is the work of a highly intelligent boy from a comfortable and happy home background. The son of a bank manager, he attends a private school, where his reports show him to be an excellent all-rounder, shining at both academic subjects and sporting pursuits.

Figure 255 (50%)

His drawing shows something else: a highly perceptive nature and some very interesting thoughts going on in his adolescent head!

Confusion over the changes in his body are reflected in his mind, where we have warmth and aggression in equal measure. It is as if each aspect of the writer's personality were competing with the other.

What keeps this young writer on his toes appears to be the constant struggle going on inside himself to try and decide whether to be warm and friendly towards his peers or sharp and aggressive. It is all to do with asserting his emerging manhood.

He compromises and shows that he can be both or either, depending on the circumstances. One half of him is warm and sympathetic, the other sharp and assertive. There is considerable activity in this boy's mind. He has so many interests and hobbies that he could turn to any one of them for his ultimate career.

But at least it is a healthy, optimistic drawing, showing no neurotic dotting within the spaces of dark shading to black any of them out altogether. Look carefully at this sketch and all sorts of coded messages can be seen.

It is the sort of doodle to be found in the hand of someone who hates wasting time and will find a variety of tasks to complete. This is a very active and rapidly developing mind.

The circumstances of the second 14-year-old could not be more different.

Figure 256 (50%)

He is a boy in long-term residential care because of behavioural problems. He is, as the experts caring for him say 'intellectually and socially challenged' which, to the rest of us means that his mental age is lower than his chronological age.

His drawing (figure 256) certainly confirms his behavioural problems. Yet this boy is managing to communicate his thoughts with remarkable clarity.

It is a disturbing and very negative sketch and speaks of real unhappiness. Note the sad little face with its down-turned mouth, the falling person with its blacked-out body and arms. And what on earth are we to make of the curiously shaped and somewhat sinister structure alongside it? Is it a chair, a bed, a cradle – or a coffin?

The poor child does not know what to do with himself. Not only is the expression one of utter bewilderment but the figure itself is asymmetrical, with oddly shaped fingers on the right hand, six of them on the left, and two odd feet emerging from one leg.

Note, too, the wisps of hair standing up on top of his head suggesting that the artist is not just bewildered, but frightened. After all, at fourteen he too is on the edge of adulthood and knows it. Unlike the artist of figure 255, who regards his developing state of mind and body as a challenge, this boy feels nothing but apprehension about the future.

The clarity of his sketch tells us that he has enough intelligence to know that the world outside can be a very intimidating place for people unable to conform to society's expectations.

The one ray of hope for this boy is that the staff running the establishment where he is currently in residence are absolutely dedicated to their work and if anyone can help him adjust with a view to eventual independent living, they can. I am grateful to Mrs MD, the principal, for supplying me with this drawing.

Index

Index

Friedrich, Dr Nikolas, 130
Friedrich's Ataxia, 130
Freud and Adler, 84–5

'g' and 'y' underloops, 43–6
gangrene, 142
gender, 11–12, 23, 195, 201
Goering, Hermann, 186
'grapho-therapy', 58
greed, 46, 68,
guilt, 9, 66, 69, 102, 103, 115, 171

Harrison, Ben, 172, 212
Harrison, Leslie, 212
hieroglyphics, Egyptian, 21
Hitler, Adolf, 184–5
H.S., Mr, 150–4
house drawings
    by grandmother, 257–8
    by hypnotherapist, 261–3
    by librarian, 256–7
    showing signs of: confusion, 260–1;
        contentment, 258–9; warmth and
        love, 259
hypertension, 131, 145
hypnosis, 84, 93, 100, 193
hypnotherapist, 261–2
hypnotherapy, 193, 208
hypnotism, 39

i-dots and t-bars, 41
immaturity, 97–8
inferiority, feelings of, 68, 107

'James' (editor), 226–8
Jung, Carl Gustav, 86

key words, 111–12
Knievel, Evil, 38

'Lady R.', 178
Latin, 9, 19, 21, 122, 202, 218
letter connections, 35
lettering, forms of, 27
letters
    'e', 83–4
    'f', 42–3
    'g', 43–6
    'i', 41
    'I', 68–82
    't', 41
    'y', 43–6
    capital, 46–7
    size of, 30
    slant of, 29
    spacing of, 33
    starting and ending strokes of, 47
Liberace, 38

London Institute of Neurology, 133
London National Hospital for
    Nervous Diseases, 133
loop breaks, 51–3
Lord, Capt., Stanley, 212–15
Lord, Stanley, 215
Ludwig I, King of Bavaria, 216–18

margins, 36
M.D., Mrs, 269
Menières Disease, 74
mental deterioration, 149–54
Mesmer, Franz, Anton, 39
'Michelle', 196–200
Michon, Abbé Hippolyte, 22
mirror writing, 59
miscarriage, 244
money signs, 69, 70
Mott, F.W., 178, 180
Mould, Dr Richard, 8, 12, 14, 15
Mouth and Foot Painting Association
    (MFPA), 8, 155–252
Mozart, Wolfgang Amadeus, 133
Murray, Dr T.J., 133, 138
music, 20, 67, 117, 123, 148,

Napoleon Bonaparte, 181–4
Nelson, Admiral Lord, 11, 13, 14, 15
nervous exhaustion, 88–90
neurological disorders
    epilepsy, 131
    Friedrich's Ataxia, 130–1
    Gilles de la Tourette Syndrome, 132–7
    multiple sclerosis, 128–30
    stroke, 131–2
Nixon, Richard, 187–8

obsessional neurosis, 87–8
Oedipus, 85
overwriting, 88, 91, 103, 104, 151, 234, 246

Parkinson's Disease, 24, 128
pen pressure, 34–5
pen trails, 56, 79, 82, 87, 136, 147, 218
personal pronoun 'I' (PPI)
    ambiguity in, 81–2
    different styles within same text, 76–9
    ear-shaped, 71–4
    foetal-shaped, 70–1
    indicating lack of warmth, 67
    PPI and parents, 63–6
    printed style, 74–5
    revealing harmony and discord, 79–81
    reversed strokes, 75–6
    showing neurotic tendencies, 82
    showing resentment, 66–7
    size and style of, 68–70
phantom limb, 120–1

271